Markets versus Hierarchies

Markets versus Hierarchies

A Political Economy of Russia from the 10th Century to 2008

Ekaterina Brancato

Senior Research Fellow, The Locke Institute, USA

Edward Elgar

Cheltenham, UK • Northampton, MA, USA

Published by
Edward Elgar Publishing Limited
The Lypiatts
15 Lansdown Road
Cheltenham
Glos GL50 2JA
UK

Edward Elgar Publishing, Inc.
William Pratt House
9 Dewey Court
Northampton
Massachusetts 01060
USA

A catalogue record for this book
is available from the British Library

Library of Congress Control Number: 2009921528

Mixed Sources
Product group from well-managed
forests and other controlled sources
www.fsc.org Cert no. SA-COC-1565
© 1996 Forest Stewardship Council

ISBN 978 1 84720 811 8

Printed and bound by MPG Books Group, UK

Contents

Figures and tables

FIGURES

TABLES

Foreword

This splendid tome deploys the cutting-edge scholarship of transaction cost economics, Austrian economics, law and economics, and public choice to offer profound insights into the evolving nature of markets and hierarchies in Russia over a period of more than one thousand years, from the early Russian Tsars, through the grim era of communism, through the short period of nascent democracy, into the current oligarchy, completely dominated by the ex-KGB agent, one-time President, now Prime Minister, Vladimir Putin. Written by a Russian émigré to the United States, fluent in both languages, the book draws deeply on relevant sources in a way that less-gifted linguists simply cannot achieve.

By probing deeply into Russia's past, Dr Brancato demonstrates that market process has never thrived in Russia, has no firm roots, and, even now, is evaded and avoided wherever possible by individuals and households that negotiate and trade through social networks (hierarchies in the sense of Oliver Williamson) rather than through anonymous market exchange. Dr Brancato identifies the weakness of such strong ties in narrowing opportunities for entrepreneurship and innovation, and in widening the reach of bureaucracy and resistance to change.

Notions advanced by Ronald Coase and others that individuals systematically seek out gains from trade by striking deals with each other (the Coase Theorem) are dominated in Russia by notions that individuals reject market exchange because of a systemic fear that unforeseen events will render them susceptible to exploitation (the Machiavelli Theorem). Dr Brancato demonstrates compellingly that the institutional history of Russia lends itself to this deeply embedded prejudice. In a country that has never enjoyed the rule of law, where the courts have never displayed independence from the will of those who rule, individuals are subjects, not citizens, and depend for protection, ultimately, on access to individuals who stand above them in the economic hierarchy, not on the primacy of the laws of property and contract.

At a time when Russia is regressing from democracy to Tsardom, is retreating from the modern to the medieval age, from rationality to mysticism, this book is timely indeed. It brings to the Western reader an understanding of the particular culture of a still-isolated Eastern people, protected from globalization by plentiful fossil fuel resources (the winners' curse) and by a long-standing tolerance for self-imposed relative poverty. As long as his government does not impede his flow of cheap vodka, and provides him with protection against anarchy, the stoic Russian male accepts the Hobbesian order, and turns away from the Sirens of Lockeian liberty. Whether the new Russian woman (think Lara in *Doctor Zhivago*) shares this docility is a matter yet to be resolved. Resolving that issue will be central to the future of the Russian people in the modern world.

Dr Brancato, who staunchly believes in individual liberty, has lived sufficiently long in Russia to understand and sympathize with her Hobbesian compatriots, even as she rejects their excessive acceptance of authority and their over-indulgence in hierarchical networks. This book is a masterpiece that could be written only by such an outstanding example of the new Russian woman: an exceptional scholar who is not betrayed by her past, nor seduced by unrealistic expectations of her promising future in the New World.

This book will help to loosen excessively strong ties in Russia and to re-awaken the West to the benefits of market exchange at a time of perceived crisis in the viability of capitalism; demonstrably the greatest instrument for wealth creation available to mankind. Read and enjoy the rich feast that Dr Brancato places before you.

Charles K. Rowley
Duncan Black Professor of Economics
George Mason University
and General Director
The Locke Institute, USA

Acknowledgements

My utmost gratitude goes to the Locke Institute for its financial support, and to its director, Charles Rowley. One of the most devoted teachers and principled men I have ever met, Charles Rowley has directed my effort in the most efficient way, and he has tirelessly emphasized the importance of integrity. Without his continuous encouragement *Markets versus Hierarchies* would have been lost in the academic thicket.

This book is an outgrowth of my dissertation, and there are numerous people to thank who helped me at that stage, but I would have never reached the dissertation stage without the unselfish support of Mrs Thelma O. Weaver, who believed in me without ever meeting face-to-face. Walter Williams, of the Economics Department of George Mason University, provided financial assistance for my latest trip to Russia, which was crucial for finishing the research.

My life and my intellectual experience have been enriched by many individuals who also directly and indirectly shaped the line of my research. They are especially those cited in this book. Richard and Anna Ebeling encouraged my initial interest in economics and Russian studies.

My special thanks to the anonymous referee for his valuable comments, as well as the participants of The 2007 Ratio Colloquium for Young Social Scientists for their insights. Of course, I bear all responsibility for the shortcomings and errors in this book.

Without the help of my family – my mother Ludmila Stepykina and my husband Kevin Brancato – this research would have not been completed. Stimulating discussions with them helped me with my understanding of the complex issues I tried to tackle.

I would like to thank my numerous respondents in Russia for their time and their frankness.

To people I cannot thank in person . . .

PART I

Introduction

1. Markets versus hierarchies

In 1937, Coase explained the difference between the coordinating efforts of an entrepreneur and the coordinating function of the price mechanism in the market and why vertical integration is sometimes necessary. There are two ways of allocating resources – one is through markets, the other is through hierarchies. The cost of market operation is more than zero, therefore, delegating the allocation of resources to an authority saves some of that cost, especially when a longer-term contract is desirable. This is when a firm emerges.

At the relevant margins, markets will end and bureaucratic hierarchies will appear when transaction costs are too high. The firm must carry out its function at less than market cost, otherwise the employees would revert back to the open market.[1] But this does not tell the full story. Williamson (1985) asserts that bounded rationality, asset specificity and opportunism play a decisive role in sustaining hierarchies.

Bounded rationality means that the agents are perfectly rational – will not do anything to violate their preferences – only part of the time. This reflects the limit of their cognitive competence. Opportunism is a calculated effort to misrepresent information to the other party for a personal gain. Asset specificity means that an asset has a lower value outside of a particular transaction. When bounded rationality, opportunism and asset specificity are simultaneously present, the form of contracting that emerges is governance. Where court enforcement is problematic, the system must rely on the institutions of private ordering.[2] This is where the role of transaction costs must be examined with special care.

Under all phases of Russian history there was no good law of contract and no good law of private property, which are crucial for development of markets. In addition, the state involvement in the economy was considerable and some markets were highly regulated; and for a period of time open markets were suppressed by the political regime. Consequently, the cost of market transactions was high, and the cost of social networking through hierarchies was relatively lower.

'[T]he economic institutions of capitalism have the main purpose and effect of economizing on transaction costs' (Williamson, 1985, p. 17). I would advance further that any economic system (however over-regulated) is going to gravitate to economizing on transaction costs as one of the main purposes. Hierarchical social networks in Russia were the institutions of private ordering that emerged to govern exchanges instead of free market institutions. Agents in these hierarchical or vertical networks had very limited exit capabilities, as opposed to firms in a free market.

Coase (1937) treats uncertainty as an insufficient reason for firms to emerge. Even if his explanation is satisfactory regarding the emergence of a firm in the West, it would certainly be short-sighted to undervalue the role of uncertainty in sustaining hierarchical relationships in Russia because limitations of open market governance clearly exist and rule of law is also lacking.

When asset specificity is bilateral, then both parties have a higher incentive to see a contract through, even though the more opportunistic partner will try to take advantage of the other. When asset specificity is unilateral or uneven, then the problem of opportunism skyrockets. In Russia this is demonstrated by the bureaucrat and citizen relations or in seller and consumer relations when third-party arbitration is impossible, especially when transactions are occasional, when the seller is a monopolist or when the bureaucrat exercises an exclusive right to dispense favours.

Non-standard contracting that is a subset of economic transactions produces one outcome, but will yield greater implications when it is economy-wide. I believe that high opportunism and uncertainty made Russians more receptive to autocracy – they viewed the strong ruling hand as a panacea for widespread opportunism. Ultimately it made them more receptive to socialism as well – idealization of forced collaboration, mistaking self-interest (in the neoclassical sense) for opportunism and interpretation of it as evil, and desire of an efficient form of governance in the face of relational contracting.

The analysis in the following chapters extends the implications of transaction cost literature to the Russian economy, where the role of social networks is very important.

NOTES

1. For more details on the nature of firm, see Coase (1937).
2. For more information, see Williamson (1985, pp. 30–32, 44–50, 52–6).

2. Theoretical background

Social networks are present in every society. As an institution of private ordering, social networks in Russia did not emerge overnight. Examination of network relationships along three characteristics – strength of ties, direction and content – identifies essential distinctions of Russian social networks. They are based on strong personalized relationships, they are dense and affect practically every walk of life, vertical networks dominate and horizontal networks are very segregated. First, I would like to discuss the theoretical background for my analysis and then focus briefly on three subjects that have played a large role in the evolution of ties in Russia – trust, autocracy and rent seeking.

TIES

Granovetter's (1973) pioneering work introduced the concept of ties and their importance in the US labour market. He proposed further that the *strength* of interpersonal ties could relate network analysis to macro phenomena such as diffusion, social mobility, political organization and social cohesion. '[I]t is through these networks that small-scale interaction becomes translated into large-scale patterns, and that these, in turn, feed back into small groups' (ibid., p. 1360). Strong and weak ties affect societies very differently. Primitively, a strong tie is found between family members or friends, and a weak tie is held with acquaintances (Figures 2.1 and 2.2).[1] Granovetter stresses the importance of weak ties because *bridges*, which are necessarily weak ties, are responsible for social cohesion. A bridge is 'a line in a network which provides the *only* path between two points' (ibid., p. 1364; original emphasis). That is, a bridge is a weak link between two individuals who belong to different closely knit cliques. Therefore, weak ties diffuse information or norms in such a way that whatever it is, it travels great social distances, reaching larger numbers of people (ibid., p. 1371):

> [S]ince the resistance to a risky or deviant activity is greater than to a safe and normal one, a larger number of people will have to be exposed to it and adopt it, in the early stages, before it will spread in a chain reaction. Individuals with weak ties are . . . best placed to diffuse such a difficult innovation. . . . An initially

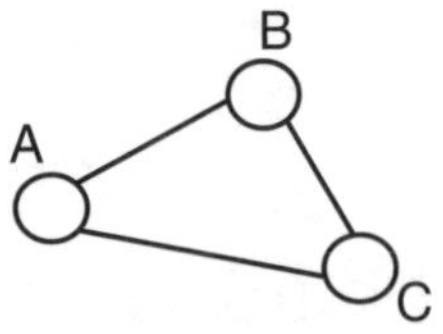

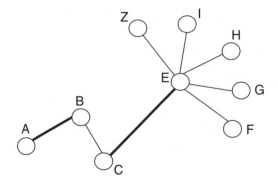

Figure 2.1   A cluster of strong ties

Note: AB and CE indicate strong ties, while BC, EZ, EI and so on, indicate weak ties.

Figure 2.2   Strong and weak ties

unpopular innovation spread by those with *few* weak ties is more likely to be confined to a few cliques. (ibid., pp. 1367–8; original emphasis)

This is crucial for spreading anonymous trust – trust in a transaction between strangers – a topic that will be taken up next. Granovetter defines the strength of a tie as 'a combination of the amount of time, the emotional intensity, the intimacy (mutual confiding), and the reciprocal services that characterize the tie' (ibid., p. 1361). '[S]ocial systems lacking in weak ties will be fragmented and incoherent' (Granovetter, 1983, p. 202). Though Russia does not lack weak ties, they are not sustaining the important economic relations and exchanges. Vertical networks, which are supported by strong personalized relationships, do that.

TRUST

The explanatory efforts of economics have been more and more focused on the puzzle of prosperity, perhaps because, with better information, we witness a large gap in standards of living around the world or perhaps because intellectuals still contemplate the social engineering of prosperity. A blend of economics, sociology, cultural studies and so on, produces a picture that is rich but too complex. At a basic level it all comes down to trust and social networks as mechanisms that generate and sustain it. Even in an extremely atomized society like the Soviet Union, networks of trust must exist because without trust there is no cooperation, and that is the only way human beings can lead an economically meaningful life.

Social capital has recently emerged as an important, if not one of the most crucial factors that contribute to prosperity of a society. Social ties, which are part social capital, are a prerequisite, not an outcome of prosperity. Societies 'have become rich because they were civic', as Putnam (1993b) pointed out, not the other way around. Literature in institutional economics indicates that trust, which develops with ties, serves as the foundation for spontaneous cooperation among members of a society. In *Trust*, Fukuyama shows that 'people's ability to maintain a shared "language of good and evil" is critical to the creation of trust' (1995, p. 270). He further shows that there is a very fine line between cultural diversity and a central cultural tradition. While there are gains to be had from diversity, in large doses diversity may be detrimental to communication and cooperation (ibid.). It would appear that Russia's problem is not the lack of a central cultural tradition, but its nature. (Russia's central traditional culture has faced the difficulty of diversity only recently.)

According to Fukuyama (1995), Russia falls under the definition of low-trust societies. The type of social relations dominant in such societies adversely affects their economic performance and lowers standards of living for an average person. But a low level of general trust does not necessarily mean that networks are weak – personal connections have been effectively used and promoted by interest groups throughout Russian history; a low level of general trust implies a peculiar structure of networks.

All ties facilitate cooperation, but inevitably there is a dosage of both 'good' and 'bad' ties in every society. The 'good' is a loose network of weak ties, which creates an atmosphere of common shared values in a society and which does not predetermine economic and social opportunities of its members by their position in the network. 'Social networks allow trust to become transitive and spread: I trust you because I trust her and she assures me that she trusts you'.[2] How are the 'bad' ties different if they apparently function the same way? Putnam distinguishes between the horizontal 'networks of civic engagement, like neighbourhood associations, cooperatives, sports clubs' (1993a, p. 173) and vertical networks based on asymmetric obligations (ibid., p. 174). Vertical networks simply cannot sustain trust for the purpose of spontaneous cooperation. In Russia, vertical and horizontal networks exist in an unhealthy blend. They are self-reinforcing and the message they spread is that it is always possible to get around the formal law. The original purpose of networks was not to cooperate in order to create but to get around the formal rule. The legacy is the culture of a people who honour personal relationships no matter how fraudulent and corrupt they are and cheat whenever they can avoid detection.

The atomization of the Russian society has not vanished with its Soviet paraphernalia. Social networks to the present day secure the much-needed trust in business and personal exchanges. They clearly impede prosperity of the whole population. They also clearly save on some transaction costs, but increase overall opportunity costs, I suspect, by a lot more. As Toshio Yamagishi notes:

> commitments become a liability rather than an asset as traders face more and better opportunities outside their current, mutually committed relationships. The levels of social uncertainty and opportunity costs for staying in commitment relations are the two fundamental factors that determine the level of the collectivist behavioural pattern of commitment formation. The third factor that affects the strength of the collectivist behavioural pattern is the level of general trust. General trust provides a springboard for people who have been "confined" to commitment relationships to move out into the larger world of opportunities. In this way general trust emancipates people from the confines and security of stable commitment relations. (in Ostrom and Walker, 2003, p. 359)

Unfortunately, there are yet no mechanisms to produce a higher level of general trust that would ease impersonal exchange. Moreover, an average Russian easily observes narrowly defined transaction costs, which can be alleviated by networking; but he rarely observes other opportunity costs associated with vertical networks. This annihilates the possibility of change.

AUTOCRACY

Does one form of government facilitate the 'bad' type of social networks more than another? Not always, but, in my opinion, Russian authoritarian rule is directly responsible for the prevalence of networks over market institutions.[3] Because autocracy rests on subordination and loyalty due to ideological or other reasons, it endorses vertical networks. Horizontal networks appear as a by-product of overly strict formal rules, bureaucracy and economic shortages, which are highly likely to be characteristic of autocracy. Whether the networks of personal connections are large and dense depends on the magnitude of bureaucratic power, economic shortages, on social norms and chance.

Social networks are better understood in the context of political organization, and it is my belief that Russia is best described as an autocracy even to the present day. In *Autocracy*, Gordon Tullock quite frankly remarks, 'I should . . . not conceal from the reader my own feeling that despotism is in essence the equilibrium state of human society' (1987, p. 190). At the core, Russia always had an authoritarian government. There have been attempts to institute local self-government, a multi-party system and liberal policies but these attempts always failed. Many believe that a liberal regime was instituted with partial success by the government of Yeltsin, that even though there were mistakes in the economic liberalization programme, and even though the constitution was not fully transparent, there *were* steps made in the right direction and that present government is continuing to make such steps. I do not think that authoritarianism is a thing of the past, and in 2008, compared with just a few years ago, there are many more people outside of Russia who would agree with this. Liberalism as a model is not appropriate for understanding Russia[4] because the Russian government has remained autocratic in nature, however much lip service it pays to democracy.

In a Russian-style autocracy there are no or weak 'buffer'[5] institutions (or in Putnam's terminology, horizontal networks of 'civic engagement') to mitigate the relationship between individual and the state. People usually lack the desire and the ability (and autocratic rule helps them lose both by consistently crushing the efforts) to form associations voluntarily, such as private clubs, trading associations, condominium associations, cooperatives and so on. As Granovetter puts it, strong ties, as opposed to weak, do not fulfil the need for 'cognitive flexibility'. They limit 'the ability to function in complex voluntary organizations', which 'may depend on a habit of mind that permits one to assess the needs, motives, and actions of a great variety of different people simultaneously' (1983, p. 205). In addition, laws usually side with authorities or, in a civil litigation, with the party of greater political or financial influence. But things have to be done even in a society like this – people need to buy food, clothes, get a job, attend cultural events, deal with bureaucracy and so on.

Throughout Russian history, formal institutions were directed primarily to subjugate the individual to the state and not to ensure the kind of peaceful cooperation that facilitates productive exchange in the market. Alongside there evolved the informal institution of personal connections, which ensured the cooperation between exchanging parties.

Cooperation seems to be the cause of a society's economic success and a lot of resources are devoted to finding out how it works. Wintrobe (1998, p. 130) says that a predominant way of thinking is that:

it is possible to organize a society in such a way that individuals will cooperate, even when that cooperation is inconsistent with their self-interest narrowly
conceived. . . . The spectre that haunts the admirer of democracy who takes this
point of view is the idea that the most likely form of social organization which
makes this cooperation possible is some form of authoritarianism.

But this would mean an oversimplified approach. Cooperation in a
democratic culture is very different from cooperation under an authoritarian regime. And autocracy necessarily creates a unique culture by setting
the formal rules, more so than in democracy because an autocratic regime
exercises more power over its citizens. Cooperation under an authoritarian
regime is exchange forced out of the legal realm of economic activity. If
markets are forced to operate where market institutions cannot,[6] efficiency
will suffer. If trust cannot be supported by the formal institutions, it has to
be signalled through strong ties, and it will be more costly to sustain.

A number of economists find it a puzzle and at the same time an inspiration
that nations under authoritarian regimes achieve high levels of economic
performance. Dictatorships often redistribute more than democracies,
and some of their economic success may be explained by the fact that they
redistribute to those who are in the position to benefit most from economic
growth.[7] Ironically, this is true of post-Soviet Russia, which I cannot call
an economic success,[8] where wealth was redistributed to those who made
the best of their networking, but not necessarily production-innovative
abilities. The division of wealth between able social and economic entrepreneurs is an ongoing process, which leads to income inequality. This income
inequality has far greater implications than are raised in the standard
literature because it is based on and exacerbates social inequality, that is,
one's position in a network predetermines his income. Or simply that more
often than not economic relationships in Russia are based on status not on
contract – a point made by Peter Boettke (pers. com., 2004).

As regards economic efficiency, characteristics of dictatorship are such
that they allow for less waste than democracies.[9] But this situation is
not so clear cut as it seems at a first glance, if we take rent seeking into
account.

RENT SEEKING

The rent-seeking literature originated in Tullock (1967), Krueger (1974),
and Posner (1975). Where monopoly promises large returns on an original investment, there will be contestants willing to bid up to the amount
of expected profits. This is primitively the essence of rent seeking[10] as
explained by Tullock.

The Russian case gets a bit more complicated because of two amendments: social networks and the absence of properly documented property rights. A Russian, whether a 16th-century peasant or a modern-day oligarch, knows that whatever he possesses may be taken away from him at the whim of whoever is in power. The Tsars and the Soviets were ruthless in this respect. Present government also does not lag behind. However unjust the acquisition of property may have been in the 1990s, it is equally unjust to take the property away from some and not from others now.

Social networks to some extent secured one's privileged position in the giant rent-distribution and rent-seeking machine and the right to keep the loot. In 'Soviet Venality' Boettke and Anderson argue that the Soviet Union could be viewed similarly to the mercantilist society of the 16th- and 17th-century France and England where mercantilism was employed to 'raise revenue through the sale of monopoly privileges' (Anderson and Boettke, 1997; Boettke, 2001). 'Strategic positions in the economy were "sold" to those individuals willing to offer the highest bid to the central authorities, either in cash or (more typically) non-cash transfers' (Boettke, 2001, p. 146). Although the difference in the Soviet period was that the party strictly controlled the 'sale' of positions of privilege (ibid., pp. 149–51), this model can be applied to the pre-revolutionary Russia,[11] and I believe that this original insight stands for the post-Soviet period as well. Personal connections have always played a role in this redistributing scheme as an effort to benefit from positions of control[12] either over the actual goods or a production process, such as in natural gas monopoly, or over the distribution of rights to trade or produce, such as in bureaucracy.

As such efforts, investment in personal networks belongs to the Tullock[13] rectangle in the standard rent-seeking diagram.[14] With an addendum. Such a rectangle could constitute a pure transfer, which is efficient from an economic point of view, when the competition for monopoly is effectively stopped by an autocrat. I suggest that most of the time in Russia this is not the case because waste occurs in the form of networking and its economic consequences.

An approximate list of what goes into the Russian Tullock rectangle is as follows: networking, political contributions, promoting and ownership of media, keeping a bureaucrat on an unofficial salary, remodelling government offices 'for free', selling new apartments at a discount to government agents who permitted the construction in the first place, accessing government funds, or government bail-outs. This raises the question whether the benefits of social networks outweigh their adverse effects. I will demonstrate that the latter are greater. While connections help get things done, they have the following very significant side-effects.

Waste comes in terms of resources not spent on other more productive activities from a society's point of view, and in terms of additional costs to society in the future. First of all, there is not just one dictator, who can be an efficient redistributor in theory, but there are *many* competing redistributors at various levels of bureaucracy.

Second, once an able 'networker' acquires a position of control, there is nothing prohibiting him from abusing his connections further. Suppose X becomes owner and/or a manager of a car factory. His business plan fails and the factory is on the verge of bankruptcy. If his connections are good (and most likely they are, otherwise, he would not have obtained the factory), he will have access to government funds, just like a state-owned and operated enterprise would. The government will stand ready to bail him out, and will look the other way when the tax day comes. Hence, there exists a double cost to society. With the government involved in such a way, non-economic forms of competition become most advantageous.

Third, with a strong hand in power there will clearly be some government takings, and there are costs to renationalization and subsequent redistribution. This will be costly not only in monetary terms, but also in terms of undermining trust.

Fourth, connections make reforming activity a lot more expensive. Tollison and Wagner (1995, p. 385) point out that even a passively acquired monopoly will be defended if the monopolist feels that he could stop the reformer. They suggest that only an overwhelming force, such as a despotic regime, could reform successfully. But in Russia even though there is no shortage of despots, even they fall foul of the networking. As long as the monopolist feels he can get the government on his side by abusing connections, the resistance will raise the cost of reforming above negligibility. This is unless the reform is meant to favour another group. Then it will depend which group offers a higher bid. In any case, this is clearly a cost to the well-being of the whole society.

To sum up, Russia has been lacking horizontal-level macro integration. Numerous strong ties are clustered; too few weak ties are bridges. To the present day, rent seeking sustains a large part of Russian society, which is supported by a flexible and viable network of vertical connections. Many important exchanges took place (and continue to do so) between actors with different levels of power. The political economy of Russia does not provide for 'the more widespread conditions under which the actual use of power is restrained so that power unequals can function effectively in their daily relationships' (Powers, 1985, p. 64).

The scale of networks that is witnessed today was not always there. Centuries ago, strong ties were exploited primarily in relations between individuals and the government. Vertical networks, based on differences in power, gained a strong foothold from the beginning. Horizontal networks, based on relationships of agents of equal social status, had limited importance.

This set a path for networking in the future. Connections permeated mundane daily routines, such as purchase of food, and in this sense they reached a culmination point during the Soviet period. Because of overwhelming shortages, in the absence of effective markets, everyone had something to offer for exchange, if trust and secrecy could be ensured. Both vertical and horizontal relationships brought in mutual benefits, vertical being the primary system and horizontal the secondary system.

Post-Soviet networks are not radically different. Those who were well positioned in vertical networks usually retained, or in many cases gained and legalized, their power, status and income. Many of the horizontal network agents were not so fortunate. However, personal connections are persistent and still thriving on many levels.

The fact that personal networks in Russia are so viable implies not only that they are self-reinforcing, but also that they have somehow achieved an efficient form of organization. I propose that there are a number of factors effectively preventing their disintegration.

First, they are decentralized, which allows for greater independence of individual agents and for more complex networks. Second, horizontal networks, which usually institute healthy norms in a society, have been overwhelmed by the vertical networks. The weakness and isolation of horizontal clusters stems, perhaps, from the fact that, historically, networking secured mostly underground transactions. And while this is no danger for the vertical ties, it prevents horizontal clusters from growing.

Third, the costs of breach are high. Janet Landa (1994) identified that the Kula ring economy developed its ring structure to raise the costs of defecting – none of the members of the Kula ring would continue doing business with the cheater.[15] One-time or small-scale cheating is no doubt common in Russia, but there are two factors that stop it from spreading. Although there is no spatial factor (like in the Kula ring economy) to take advantage of, there is a psychological one. The members of network personally identify with one another and thus prevent dishonesty – it is much harder to betray a person you have a history with.

The second factor is that there is little or no competition between the illegal providers of goods or services in vertical networks. For instance, members of industrial networks are usually limited in their choice of suppliers or government officials; similarly, small business is assigned a local tax inspector. This, for sure, facilitates unilateral cooperation and prevents cheating on the part of the lower links in the network. The 'monopolist' in this case is at an advantage and could cheat, but since ties sometimes facilitate underground transactions and always take time and effort to establish, the 'monopolist' usually honours the agreement. In the Soviet period, networks were so complex and specialized, and shortages were at some point so overwhelming, that even a lower link could offer a connection that the 'monopolist' did not have.

Fourth, networks rely on and reinforce social norms, which are more persistent than policies. This allows agents to adapt to differing political and economic circumstances successfully, and makes the networks viable through the changes as drastic as those of 1917 or 1991.

Fifth, Emerson (1972) suggested that networks are embedded in broader contexts, for example, in exchange. In Russia it is the other way around – markets are embedded in social networks – which at least partially explains their persistence.

The sixth factor is the uncertainty of the environment. Relationships are invested in to solicit reciprocity; the weaker the tie the lesser probability of reciprocity. If the environment is highly uncertain, then we can expect that people will invest more in strong ties as opposed to weak. Higher uncertainty about the future implies a denser network, stronger ties and greater investment in relationships; the opportunity cost of being an outsider is too high.

NOTES

1. This line of research has been complemented since by the empirical analysis of interpersonal relationships; for a summary, see Granovetter (1983); and also by the work of Burt on structural holes or the social structure of competition where Burt investigated 'how competition works when players have established relations with one another' (1992).
2. Putnam (1993a, pp. 168–9) gives an example here of Mexican rotating credit associations. For another discussion of social capital and how interpersonal networks facilitate cooperation, see Smith (2002).
3. Wintrobe states, 'The simplest explanation for the legendary shortages characteristic of Soviet-type systems is that the shortages create rents, the distribution of which is controlled by the Communist party, which can then use them to garner political support' (1998, p. 152). I do not believe, however, that the shortages, and networks, which were used to take advantage of the shortages, were intentionally created and sustained by the party. Purposeful creation and administration of such a thing requires knowledge that central planning does not have. To me it is a spontaneous, though not an unexpected outcome of the system.
4. Boettke (1993, pp. 130–31) believes that democracy is not a necessary condition for liberalism. But authoritarianism promotes primarily vertical networks and disjoint horizontal, which are not enough to generate and sustain impersonal trust necessary for markets.
5. Richard Ebeling (pers. com., 1997).
6. Peter Boettke (1993, p. 69) writes, 'the Soviet economy was not a centrally planned economy radically different from any other economic system witnessed in history. It was over-regulated, abused and distorted, but it was, nevertheless, a market economy'. I am very reluctant to stretch the definition of a market economy that far, although I agree that markets operated in the Soviet Union. The 'propensity to truck, barter,

and exchange' aided by the crooked system of personal connections did not constitute market economy in the USSR. Nor does it now, even with an addition of a few half-way implemented liberal reforms and lip service to democratic values.

7. See Chapter 7 in Wintrobe (1998, especially p. 149).
8. There is a different point of view. Shleifer and Treisman (2004) call Russia a 'normal' economy in the sense that it is no different from other countries trying to implement liberal reforms and that it is entitled to its share of stumps and falls. I would have agreed if those stumps had moved wealth-generating activity of the population from network-ing into competing in the market. For a brilliant rebuttal, see Maly (2004). Shleifer and Treisman's claim that Russia ended the 1990s as a normal, middle-income capitalist economy is also open to questions. Standards of living in contemporary Russia are discussed in Chapter 9 in this volume.
9. Originally this point was made by Tullock (1998), who wrote, 'a powerful king sells the monopoly privilege in a manner designed to avoid competitive waste and takes the rent-seeking outlay as a personal transfer. There is no waste in such a transaction', see http://www.thelockeinstitute.org/journals/luminary_v1_n2_p2.html.
10. The term was used by Krueger in a 1974 article.
11. As it is pointed out in the article, 'Tsarist Russia already developed a kind of neo-mercantilist economy before the Russian revolution. The new Soviet rulers reallocated the monopoly rents, but otherwise needed only to modify the existing mercantilist system to serve their own purposes' (Boettke 2001, p. 147).
12. Money alone, though increasingly important nowadays, still rarely secures a monopoly right in Russia. Government officials who usually distribute monopoly rights cannot do so legally and openly, therefore bidding requires connections. Market monopoly would be the traditional example, but really any position of power, especially in bureauc-racy, can be successfully auctioned off. These positions include tax inspectors, police, construction inspectors, administration, directors of trade complexes, both public and private and so on.
13. The 'Tullock rectangle' is the profit rectangle, area directly under the Harberger trian-gle, which is the standard loss to society under monopolistic conditions. The rectangle may have to be added to the potential loss of welfare under monopoly. In Tullock's words 'Rational entrepreneurs should be willing to invest resources in attempts to form a monopoly until the marginal cost equals the properly discounted marginal return. Under certain assumptions . . . the competitive outlays to establish a monopoly will exactly equal the present value of the profit rectangle. The winning firm of course will secure an above-normal return on its investment, exactly offset by the losses of those who fail to secure the monopoly' (Tullock, 1998).
14. Peter Boettke (pers. com., 2004).
15. More details in Landa (1994, Chapter 7, pp. 141–70). The Kula ring is a ceremonial exchange system in one of the provinces in Papua New Guinea. The system spans 18 islands. This exchange is differentiated from market exchange (barter) and is used to reinforce status. Participation is not automatic; people buy their way in. The rules of gifts and counter-gifts are very complicated; the system is based on trust since rules are difficult to enforce legally. Higher status, which is achieved through successful offerings, guarantees a higher level of privileges in the other form (market) of exchange.

PART II

The Pre-revolutionary Period

3. The dominant role of the state in governing economic and political affairs

Part II of this book examines the rise of vertical networks throughout the pre-revolutionary period, weakness of civic institutions and resulting relative economic backwardness of Russia. The dominant role of the state in the economy, social attitudes within Russia and the peculiar social and economic position of the merchants resulted in hierarchies being more important than market mechanisms in the allocation of resources. The timing of the rise of the Tsarist state and the dominant role it played thereafter in governing economic and political affairs were the two principal reasons why the institutions of civil society never grew out of infancy while hierarchical networks became the ultimately powerful tool in official and informal relations during the pre-revolutionary period.

Why did the state become and stay strong and the civil institutions weak? Geographical factors are usually treated as leading candidates to present an explanation. Patterns of migration and exogenous factors, such as invasions and neighbouring cultures, are next.[1] However, it is undeniable there is some role of chance that combines all these factors at a crucial point in a people's history in such a way that a path is set for the future.

THE ORIGIN OF THE SLAVIC STATE, THE ROTA AND APPANAGE SYSTEMS IN KIEV RUS', THE TATAR-MONGOL YOKE AND THE RISE OF THE MUSCOVITE STATE

The review of literature leaves many details of this period unclear, but it is not my purpose here to solve the historical debate; it may never be solved. For instance, there is disagreement about when exactly the Vikings appeared among the Slavs. There is no question though that they did.[2] For the whole period covered in Part II, data in economic form are scarce. Though data in physical form can be found, the difficulty of compilation still leaves some gaps, and statistical analysis is not the purpose of this book.[3] Instead I try to analyse how the interaction of Russia's geography, the state policy and social norms produced particular economic outcomes.

Defence was one of the most important functions of the Slavic state; and the reason for creating the Muscovite state was first and foremost military. In addition, the split between the southern and the north-eastern Rus' as well as the circumstances of the colonization of the north-eastern territory cleared the path for political authoritarianism rather than for independent local self-government.

The Slavs most likely knew a different form of political organization before the Vikings were summoned. There are two points of view among the historians. The first one, which originated with a German scholar Schluezer and was later supported by the Russian historians Karamzin and Solov'ev (1959, 1960), maintains that before the second half of the 9th century, that is, before the Vikings came, the territory bound by Novgorod in the north and Kiev in the south along the Dnepr river had been populated by isolated warlike tribes, who had no idea how to govern or to be governed (Solov'ev, 1959, Book I, Vol. 1, p. 108).[4] This point of view has some support from the *Ancient Chronicle*.[5]

The second point of view, proposed by Russian historian and archaeologist Zabelin ([1876] 1908, [1879] 1912), maintains that the counting point should be almost as early as the times of Herodotus, and that before the Vikings were summoned in the middle of the 9th century the Eastern Slavs had already begun to form an alliance. Some contemporary foreign chronicles document that a short-lived alliance existed as early as the 6th century.[6] Moreover, we can reasonably speculate that in the trading towns of the southern Rus' *veche* (a meeting of all free males, mostly the men of local political and economic importance, for instance, merchants and large landowners)[7] had existed before the Vikings; otherwise *veche* would not have had that much leverage over the princes in the beginning of their governing careers.[8]

Kliuchevskii reasons that even though the ruling elite – the Vikings and their armed retinue – was recognized by the local population, passed a genealogical right to power, collected taxes and represented the land's military force, it was nevertheless only a temporary ruling elite. Even the princes viewed themselves as such, hence, their cooperation with the towns' *veche* and the towns' elected leaders, for instance, chiliarch or *tysiatskii*. The reversion of power back to *veche* when the princes were engrossed in family disputes in the 11th and the 12th centuries is one example. Another is that there were cases when princes were banished from towns by *veche*. In addition, the rules of the rota system of governing – in which the throne was passed laterally from brother to brother until the fourth brother and only then to the son of the oldest brother – did not enthrone any one prince in any one town. The princes moved around.[9] Thus, the civic institutions of the Slavs did not weaken suddenly and the state did not grow strong overnight, nor was a powerful state imposed by force. It was a gradual process, the main steps of which I describe next.

After its rise as the trade and political centre of Kiev Rus' or Rus'[10] in the 9th century, Kiev subdued the neighbouring Slavic and aboriginal Finnish tribes step by step. If a common interest (commerce in this case) and military force were the conditions under which the Russian state formed (Kliuchevskii, 1956, Vol. 1, pp. 147–9), the latter seemed to bear more weight. Located at the crossroads of main merchant routes, Kiev had an advantageous position for trade; at the same time this geographical position made it vulnerable to invasions. This necessitated the presence of a protective military force, which later became the political elite.[11]

There is not enough evidence to conclude that the Vikings' presence and position reflected the backwardness of the Slavs at the time. Although the Vikings might have been more advanced in military organization, quicker at taking initiative and venturing further in the pursuit of profit, this alone does not explain their relative superiority in trade and social organization. A Viking prince – a leader in times of war and an administrator and judge in times of peace – could have been just a third, allegedly impartial, party to conflict resolution (Solov'ev, 1959, Book I, Vol. 1, pp. 128–9, 222–3). The rule of the Viking princes and their armed retinue (*druzhina*)[12] was only a small step on the way to a more pronounced state power – at the time they neither imposed their own customs nor abused their power in any other way but rather 'became gradually absorbed into . . . a class socially akin to them – namely, the class of merchants who were also men-at-arms' (Hogarth, 1911, Vol. 1, p. 60).[13]

Although it is a significant fact that only under the leadership of foreigners[14] Slavic tribes organized into one polity, it is not meaningful to talk about a powerful state in Russia until the unification of princedoms under the rule of Moscow towards the end of the Tatar-Mongol Yoke (see below). In Kiev Rus' the princes still counted themselves as members of the same clan or stock, considered themselves temporary leaders and accepted local ways rather than imposed their own. Therefore, they ruled regions in turn according to the rota system, which ensured that the oldest relative in the family governed a prestigious town first[15] and were also subject to exile by *veche*. Constant turnover prevented the princes from viewing a particular town and its principality as their private property. As the family grew bigger, the princes quarrelled more and more about the order of turn, especially for prestigious commercial centres such as Kiev. Many, like Andrei Bogoliubskii, moved to the north-east and built their own towns to rule.

The colonization of the north-east brought the rise of the princes' power[16] and the decline of *veche*. The circumstances of this migration had far-reaching consequences for the relationship between an individual and the state. The population that moved north-east was, by and large, peasant. In addition, already declining Kiev fell completely under the Tatars. Without the main merchant centre, and with the trading routes interrupted, there was no longer a unifying economic interest; and the merchant class that supported it lost its political influence.

The peasant population of the north-eastern Rus' had very different – and relatively low – economic ambitions. It sided with the princes in their fight against *veche*, where it could still be heard.[17] In this political void the north-eastern princes came to view the land where they had settled as theirs to own. This proprietary attitude was reinforced by the fact that this time land was colonized under the princes' auspices, that is, they were masters of the territory first, not invited rulers. At this time we find evidence of hereditary transfers of land (Kliuchevskii, 1957, Vol. 2, pp. 29–30), and features of the appanage system, in which each principality was linearly passed from father to son.[18]

The legacy of the Tatar-Mongol Yoke (1236–1480) was the expansion of the centralized Muscovite state,[19] which crushed and subordinated the remaining small merchant element (Baron, 1978) and the whole population as well. Centralization, and the subordination of individual initiative to the wishes of the state, was necessarily a key factor to survival. The Moscow prince, Ivan Kalita, used the Khan's help to subjugate other princes; in return he promptly collected the tribute for the Golden Horde.[20] As Moscow acquired more and more political power (and safety within the borders of its influence), the population of other princedoms gravitated towards Moscow. Kalita's rule brought the long-strived-for break from the Tatar extortions and mass executions (Solov'ev, 1960, Book II, Vol. 3, p. 242). Simply a consequence of autocracy, this fact notwithstanding swayed the popular sympathy towards absolute rule. This tendency can be clearly traced to around the middle of the 15th century, which is also when Russia began to be viewed as a nation-state.[21]

The new political status, broader – and more vulnerable – geographical boundaries reinforced national defence as the state's main function. The southern, western and even south-eastern borders were constantly under attack. Out of 90 years (1492–1582), for instance, not less than 40 were spent at war (Kliuchevskii, 1956, Vol. 2, p. 118), out of 70 (1613–82) 30 years were spent at war sometimes with more than one opponent simultaneously (Kliuchevskii, 1957, Vol. 3, p. 126).[22] (Appendix A at the end of this book contains tables of Russian wars through the 18th century.)

While the population had to rely more and more on the state's protection, the Moscow prince began to entertain the idea that he not only owned the land, but the people as well. This led to a firm expression of the divine origin of the prince's power by Ivan III towards the end of the 15th century (Kliuchevskii, 1957, Vol. 2, pp. 126–7), and popular acceptance of it.[23] The title 'Suzerain Prince of Moscow' transforms into 'Tsar of all Russia' (Solov'ev, 1960, Book III, Vol. 5, pp. 144–5 and Kliuchevskii 1959, Vol. 6, pp. 137–9), though with a short and insignificant relapse during Ivan IV's rule who called himself 'Moscow prince' at one time but entertained powers far greater than suggested by this humble title.

The strong need for the state's safeguard from the outside provided just enough justification to open the back door to a dominating state presence in domestic affairs, such as administration, taxation and so on. The merchant class, formerly the main participant in deciding domestic and foreign affairs, had lost its political voice by the time the administration of the Muscovite state was being formed. A new, potentially powerful class emerged comprising boyars of various ranks, who were either former princes of small principalities or their retinue,[24] in other words members of the court hierarchy. This was a class of people who did not possess any professional skills and who traditionally lived off the tribute from their lands or service pay from the Moscow prince.

During the appanage years, boyars simply hired themselves out and could choose at any time to change masters. After the Muscovite state grew stronger, but not until a few centuries had passed since the appanage period, the boyars and commoners as well were finally compelled to stay put. The boyars were given a title, so now it was status based on heredity – a position in the social hierarchy – that determined one's position at the court (Kliuchevskii, 1957, Vol. 2, p. 144).

This was reflected by the system of *mestnichestvo*, from Russian *mesto*, which means 'place'. This system assigned a rank at the court based on lineage rather than personal qualities. There were ways to calculate such position arithmetically. Perhaps, it could be best described as relational hierarchy because the same person did not always keep the same rank.[25] For instance, count A could be captain in a military unit X, but become major when transferred to unit Z because count B, whose family stood higher on the genealogical ladder, had already taken the rank of captain in unit Z. This system built a hierarchy of power among the higher ranks of aristocracy; the perks distributed among members were controlled by the Tsar. This way, the Tsar had political and financial control over the class that had the greatest potential to oppose his power.

Gradually the same principle was applied to the lower ranks of nobility (gentry or *dvoryane*) and then to all who served the state. Still, *mestnichestvo* as applied to the higher nobility was a nuisance for the Tsar because recognition of pedigreed boyars interfered with the establishment of his absolute power. Therefore, later *mestnichestvo* was abolished and pedigreed clans substituted by lower ranks of servitors – gentry. But the principle of hierarchical ranking stayed.

As expected, over the years there was tension between boyars and the Tsar,[26] but, curiously, boyars never entered the arena of the real political power struggle. Even after a number of them had been beheaded and a great deal more had been exiled, they always acted in consort with the Tsar when it came to decisions concerning the nation. That is, they let the prosecution happen. While the Tsar had popular support, boyars had the military force on their side. The Tsar also had only a handful of supporters at the court. Knowing apathy of the general population towards politics and inability to act effectively in large groups, it is somewhat surprising that boyars did not attempt a coup d'état.

Perhaps, their fear was too great and their own organization too weak. Unlike Western Europe, Russia knew no form of contract that could be enforced through a third party. For example, during the appanage, if a boyar was unsatisfied with how the agreement of service was fulfilled, he could leave the prince. But that is *all* he could do, because the terms of an agreement could not be disputed and mediated. Even then members of his family were often mistreated and his possessions taken away. The authority was above the law.

Constant threat of invasions from the outside of Russia's borders, and the need for a larger administrative system within, pressed for a yet quicker centralization of power. There was no time for reorganization of formal institutions, and the principles of the appanage system survived in a centralized Muscovite state. The relationships between princes and population during the appanage years had very far-reaching consequences. An appanage prince enjoyed little public authority. There existed an economic but not a political relationship between him, boyars and black peasants – living on black, taxable as opposed to white, non-taxable, land (Pipes, 1974, pp. 47–8). 'It is for this reason that one can speak of Russian statehood acquiring from the earliest a decidedly patrimonial character; its roots lie not in relations between sovereign and subjects, but in those between seigneur and the bonded and semi-bonded working force of his domains' (ibid., p. 48). Just like an appanage prince, a Tsar viewed Russia as his personal estate (Kliuchevskii, 1957, Vol. 2, p. 332).

There was little concern from below – from the local self-government – about law, order and well-being of the Russian society. There was even less concern from above. In fact, as far as efforts of building a cohesive society went, ever since the Vikings came to rule there existed 'an unusually sharp gulf between rulers and ruled', Pipes (1974, p. 34) notes. 'The Kievan State and Kievan society lacked a common interest capable of binding them: State and society coexisted, retaining their separate identities and barely conscious of a sense of commitment to one another' (ibid.). This relationship was only to be reinforced through the centuries to come. For a Tsar, the courts, the police, even partially legislation were simply venues for collecting dues for the state. He hired agents from the population to collect trade, court, marriage and other tolls, and these agents automatically became part of the administration – a quite elaborate prototype of a later-day bureaucracy.

Practically every decree of a governor-general (*namestnik*) instituted additional tributes to the treasury; in this sense, regional administration was only managing taxes and had little to do with administering the law, effectively solving civil disputes, or providing public goods. Hence, this position of a governor-general was called *kormlenie*, in Russian meaning that the governor was literally feeding off the governed (Kliuchevskii, 1957, Vol. 2, p. 335; and 1959 Vol. 8, pp. 78–9).

Bureaucratization proceeded quite rapidly. Already by the end of the 16th century Kliuchevskii notes no less than 30 different government agencies in Moscow (Kliuchevskii 1957, Vol. 2, p. 341). The majority of them were dedicated to the state administration and management of the Tsar's personal needs and those of the court. There were very few agencies dedicated to the provision of public goods. Out of the existing ones some were very small, like the pharmaceutical or printing departments; others served the needs of bureaucracy, like the postal department (Kliuchevskii, 1957, Vol. 2, pp. 342–3).[27]

The process of centralization is in theory opposed to the evolution of self-government. In Russia this relationship is rather complicated because autocracy used the latter for its own purposes. Russian local self-government with its elected representatives was no more than a hub in the central administrative apparatus. Elders (*zemskie starosty*) collected direct taxes. Indirect and other taxes (customs, for example) and exploitation of the state property, such as production of spirits, salt and fish farming, were given to representatives 'in good faith' (*na very*). This meant that localities elected representatives to collect taxes from such ventures – work that yielded no direct financial compensation. These representatives vouched their personal property for good performance.

In addition, the electorate carried a financial responsibility as well (Kliuchevskii, 1957, Vol. 2, pp. 366–7; 1959, Vol. 8, pp. 98–100; 1959, Vol. 6, pp. 414–15) – the so-called collective responsibility (*krugovaia poruka* is the Russian term). New expenses were readily covered by new taxes out of the Russians' pockets. The purpose of self-government from the start was limited to serving the state, and there was no chance to voice opposition because elected representatives did not serve the needs of their elector-ate. Therefore, it is not surprising that *sobor*,[28] a representative assembly gathered in Moscow at the call of the Tsar, was an obedient puppet in his hands. Representatives came to Moscow not to voice the opinion of their electorate, but as servants of the state.[29]

Thus, responsibility before the state conveniently replaced civil respon-sibility.[30] Classes in Russia differed not by their rights but by their obli-gations to the state. There were those who defended the state and those who worked for the state, that is, fed the soldiers. There were soldiers and workers in Russia, but no citizens (Kliuchevskii, 1957, Vol. 2, p. 397).

It is important to note, before I proceed further, that historians have yet to agree on the degree of state intervention in the early period of the Russian state. In the 16th and 17th centuries, for instance, contemporary foreign observers stated that 'Russian government was excessively involved in economic enterprise' and that it hindered private business through exten-sive regulation. Others, for example historian Pokrovsky, say that rise of commercial capitalism was primarily due to the rise of the merchant class in the 16th and 17th centuries. The truth, as I shall attempt to show, probably lies in between, and this debate does not diminish the relevance of govern-ment involvement in the Russian market place.[31] For instance, though the state is documented as a 'price-taker' in the 17th-century statistics, its control over domestic markets and foreign trade is undeniable because of its major role in factor markets (Hellie, 1999, pp. 628, 636–45). Even if, according to McKay (1970), the state did not intervene into the economic development of the late 19th/early 20th century, except for a major public relations campaign to lure foreign capital into Russia, the individual rep-resentatives of the government still had a great deal to do with who got the concessions, as I shall attempt to show.

STANDARDIZATION: DEFINING ESTATES, TYING TO LAND AND EFFECTS ON INTERNAL LABOUR MARKETS

An all-encompassing dictator (in McGuire and Olson's 1996 terminol-ogy)[32] in an ideal world would like to know exactly his subjects' where-abouts, what they own and by what means. This would ease taxation and the provision of public goods. Happy with the state's care, the subjects would create more wealth, contribute more to the treasury, make the dic-tator richer and in turn increase government provision of various goods, services, infrastructure, military protection and so on. This idyllic situation did not and could not happen in Russia.

That is, the second part of this scenario miserably failed. And the first part could not come close enough to its ideal. Despite the fact that the Russian state had relatively extensive knowledge about the residence and property[33] of its subjects and that it had great control over the flow of financial capital and over social organization, both external and internal pressures handicapped its ability (although not always its desire) to provide for economic infrastructure. Continuous wars, sometimes on several fronts (Appendix A provides war tables), territorial expansion, which required a large bureaucratic apparatus and modernization of the economy, which was thought to be the task of the state – all drove the treasury into perpetual deficit. These pressures came about incessantly, so that the surplus of funds could never be accumulated, but the deficit could only be covered by tax increases.[34] As a result, many policies, packed with wealth-creating incentives, had to be reverted or left unfinished. The expectation of a large mismatch between what was promised and what actually happened was justified every time new policies were attempted. Naturally, the general distrust of the state increased when this happened.

The Tatar Yoke left the north-east of Russia in social and political disarray. The Muscovite state matured before the society did.[35] Consequently, the state created some of the society's institutions and influenced the formation of others. Hunting for additional revenue, the state made the practice of assigning legal status from above the norm, and cases of corporate bargaining for status and rights were few.[36] Legal status should have become 'a function of residence, occupation, and way of life whereas Russian law tried to make residence, occupation, and way of life a function of legal status' (Jones, 1977, p. 428).

This is important because individuals strove first and foremost for status in a hierarchical network. Entrepreneurship of an opportunistic kind, such as networking, crowded out entrepreneurship of an economic kind. Second, the state constantly meddled with local administration and civic institutions,[37] shaping them in such a way that they would first serve the needs of the government and only then, if at all, the needs of a locality. For instance, the subjects were recruited to work, often for free, as state agents. Levied on the community as a whole, taxes reinforced and in some cases imposed a system of mutual responsibility. This system integrated well where communal ownership existed, but conflicted with individual ownership as in the case of freeholders.[38] Third, all reforms were barrels with false bottoms: policies directed at improving public welfare hardly delivered any improvement for an average person but were instead full of concessions to interest groups and provisions to safeguard the state finances.

As the territory grew disproportionately faster than the capacity of the bureaucratic apparatus, it became clear that, for revenue-raising purposes, the government must split the population into well-defined groups, choose an easily identifiable taxable unit and fix it to land so that the subjects could not escape the dues. The process was by no means clean and swift, nor was it confined to any particular social group (although enserfing of peasants is the most obvious step because of their large numbers).

Social rigidity became paramount in the 16th and 17th centuries. First, all the subjects had to be accounted for. In 1646 the state conducted a mandatory census of the taxable population. Upon its completion the population was assigned into three main estates: those who served the state either through military or office career, town – *posad*[39] – residents and agrarian population.[40]

The gentry were given land tenure conditional on their service to the state, although service obligations without land tenure had already existed for a century (Kliuchevskii, 1957, Vol. 2, pp. 226–7).[41] They were also made accountable for their serfs: a landowner conveniently turned into a state supervisor responsible for law and order in his estate and for tax collection in the peasant commune (Kliuchevskii, 1957, Vol. 3, pp. 184–5).[42]

Town residents were the only category allowed to engage in commerce and industry. All others who had property in towns had to sell it – peasants could only trade in towns from a wagon and were not permitted to own or rent shops. This provision was hardly enforceable, so concession remained a concession on paper, as much as the treasury would have liked to benefit from increased wealth of the townsmen. At the same time civil liberties of town residents were restricted.[43] A decree of 1658 stated that townsmen who left their residence without special permission were to be punished by death; even those who married out of town were prosecuted (Kliuchevskii, 1957, Vol. 3, p. 161).[44] '[T]he natural mobility of the townsman and merchant, who might find better opportunities for his special craft or trade in another location, revived the interest of remaining townsmen in returning such runaways to their legal residences'.[45] Some individuals, who were still hard to place in any one particular category, continued to evade taxes for the time being.

Peter the Great's reforms over half a century later abolished the intermediary classes (Kliuchevskii, 1958, Vol. 4, pp. 93–4, 100). Thus, social status became hereditary (Pipes, 1974, p. 87). All individuals, from nobility to serf, were limited in their ability to move between social classes, change professions or places of residence. Advancing from the very bottom or even from the middle of the hierarchy to its top proved extremely difficult unless one served the state needs.[46] Those who pursued wealth creation through economic entrepreneurship were turned into state agents indirectly – the collective responsibility among small communes of artisans, townsmen and so on ensured that they watched and reported those neighbours who concealed income or moved. An ingenious, though not an especially planned move, it mitigated lack of official agents and corrupted institutions of the still infant civil society.

SERFDOM

The effects of government policies of the middle 17th century are usually considered quite devastating when applied to the agrarian,[47] especially the enserfed, population. However, as Pipes (1974, p. 144) rightly notes, before the emancipation serfs accounted for only 37.7 per cent of the population.[48] The question then becomes whether the institution of serfdom affected socioeconomic opportunities for the other two-thirds of the population.

The answer is that it did because serfdom permeated many vital institutions. First of all, there were about as many state peasants[49] as there were serfs (ibid.). State peasants were bound to land, much like the serfs; they were also regulated by the commune, bore collective responsibility before the state, were limited in their ability to move about the country, were obligated to provide recruits for the army and to perform public services, such as maintenance of roads and bridges, for free (Mavor [1925] 1965, Vol. 1, p. 259).[50]

Serfdom had such pronounced effects because pre-revolutionary Russia was by and large rural – in 1678 the population was estimated at 10.5 million, 9.6 million out of which were peasants (Pososhkov, 1987, p. 29); at the Third Census (1762–66) *bonded* peasants were 14,800,000 or seven-ninths of the total population (Mavor [1925] 1965, Vol. 1, p. 192);[51] in 1797, 96.4 per cent were rural, in 1897 agrarian population constituted 112,700,000 or 87.4 per cent of total population (Riasanovsky, 1968, p. 263). Just before the 1917 revolution, four-fifths of the population was officially classified as peasants (Pipes, 1974, p. 141).

The institution of serfdom affected other social groups as well because the whole system was built around it:

[T]he general result of the expansion of bureaucratic administration during this period, especially at the provincial level (where gentry estates had been created and had been given general administrative functions), was to make gentry domination over the peasants ever more encompassing. Serfdom was, in fact, the "law of the land," and all State institutions – the courts, the schools, the army, the tax system – were all organized in accordance with it. (Emmons, 1968, p. 42)

The institution of serfdom handicapped labour mobility, formation of the industrial class, merchant class, independent institutions of self-government, and ultimately, free markets. Therefore, the investigation into the origins of this institution will shed some light on the causes of Russia's relative economic backwardness.

Unfortunately, detailed statistics from this period are sketchy, and written accounts by peasants of that time simply do not exist.[52] From the quite variable and often contradictory social portrait of the peasantry[53] several common features of peasant life can be traced through most of the accounts.

Historically, peasants were dependent on their landlords. As the colonization of the north-east proceeded, peasant families settled with the permission of large landowners on their land and took loans from them, either in money or in kind because a peasant usually did not have enough income to sustain even a single family household (Kliuchevskii, 1957, Vol. 2, pp. 300–302). Since hardly any peasant earned enough to pay back both the loan and the rent, they typically bound themselves to the landlord for life. Rarely better off than their parents, children honoured the same arrangement.

Various government provisions restricted peasants' movements, although they could leave one landlord for another around a certain time during a year. Gradually abolished, but even while it existed, this privilege allowed peasants only to change one master for another.[54] Serfdom occurred earlier in practice than on paper. Government decrees provided that runaways be returned and pay a penalty.[55] But until the 1640s agreements between landlords and their tenants were a matter of their private business. Gradually though, an alarming (for the state) tendency emerged – peasants started selling themselves into slavery.

Slaves (*kholopy*) were an inconvenient category of the population because they bore no responsibility before the state, while indebted peasants still had to pay taxes. The right to sell oneself into slavery (ironically the only right to exercise freedom that a person had) was prohibited.[56] The state had changed the nature of even this most minimal of contractual obligations in Russian society both through official law (1597) and by encouraging informal hierarchical practices.

In the appanage period all contracts between free persons could be terminated, specifically, a contract between an indebted peasant and his landowner-creditor could be terminated before the agreed deadline, if the peasant paid off the debt. Once the nature of servicemen's obligations to the state became permanent and hereditary, they thought it only just that the nature of peasants' obligations to them be the same.[57] Peasants had been subject to landowners' arbitrary power before, but after the decree of 1649 their conditions were closer to those of former slaves. The majority owned nothing; even the equipment belonged to landowners.[58] Nowhere did peasants own the land that they worked.

The unifying motive for the peasant commune *mir* was not land but a collective financial duty to the state – *tiaglo*. The commune divided the land between households on the amount of labour force in each household. Taxes were assigned proportionally to the size of the plot, but not according to the expected crop, which depended on the quality of soil. A peasant family could not refuse the plot, no matter how poor its quality. Thus, the incentives for productive cultivation were adversely affected in the village, as were the incentives for the efficient application of peasant labour elsewhere.

It is true that in spite of regulations, peasants continued to work as artisans and to trade their produce and crafts in towns, most of the time illegally or by working under the protection of tax-exempt landowners. But how far did they go? Only a handful travelled and settled far away; the majority did not travel beyond a nearby town. Their social and economic connection to the village was never severed, and remained the main impediment to the mobility of this social group, which together with the state peasants, constituted the largest labour resource in the country.

As more and more factories appeared by the early 18th century, with labour supply falling far short of demand, the government saw no other way but to assign large numbers of peasants to permanent factory work. These new factory workers came from the state peasants – now called 'possessional serfs' – and became an inalienable property of the factory itself (Zelnik, 1968, pp. 161, 168–9).[59] This happened frequently, but the numbers here are less important than the fact of uncertainty, given that factory owners purchased[60] whole villages with little or no warning to the inhabitants.

Partially because peasants strongly preferred their traditional social role, partially because no institutions existed to ease the integration of peasants into urban life (ibid., p. 181), the newly fledged factory workers vehemently opposed their latest status. The peasant–worker tension prevented a class of industrial proletariat from emerging until the very end of the 19th century (Mavor, 1925, Vol. 2, p. 364), and even then most workers remained perpetual migrants between town and village.[61]

Eventually something similar to a village commune emerged in the factory as well. Initially, the employers imposed mutual responsibility among groups of workers, who themselves welcomed this practice. Peasants preferred to be hired into a commune of their fellow villagers (Wirtschafter, 1997, p. 148). The government too encouraged this practice for reasons of social stability. This 'urban commune' cushioned the transition to urban life in the short run, but reinforced the ties with the village.

In the reports of St Petersburg police, workers and peasants are rarely differentiated from one another; this shows that the official perception of them was also of at least very closely related categories (Zelnik, 1968, pp. 180–81).[62] Even the industry expansion was supplemented only by a quantitative rather than qualitative change in labour force (ibid., p. 181). The government, worried about social stability and scared by the revolutions of 1848 in Europe, was opposed to creating a skilled, educated labour force and reluctant to give workers a legitimate separate status.

In addition to being afraid of a new independent stratum, the government thwarted workers' participation in urban public institutions because it 'preferred a bureaucratic presence in the factory' (Wirtschafter, 1997, p. 154).[63] Even private efforts to develop 'institutional channels through which workers' grievances could be aired' were looked upon as counter to the state policy of paternalism, which treated factory peasant-workers as peasants (Zelnik, 1968, p. 184).

'Hyphenated' peasants (peasant-tradesmen, peasant-coachmen and so on) constituted over 30 per cent of St Petersburg's population in the decade after the emancipation (ibid., p. 187). In the 1890s, over 6 million peasants in European Russia engaged in off-farm work, but the majority preserved their ties with village and eventually returned. In addition, in the early 20th century as much as 65 per cent of workers and 65 per cent of factories were located outside urban centres (Wirtschafter, 1997, pp. 115, 133–4). Townsmen migrated to rural areas in search of work as well.[64]

In essence, the 'freely hired' labour, which constituted probably two-thirds of the workers by the 1860s (Mavor, 1925, Vol. 2, p. 368), were manorial serfs on quitrent, possessional serfs or state peasants, all of whom not only had major difficulties in changing their permanent residence and status but also wholeheartedly opposed the permanency of this change. This freely hired labour, especially manorial serfs, had a poor work ethic. Enterprising merchants accused them of theft and laziness (Kliuchevskii, 1958, Vol. 5, p. 98).

In addition, bondage to the land in effect slowed down internal labour markets and prevented more efficient land cultivation. Originally, the majority of the peasant population concentrated in the central region around Moscow due to the threat of invasions when the Muscovite state was formed. There, land was much less fertile than in the south, but the law of 1649 kept these lands overpopulated relative to land productivity, while keeping the lands in the south underpopulated.[65]

The Emancipation Edict of 1861 had very little enforcement power to change existing institutions.[66] As before, most peasants had no accumulated income to resettle elsewhere, as most land they toiled still belonged to the gentry. On average, nobility retained 45 per cent of the best land (Volin, 1960, pp. 294–5), that is, plots best suited for farming. Although there were significant variations between regions, in many cases peasants suffered reduction of land relative to what had been allotted before the emancipation.[67] The emancipated peasants held a total of 33,755,658 *desiatinas* (unit of measure) of land while the landlords held 73,163,774 *desiatinas*.[68] A heavy redemption price for land,[69] which exceeded its actual market value (Wirtschafter, 1997, p. 111), restricted their mobility even further. The property title to the plots was initially given to the commune, presumably to ensure the redemption payments, when ex-serfs bought the land.[70]

As a result, the peasant commune *mir* took over the fiscal responsibility. Because the main principle was one of unlimited collective responsibility of the whole membership, the pressure was directed at keeping peasants in the village. It was especially hard for the members to break away now since the government transferred police authority, which had previously belonged to landlords, to *mir* as well (Volin, 1960, p. 295).[71] The commune was now empowered with the right to grant and renew passports without which peasants could not legally travel. The number of long-term passports for extended leave was only an average of 59,200 per year in the period between 1861 and 1870. During the industrial expansion of 1891–1900 it increased to 184,500 per year. This was a small number given that emancipation left at least 4 million landless or poorly allotted peasants eager to work in industry (Gliksman, 1960, p. 312).[72]

The peasant commune was ruled by 'its more prosperous or more aggressive elements' (Volin, 1960, p. 296), but even those stood little chance of defending community interests before the local bureaucracy, which grew ever stronger in the second half of the 19th century. Instead of direct control by the landlords, peasants now answered to *mirovye posredniki* (mediators), who were appointed by the government from the list drawn up by local gentry, and to various government officials. Both of these had 'wide power of both formal and ad hoc nature over the organs of peasant administration' (Emmons, 1968, p. 46). The administrative partitions including several peasant communities (*volosti*):

> had to be created from scratch and their officials – elders, deputies, and judges – elected by the participating peasant communities. . . . Even though peasant officials were elected by the peasants themselves, from the government's point of view . . . they were regarded primarily as instruments for controlling and disciplining the peasants. They were the links that connected peasant Russia with bureaucratic Russia. (Emmons, 1968, note on p. 53)

Yet another circumstance precluding peasants from leaving the village freely was the joint family ownership of the peasant household. Under this form of ownership individual incomes flowed into one common pool long after those individuals worked and lived elsewhere.[73] Ties to villages hindered the division of labour, thus contributing to lower wages and inferior productivity.[74] A very comprehensive micro-study of peasant households by Kolle (1995) demonstrates that large peasant households, which often included parents and married sons with children, were quite common in the areas where agriculture remained a primary occupation after the emancipation. Where peasants supplemented with industrial income more actively there was a tendency to subdivide into smaller family units.[75]

The Russian peasant became a freer individual only after 1905.[76] The government abandoned its policy of supporting *mir* and encouraged transferring land to individual peasant households because in the commune a peasant had a right to land, but could not keep a particular lot forever; they also could not sell land. Still, about two-thirds of the peasant households were clinging to the commune in the decade before 1917 (Volin, 1960, p. 303), even though individual land ownership among peasants did increase.

The distinction between taxable estates was good for the treasury in the short run but bad for economic growth. By creating artificial barriers for individuals who wanted to change their place of residence, profession or social status, the state prevented the country's labour resources and entrepreneurial talent from being applied in the most efficient way. Even though several relapses occurred in this grand scheme of standardization (mainly because it was a trial-and-error process), these did not ease the circumstances of the majority in any significant way. The general direction of policies remained the same, and it always assigned more weight to the state's current financial needs.[77]

North-eastern Russia had little social cohesion from the beginning. Standardization had an unintended consequence[78] of alienating members of the Russian society even further. Such was the precedent for strengthening vertical (hierarchical) and weakening horizontal networks as the bureaucracy grew and agents began to exploit their positions in the system for their own private benefit.

URBANIZATION

Russian urbanization has not escaped some controversy in the historical literature, much like serfdom. Again, evidence on how many towns there were and what their population was is scarce,[79] and available facts are subject to individual interpretation. Macro data on urban growth alone provide no explanation for lame urban institutions and slow economic advance. Urban networks usually harbour the most socially and economically progressive elements of the population, who ultimately acquire political influence to set limits on the power of central government. Horizontal urban networks also nurture relationships between individuals and social groups that form institutions of self-government.

Russian urban centres, though in numbers and function similar to Western Europe,[80] had peculiar characteristics, which impeded the emergence of a politically strong bourgeoisie and the development of effective institutions of self-government. Here, I mean self-government independent from the state. Many institutions in Russia bore the name of self-government, but only due to the overall appearance. Their internal structure and a small degree of functional autonomy were not characteristic of self-governing.

First, Russian towns and townsmen had a special relationship with the state. Throughout the pre-revolutionary period, the princes and later on the Tsars perceived towns as a substantial source of revenue. This determined the vacillating policy of the government towards urban centres and uncertainty of the legal status of a townsman, which ultimately impoverished him. Second, the geography of towns, the absence of juridical distinction between townsmen and other social groups, and pattern of taxation influenced the specifics of internal trade relations, the development of artisanry and division of labour, as well as the formation of networks of civic engagement.

Usually, urbanization is positively associated with economic development. Most historians agree that urbanization in Russia had some degree of backwardness.[81] A closer look at the evidence demonstrates that in all likelihood the towns were quite numerous and relatively large,[82] but lagged far behind Europe in economic and organizational advance. In the 14th and 15th centuries there were about 68 towns, 29 of which undoubtedly had significant political and social importance as well as diversity of crafts and stone buildings (Sakharov, 1959, p. 128). Moscow in the 15th century had between 50,000 and 100,000 inhabitants, Novgorod may have had between 25,000 and 50,000.[83] In the early 16th century there were 96 and a century later 226 towns, climbing up to over 220 by 1650 (Hittle, 1979, p. 21).

Findings that Russia had more than 8 per cent of its population residing in cities by 1780 are quite convincing. Several administrative regions had even 10–15 per cent, while most regions had more than 5 per cent (Rozman, 1976a, pp. 77–9). According to Rozman, Russia before the 1800s was closing in on Western Europe in terms of urban growth (ibid., graph on p. 84) and in some other respects. He provides a very detailed study of urban networks between 1750 and 1800, and puts Russia in perspective with England, France, China and Japan. Russian towns functioned as administrative, political, military, fiscal and commercial centres.[84] Rozman's conclusion is that Russia was not backward after all, and *macro*-level numbers on urban growth support his hypothesis.

Pipes' take on Russia's backwardness is quite different:

> There is no indication that in the eighteenth century Russian cities gained in economic importance. Leading authorities on urban history believe that the extremely low level of urban activity, characteristic of Muscovite Russia did not change in the eighteenth century, largely owing to the steady shift of trade and industry from town to village. Nor did the population structure of the cities change. In Moscow of 1805, there were still three times as many peasant serfs as merchants. (Pipes, 1974, p. 216)

In addition, the urban population was spread very unevenly. The two Russian capitals came far ahead of other cities in population growth by the end of the 19th century, but already in the 16th century Moscow contained as much as one-third of all urban population (Blackwell, 1976, p. 301). In 1897, St Petersburg had 1,330,000 with additional 134,000 in the suburbs (Mavor, 1925, Vol. 2, p. 397). In the beginning of the 20th century there were around 120 cities (Thiede, 1976, p. 129); and the official urban population in 1914 was 15.3 per cent in European Russia (Wirtschafter, 1997, Note 142 on p. 133), although by comparison, the population of England was 50 per cent urban by 1850, and of the United States 20 per cent urban by 1860 (Blackwell, 1976, p. 306). Still, if Russian towns were not that dissimilar in major characteristics[85] to pre- and post-industrial towns of Western Europe, what was different?

As already mentioned above, the towns of north-eastern Russia varied greatly from the ones in Kiev Rus': the former were originated under the auspices of princes[86] and were looked upon as their patrimonial (*votchinal*) property;[87] they also lacked a larger influential merchant class and independence from the state urban institutions.[88] All those important urban functions that made them look like Western European towns – administration, collection of dues, court system, military defence, minting of coins, police – were in the hands of the prince (Hamm, 1976a, p. 24), and later in the hands of the Tsar.

Veche was gradually silenced during the period of the Tatar-Mongol invasion,[89] with a short rise during the 13th century, but a sharp decline in the second half of the 14th (Sakharov, 1959, pp. 203–20 and Solov'ev, 1960, Book II, Vol. 4, pp. 516–17). At this time the princes' power was already on the rise, but potential for urban economic growth had only started to accumulate. Throughout the 14th, 15th and 16th centuries townsmen had no self-government and no provision that they could be self-governed; they were regulated either by large landowners or by a prince's appointees (Sakharov, 1959, p. 223).[90]

Moreover, unlike Western European cities, artisan cooperatives (*arteli*),[91] institutions of urban governing and merchant organizations now evolved *along* with the nation-state (Hittle, 1979, pp. 11–12). Even the Soviet historians acknowledge that there were no guilds (*tsehi*) in Russian towns in the

14th–15th centuries (Sakharov, 1959, p. 143),[92] although *sloboda* – a settlement organized by a prince or a landowner with the incentive of privileges granted to the settlers of the *sloboda* – bore at least some resemblance to them.[93] *Tsehi* did not appear until much later and only due to the process of intensive centralization; that is, when Peter the Great created craft organizations 'to regulate artisans and incorporate them into the taxed population' (Wirtschafter, 1997, p. 131).[94]

The state needed townsmen: they provided by far the largest share of taxes.[95] But the government's choice of policies, by and large, favoured its own fiscal needs. 'The dilemma for the State in its relationship with the townsmen was to find a way to nurture the cities and increase the income from Russia's own urban milieu while both maintaining the support of other elements of Muscovite society and continuing to encourage and to expand lucrative foreign trade between Muscovy and Europe' (Miller, 1976, p. 38). A major influx of foreign merchants in the 17th century, for example, stymied attempts by townsmen to control the city (ibid.).

But throughout the 17th century, the town remained the main source of the state's revenue (ibid., pp. 34–52). Therefore, the reforms of 1649 made certain concessions to the townsmen:[96] they trumped ecclesiastical privileges by confiscating land, households and people from the church and monastic establishments. The state treasury gained as well: 10,095 town households were added to the tax rolls (ibid., pp. 41–2).[97] Even though several decrees (of 1658, 1677 and early 1680s) prohibited purchase of townspeople's property by tax-exempt population, they had no effect de facto. By the end of the 1680s, government recognized this fact openly and came to terms with tax-exempt entities and persons (ibid., p. 45), reneging on its promise to the *posad* population.

Another urban reform of 1699 promised to close the city doors to competition from Russians of other social groups and foreigners, but once again the enforcement of provisions was delayed and inconsistent (ibid., pp. 47–50). Instead, in 1745 peasants were legally permitted to trade (although in villages) a limited number of items. Further, in 1753–54 internal customs were eliminated, which greatly eased small-scale commerce and boosted peasants' competitiveness (Hittle, 1976, pp. 62–3). This blurred the juridical boundaries between social status and economic occupation even more. 'The city as a body of men enjoying rights not shared by the rural population is a phenomenon peculiar to the civilization of western Europe' (Pipes, 1974, p. 199)[98] and never occurred in Russia.[99] Maximization of the population's income on the one hand and maximization of tax revenue and central power on the other were incompatible goals in practice. Peter the Great appeared to allow for more autonomy through provincial reforms, but his goal was not decentralization. Instead the goal was once again – maximizing state revenue (Hittle, 1976, pp. 57–61).[100]

It is true that in the 18th century *posad* obligations diminished, mostly because no more agents were needed for internal customs points and because the state began granting contracts to private individuals outside *posad* for collection of liquor taxes – an obligation that previously fell exclusively on townsmen (Hittle, 1976, p. 63). But the city remained a service element of the state.[101] 'The State exercised ultimate control over the land on which the townsmen lived and worked; it established the dimensions and character of the townsmen's tax and labour-service obligations' (Hittle, 1979, p. 10).

Catherine II faced the nascent failure of this city service system: the city could no longer cope with the state's increasing needs. She found that there were simply not enough cities in the right places in order to take on the administration of ever-increasing territory and the growing population of the empire. She ordered some new cities to be created in prescribed locations and some suitable villages elevated to the status of a city (Pipes, 1974, p. 216; Hittle, 1976, p. 64; and Kahan, 1985, pp. 15–30). The result of this reform was as pitiful as the centralized plan for a decentralized administrative apparatus itself.[102] In 1775, the state split the mercantile population into two categories based on wealth – merchants and *meshchane*.[103] The reason again was to boost tax revenue. It shattered whatever informal commonality townsmen had through communal responsibility (Hittle, 1976, p. 65).

Uncertainty created by the state's vacillating policies promoted self-sustained existence. Townsmen supplemented with agriculture as much as peasants supplemented with trade; and both supplemented with works (*promysly*), such as hunting, cottage industry, fur trade, fishing, salt-works and so on. There is clear evidence of cattle breeding in towns in the 14th and 15th centuries (Sakharov, 1959, p. 139).[104] Even in the 1860s in more than half of almost 600 cities in European Russia the population engaged almost exclusively in agricultural work (Hanchett, 1976, p. 91). Investigation of the early 1860s revealed that in 30 out of 69 southern and south-eastern cities a significant proportion of income came from agriculture. Farming remained an essential feature of urban life well into the 20th century.[105]

Hittle notes that the great distance between urban centres prevented dynamic inter-regional trade and exchange and reinforced a self-sustained lifestyle. Towns were spread throughout the territory unevenly and far apart (1979, pp. 21–2).[106] There is no evidence in the 14th and 15th centuries that independent artisans produced for the market (Sakharov, 1959, pp. 133–4). Artisans working under the church auspices were exempt from dues to the Tatars, which attracted larger numbers into church artisanship, but church artisans still did not produce for the market (ibid., pp. 135–6).[107]

A Russian town of the 14th and 15th centuries was a centre of trade and exchange but not of production.[108] The same stands for towns of the 16th century, which Solov'ev calls 'fenced in villages' (1960, Book IV, Vol. 7, p. 298). The estate system of land tenure severely undermined the growth of urban population and specialization. The estates lured service people away from the cities into the countryside. Landed gentry preferred to hire craftsmen to work on their estates, so that a trip to the local town market would not be necessary. Thus, the *posad* was deprived of its main source of demand, which resulted in slow growth of urban industry throughout the 17th century (Kliuchevskii, 1957, Vol. 2, p. 240).

Throughout the pre-revolutionary period, townsmen generally fared better with commerce than with production. To give proper balance to internal factors, such as the role of the state, and the external, such as the Tatar Yoke, one must admit that the latter handed a severe blow to the organized production of goods. Handicraft requires that personal skills be continually transferred from artisan to apprentice (Sakharov, 1959, p. 202). This link was broken with the destruction of urban networks during the Tatar Yoke.

Weak division of labour produced no comparative advantage for Russia: there is very little evidence that in the pre-Muscovite period (the 14th–15th centuries) Russian artisans exported their products abroad (ibid., p. 171). In the following two centuries commercial activity was flooded by all categories of population, some operating under more favourable conditions than others. The *posad* commune faced further competition, which came from its own members.[109] Through commendation some of them shed their status as townsmen and were no longer responsible for taxes, but continued to pursue crafts under the protection of tax-exempt landowners, the largest of which was the church. These former townsmen continued to engage in trade and crafts and participate in a town's economy in all other ways, but the burden of dues was shifted on to the shoulders of the remaining members of the *posad* commune. Since the tax was levied on the community as a whole, the *posad* had to pay for those who left until the next census.[110]

Even if the cities' trade thrived, it was through commendation, while real independent commercial activity never formed.[111] This sort of an anti-city within the city posed a very serious competition based not on a market advantage but on a network advantage. It pushed more and more urban residents to evade their legal status and flee (Miller, 1976, pp. 36–7).[112] Serfdom inhibited population flow into the cities:

> The self-contained character of the estates populated by bonded peasants hindered the growth of towns, because the proprietors purchased little and the peasants almost nothing. The richer proprietors patronized the town merchants, but almost exclusively for goods imported from abroad. The development of miscellaneous manufacture for consumption within the country is thus in Russia a comparatively modern affair. (Mavor [1925] 1965, Vol. 1, p. 431)[113]

It is likely that after 1861 off-farm work increased because of cash and land shortage (Wirtschafter, 1997, p. 114).[114] But only by 1900 self-sustained existence was on the wane: by 1900 a peasant covered between a quarter and a half of his needs from farming (Pipes, 1974, p. 167). Only now there was a push either to use more land or to go elsewhere.

Urban institutions, both formal and informal, left much to be desired in terms of autonomy and efficiency. The state's involvement from the beginning created social fragmentation of the town community. Was there a *posad* mentality or a unified *posad* community? If most of the customs and traditions are not indigenous to a community, what sort of social cohesion can we speak about? The *posad* was a separate city quarter in the earlier years of Muscovite Russia. It is where the market place was situated and where artisans and merchants resided. But very quickly it became more legal than territorial unity because the state handed out land within the *posad* geographical location to tax-exempt persons. A prince and later a Tsar owned real estate in the *posad* as well. It should be noted that there were no private cities in Russia; all land was held conditionally, and really belonged to the crown (Pipes, 1974, p. 200).

The state conveniently blended the legal boundaries of the community to suit its own needs and the needs of interest groups. As a result, the *posad* 'had no intrinsic connection with the city', and many *posad* communes were situated in the countryside (ibid., p. 201). Horizontal networks were primarily based on communal responsibility for taxes. Thus, they were at most forced upon the people from above or at least associated with a negative duty.[115]

In the 18th century, in spite of all restrictions, the urban population grew from 3 per cent to over 8 per cent of the total population while the *posad* population remained constant at about 3 per cent (Hittle, 1976, p. 62). So the competition from other urban categories – including the unbeatable competition from foreigners, from the greatest merchant of Russia (the Tsar himself) and from other privileged members of the Russian society – increased, but the tax burden on the *posad* at least remained constant and perhaps even increased. The most successful members of the *posad* commune were left with only one alternative – to escape the *posad* ranks.

Merchants often entered the ranks of the bureaucracy, where they secured privileges for themselves in the same economic occupation but juridically ceased to be a part of the *posad* and share tax payments. Needless to say, such use of hierarchical networks fostered animosity between individuals of the urban community, as everyone was a potential tax shirker.[116]

Initially, urban administrative and commercial functions were disjoint. Later the government tried to combine them by imposing broader administrative duties on the elected representatives of the *posad*. For instance, since 1677 townsmen carried the responsibility 'for the audit of income ledgers for customs and tavern collections' (Miller, 1976, pp. 46–7). Since 1679 elected city elders were personally responsible for the collection of the household tax and its direct payment to the treasury (ibid.). But this integration only reinforced the vertical link between the city and the state, giving no real autonomy to the urban legislative and executive body (*duma* – after 1906 Duma became the name of the Russia's first elected parliament).

The arrangement where the population both paid and collected taxes 'worked against the development of any intermediate-level institution, such as a town council, that might harbor aspirations of its own' (Hittle, 1976, p. 55).[117] The urban society was socially fragmented, which prevented the formation of horizontal networks. There was no one institution where all the social groups were represented; instead, each social group was administered through a separate central agency – *prikaz* (ibid.).

Catherine II sought to create local town administrations by involving all estates, but the opposition her reforms were met with shows how well the estate distinction had been engrained in the mentality by the end of the 18th century. Besides, by that time rapidly growing bureaucracy had already overwhelmed local initiative (ibid., p. 66).

The municipal statute of 1870 gave more local autonomy to the cities, but even under this statute:

> the rights and duties of the mayor were defined in the statute in such a way as to create an executive officer with sufficient powers to restrain development within the duma of opposition to the central authorities. For example, no proposal could be discussed in the duma unless the mayor had been notified about it at least three days prior to the session and no councilor could speak in the assembly unless he had informed the mayor of his intention before the meeting opened. The duma itself had no right to override its presiding officer if he denied a councilor the chance to speak. If a mayor or the presiding officer failed to exercise these controls he himself was subject to State punishment. (Hanchett, 1976, p. 100)[118]

The sphere of a city *duma* activity, centralizing economic issues, was rather broad. However, its operational power was limited (ibid., pp. 102–4). The fact that police remained under the central state control significantly undermined the role of self-government in Russia (ibid., p. 106). As a link in the autocratic apparatus Russian municipal governments always had to carry out obligations imposed by the state. They had no freedom *not* to act on these matters (ibid.). The municipal statute of 1892 featured a counter-reformation to the limited freedoms granted in 1870 and proved to be long-lived.[119]

By the beginning of the 20th century, Russia's economic development was catching up with Western Europe, but the lameness of its institutions, and in particular, of its urban institutions, prevented it from doing so fully. The urban environment was clearly in a poor condition,[120] which mirrored the low income of the majority of its inhabitants. Germany, for instance, spent 'five times more per capita than Russia on urban amenities and services in cities under 100,000 and about four times more per capita in all her cities combined' (Hamm, 1976b, p. 185). While St Petersburg was spending 32 rubles per head, Vienna was spending 50, Paris, 60 and Berlin, 70 rubles. '[T]he budgets of Paris, New York, and London *each* exceeded the total budget of all Russian cities combined on the eve of the war' (ibid., pp. 185–6).[121]

The city governments were under an obligation to subsidize services of the state, and therefore, had little money to spend on urban development projects. For example, the statute of 1892 required city governments to pay the cost of quartering imperial troops. This together with other obligations consumed anywhere from a third to nearly the entire budget in many cities (ibid., p. 184).

The face of the 'new city' of the late 19th and beginning of the 20th century contained old (permanent) residents and an overwhelming number of migrant villagers, all in constant flux. Out of the old residents the number of impoverished artisans and traders were so numerous that in the end of the 19th century the St Petersburg police prefect said that only a quarter of them were 'more or less prosperous economically' (Brower, 1990, p. 66).[122] Ninety per cent of hereditary guild artisans were excluded from artisan society elections because they could not contribute a minimum payment of tax on their property.[123] The majority of wealth was concentrated in the hands of a very small group of urban propertied elite, including a handful of successful merchants (Brower, 1990, p. 69).

The government's extortionist fiscal policy, continuous involvement in social relations between individuals and zeal for regulation undermined urban economic potential and generated social fragmentation. Townsmen lacked 'firmly articulated and effectively defended personal rights' (Hittle, 1979, p. 14). The *posad* tried to secure its legal status by being the state's 'gofer'. The state's fiscal needs on the one hand and economic and political weakness of the *posad* on the other created interdependency, which was detrimental for the latter.

STATE INTERVENTION INTO ECONOMY

After the breaking of the Tatar Yoke in the 14th century, the economy had gradually, though unevenly, advanced in medieval methods and technology. From then on heavy taxes accompanied the life of Russian producers and consumers. In addition, the state controlled the most profitable ventures (Baron, 1978) and exercised the sole power to grant monopoly privileges to individuals, families and interest groups.

This exclusive control fell into the hands of Moscow princes by different means. Partially it was inherited from an older order of things, such as in the case of collection of dues, monopoly on foreign trade and state ownership of land. Partially it was acquired by force. But often a ruler simply announced his property rights over a natural resource, economic activity or method of production.[124] Because the population in north-eastern Russia was politically and socially more dependent on the princely power than in Kiev Rus', potential contestants usually remained silent.

In the 14th and 15th centuries the suzerain prince of Moscow already had a monopoly on salt mining and production (*solevarenie*). In order to repay the Orthodox Church's support of the princely power, he granted the exclusive right to trade salt and fish to the monasteries. Accordingly, town markets in the 14th–15th centuries were heavily dominated by the ecclesiastical powers (Sakharov, 1959, p. 147),[125] represented by such monasteries as Troitse-Sergiev, Kirillov Belozerskii, Ferapontov, Simonov and Spaso-Evfimev (Hamm, 1976a, pp. 22–3). Over the course of the next two centuries the state declared a monopoly on many other ventures, including quite importantly retail trade in spirits.

For a variety of reasons, such as supporting the military, the state actively engaged in industrializing the economy starting from the 18th century. The main goal of Peter the Great's economic policy was to boost the economy in order to finance a more aggressive foreign policy.[126] As a strong leader who had an expansionist vision for his country and no patience with an economically backward population, Peter initiated government-orchestrated and government-enforced industrialization and education. He did not expect people to respond to initiatives voluntarily. But in his mind the end was worth any means: factories were ordered to be built without calculations of their cost effectiveness.[127]

Russian entrepreneurship disappointed Peter. For many projects, for instance to build a trade fleet, no volunteers were found; yet other ventures went bankrupt because of poor management. For example, the White Sea fishing partnership founded by Peter's favourite Men'shikov could not stay afloat even after it sold fishing privileges to merchants at a price much higher than it had originally paid to the state (Kliuchevskii, 1958, Vol. 4, pp. 117–8, 125).

Usually Peter the Great built a factory at the expense of the state and then leased it on propitious conditions to, or often foisted it on, private entrepreneurs. Naturally, under such circumstances the industry was closely supervised, which limited free initiative on the part of managers, created yet another mandatory service for the state, and also produced a greenhouse environment for cooperation between the supervisors and the supervised – bureaucrats and entrepreneurs – thus, promoting hierarchical networks. Another serious problem for the development of industry was capital flight and capital waste. Seeing frequent arbitrary changes in economic regulation, people were afraid to invest. Peasants and factory workers buried valuables in the ground; others, starting from customs inspectors to the Tsar's favourites hid them at home or in foreign banks.

Thus, potentially useful capital was absent from turnover, which angered the government because it collected a 5 per cent fee on all capital return. Eventually it led to a law that encouraged informants to report those who hid money. But when the state managed to locate and confiscate these valuables, it did not invest them properly or in time.[128]

The pitiful state of government finances prompted yet another way to institute more taxes. The state ran out of ideas for new items to tax, so it decided to financially reward those who think up new dues, also known as 'profits men' (*pribyl'shchiki*) or 'devisors' (*vymyshlenniki*).[129] As a result, a tremendous amount of direct and indirect taxes, often consuming up to one-quarter of income, was levied on Russian producers.

There were over 30 different taxes during Peter's reign, some of them carrying high excess burdens: boot dues, tax on variety of headdress, tax on weights and measures, tax on horsehide-tannings, bathhouse tax, tax on leather, rent tax, tax on leasing housing, tax on firewood, tax on stove-pipes, tax on watermelons, nuts and cucumbers, tax on beards and moustaches, tax on Old Believers (see Notes 15 and 16, Chapter 5), marriage tax for the unorthodox (such as the Tatars and the Mordva), tax on fishing, tax on bees, tax on birth, death and burial (Kliuchevskii, 1958, Vol. 4, pp. 131–3).[130] And this is only monetary extortions; there were also dues paid in kind – bread, horses and so on (ibid., p. 145).

Most damagingly the state levied them without any notice, so that not only profit margins and for many, subsistence levels were shrunk, but also any kind of business and household planning was thrown off by the policy's unpredictability. The budget of 1724 reveals the pitiful state of the economy: most taxes were received from the soul tax[131] (53 per cent) and from government monopolies; income from independent private business was miniscule.[132]

Instead, entrepreneurship efforts went underground. Latov suggests that anti-government informal economic activity, which develops as a response to government monopoly, and usually utilizes social networks, first originated in Russia in 1652 with the establishment of the state monopoly on the retail trade of spirits. It was impossible to stop underground production. The first government campaign to expropriate moonshine casks (devices) was attempted as early as the beginning of the 18th century, but was apparently unsuccessful (Latov, 1999). Even monasteries in the 1720s and the 1730s undertook moonshine production for profit (Volkov, 1979, pp. 32–4).

Latov cites Polianskii on the fight against the 'undirected production' (*neukaznoe proizvodstvo*) in Russia after Peter the Great (Polianskii, 1983, pp. 167–220). This second campaign lasted for nearly 30 years (from 1737 to 1767) and was directed to stop the new wave of underground production, which now included everything from iron to various kinds of tinsel. This new wave was itself a response to the introduction of new monopoly privileges. To existing government monopolies (resin, potash, rhubarb, glue and so on) new ones were added: salt, tobacco, chalk, tar, fish fat, oak coffins, games like cards or chess (Kliuchevskii, 1958, Vol. 4, p. 134). Because of sheer numbers, this informal activity could not remain unconnected and free of corruption.[133] Little by little, small businesses developed *sviazi* (personal connections) with local bureaucrats, whereas larger ventures had already been bonded with federal government from the start.

After the unsuccessful attempt to trump the informal production some special privileges for monopolies were abandoned. This had an overall positive effect on the industry growth, including small artisans. At the beginning of Catherine II's reign there were 984 factories and workshops, at the end, 3161 (Mavor [1925] 1965, Vol. 1, p. 491).[134] But the fiscal deficit crept up after Peter's death, and the beginning of the 19th century saw a twofold increase of most taxes (Kliuchevskii, 1958, Vol. 5, p. 226).

Even though officially monopolies were now not encouraged, the areas of the economy that developed were the ones with monopoly-like markets or the ones with quick turnover of capital. The majority of industrial capital went into the exploitation of minerals and metal manufacture, which met little competition. Merchants preferred to invest in commerce where turnover of capital was quick, fearing high-risk long-run ventures. Landowners naturally preferred to invest in agriculture, as they had cheap labour at hand. Some of them invested in industry, but again, because cheap labour – serfs – was available. Large-scale industrial production in textiles, which faced competition from every peasant household, was, on the other hand, very poorly developed in the 18th century.[135] The percentage of urban population in trade cities as opposed to industrial cities shows that the latter lagged behind (Table 3.1).

Table 3.1   Percentage of total urban population in trade and industrial cities, 1859–1910

	Percentage of total urban population		
	1859/64	1897	1910
Trade cities	76.8	72.7	68.7
Industrial cities	23.2	27.3	31.3

Source: Thiede (1976, p. 133).

Even then, it was not the trade of the times of Kiev Rus'. Tea, cotton, iron and a few luxury items exhausted the list of imported goods (Mavor, 1925, Vol. 2, p. 363); local markets traded mostly produce and cattle.

In the post-Petrine period the share of state-owned enterprises in total manufacturing output diminished, but the state control over private enterprises increased. This led Kahan to conjecture (which I support) that, while endorsing that state regulation and state ownership are substitutes, policy-makers decided in favour of regulation, perhaps because they thought it less costly. The major areas of control included 'the requirement of accurate reporting and punishment for report falsification; control over size of operation; control over some sources of raw materials and labor; control over the functioning of establishments; control to stimulate growth of particular industry branches' (Kahan, 1985, p. 160).[136]

Despite Peter the Great's costly achievements pre-1860s' Russia displayed economic conditions unfavourable to industrialization.[137] Apart from issues with labour supply, the Russian way of life was still self-sustained. Even the nobles who lived in Moscow and St Petersburg in the winter months transported almost everything they needed from their estates (Mavor, 1925, Vol. 2, p. 363 and Hellie, 1999, pp. 633–4). So towards the end of the 19th century, the government once again engaged in rigorous stimulation of the economy: through the state bank it financed industrial enterprises and gave land and other production concessions to those who were willing to undertake the task (Mavor, 1925, Vol. 2, p. 365). The golden age of Russian industry was made by the high protective tariff, reaching its peak in 1891, government-sponsored banks, foreign capital and the railroad.[138]

The 19th-century industrialization remade urban landscape and the nature of production only in the Urals manufacturing towns. Other towns, where factories were often situated on the outskirts (Brower, 1990, p. 63), maintained their half-agricultural lifestyle. Mechanization of industry was still far from complete even towards the end of the 19th century: cotton-spinning factories in northern Russia had 25,000 power looms along with

20,000 hand looms (ibid., p. 64). Small workshops and cottage industry – *kustarnoe proizvodstvo* – were still the dominant source of jobs in most towns (ibid., pp. 64–5), although petty artisans and traders were not experiencing high profit levels.[139] The banking system could not accommodate them with loans for expansion and technological improvement.[140]

Railroad construction in the 1860s had an unequivocally positive effect on the economy (ibid., pp. 43–4, 47–52). It also rendered state urban planning obsolete. Land speculation based on the proximity to the railroad station now mastered the urban landscape (ibid., pp. 52–3). But the means employed in the railroad construction deserve a special note. The railroads were owned and operated by private companies that were subsidized by the government through low-interest loans. Most importantly, personal contacts that developed between the enterprising merchants of Moscow and high-placed government officials in the late 19th century had their foundations established precisely through the railroad project.

Initially, foreigners and foreign capital played a large role in the construction of the first rail line between Moscow and St Petersburg, but nationalistic-leaning leading Moscow merchants together with certain intellectuals engaged in a campaign to take over the Russian railroad. A complicated battle of interests ensued.[141] During this battle merchants had periodic though irregular personal contacts with government officials. In the end however, when they managed to secure railroad operation in their hands, those personal contacts became quite regular because the government officials voted on the ownership and dispensed credit through state-dominated banking system.[142] Evidently, in the decade following 1870 these contacts developed into more stable personal relationships as merchants became more experienced at intriguing among high bureaucrats at court (Owen, 1981, p. 59).

The tariff war that followed the Crimean War (1860s) was also a very important step in the development of hierarchical networks, specifically, in the relationship between the business elite and the government. In the 1850s and the 1860s free-trade ideas started becoming more and more popular among Russian intellectuals. One of the proposals was to lower import tariffs, which captured sympathy in the Ministry of Finance.

Moscow merchants, especially textile industrialists, successfully fought off the free-trade threat during two episodes, in 1864 and 1867. Every possible means was utilized – official petitions, personal appearance of the most articulate merchants in front of the State Council, alliance with heavy industrialists of St Petersburg. But in the end, victory was secured through the personal efforts of merchants' intellectual allies. These allies were Slavophiles – members of the 19th-century intellectual movement who wanted Russia to develop according to its early traditions and who vehemently opposed any Western influence.

Many Slavophiles held high bureaucratic posts or exercised influence at the court. One of them, Prince Dmitri Obolenski, was directly in charge of the Department of Foreign Trade. Babst, who was economics teacher to Grand Duke Vladimir, secretly presented the protectionists' appeals in a favourable context to the future Alexander III. He arranged a meeting between Chevkin of the State Council and the industrialists, and also two meetings with the Crown Prince Alexander.

As a result, a 'special group' within the State Council was formed to decide the fate of the tariffs. It consisted of Chevkin, the Crown Prince, Finance Minister Reutern, two former ministers and Nebolsin, head of the Tariff Commission. Its decision was to stop the downward trend in import tariffs.[143] To guard their interests in the future Moscow merchants established the Russian Industrial Society (RIS) under the protection of government officials (Owen, 1981, pp. 64–70). All would be well, since the Russian bourgeoisie for the first time in its history gained independent representation and influence, if not for the character of this organization's demands. This society very quickly became the leading proponent of protectionism and state-sponsored economic growth.

The RIS promoted creation of two other organizations, which replaced manufacturing and commercial councils and which membership now included not only bureaucrats but also merchants (ibid., p. 68). The fact that merchants had to sit together with bureaucrats on the councils probably reinforced their ties. Such a big threat as changes in tariff policy made the merchants overcome their apathy to the state policy and instead become active makers of it. For the first time they entered the political arena not as individuals, but as a large interest group.

Indebted to the autocracy for their economic prosperity, merchants were hardly interested in reforming the political institutions to create a freer civic society. Though demanding abolition of state regulation in the industry, they depended upon the state's military force to conquer new territories to expand markets, on the state's financial support and on protective tariffs. The idea of laissez-faire was culturally and practically remote, but the promise of Finance Minister Reutern to consult merchants on all state economic policies from now on was sure to bring real benefit (ibid., p. 70).

Industrialization could not occur in Russia spontaneously. Finance Minister Witte believed that Russia was stuck in a vicious circle – since supply of entrepreneurship and knowledge grows with industry and the development of industry is dependent on entrepreneurship and knowledge (McKay, 1970, pp. 10–11). All the building blocks of economic advance were either controlled or impeded by the government. When industrialization as well as urbanization, which lacked a causal connection, did occur in Russia, they were processes orchestrated by the state. Russian industrialization failed to direct capital to support urbanization. As a result, the needs of a growing urban population could not be accommodated by either central or local governments, which had enough trouble covering other expenses such as war. Rapid industrialization and urbanization (similar to those in Europe) took place only towards the end of the 19th century.

ALL-ENCOMPASSING DICTATOR: AN INEVITABLE FAILURE?

As a rational personal wealth maximizer an all-encompassing dictator assists his subjects in creating wealth by building the economic infrastructure. With the exception of a slight positive trend in the end of the 19th and at beginning of the 20th century, Russian Tsars failed to do so. Risking giving support to the notion that Russians are fatalists, I must nevertheless acknowledge the deterministic nature of some of the circumstances that led to this failure.

Essentially, from the start the Muscovite state had to run a war economy.[144] To give away economically important territories, or to lead an expansionist war, were the choices every Tsar faced. Nomadic incursions of the southern and eastern borders were a persistent threat; foreign states in the west and in the north-west were always looking to grab a piece of territory. Some Tsars settled for peace treaties but most chose an offensive strategy because Russia lacked trade outlets in the west and in the south and because the war policy did not meet any significant resistance from the population.

Naturally, the war economy had profound implications on the social and economic relations among individuals and between individuals and the state. As Kliuchevskii notes, the population was dispersed by the government so as to create rings of military defence around Moscow (1959, Vol. 6, pp. 407–8 and Appendix B of this volume). The estates were formed and assigned obligations with the idea of exerting the maximum amount of service to the state. Rights were the last thing the legislature was concerned with in the face of demanding tasks of national defence. The state imposed more financial duties without knowing how they would be paid. The hardships of average people were blatantly ignored (Kliuchevskii, 1958, Vol. 4, p. 55). Surprisingly, the formula 'to demand the impossible [from the population] in order to receive most from the possible' (ibid., p. 133) worked.

War was very costly. Even under what many consider positive changes in domestic and foreign policy under Peter the Great, ten years of war cost a

14 million population more than 300,000 men or about 2.1 per cent (ibid., pp. 67–8).[145] Out of 35 years of Peter the Great's reign only one was a year of continuous peace; and out of the rest there were hardly 13 months of peace in total (ibid., p. 50 and Appendix A of this volume). The army was now completely financed out of state budget. By 1725 it consumed no less than two-thirds of yearly income (ibid., pp. 69, 142). Just two years of the Seven Years' War under Catherine II cost nearly as much as the yearly budget (Kliuchevskii, 1958, Vol. 5, p. 315).

It is usually counterproductive to implement domestic reforms in war time. But this is exactly what happened in Russia. Peter the Great left the social and economic reform incomplete.[146] He thought the bureaucratic apparatus would complete it, but creation of a highly centralized administration with discretionary powers also laid the foundation for a police state and an auspicious environment for corruption. Bribery had already been deep-rooted in the system by the 1700s, and bureaucracy actively stalled progressive reforms. Peter the Great, who was trying to crack down on corruption, was once told by a prominent member of the Senate that if he had removed everyone who took bribes, there would be no one left in the administration (Kliuchevskii, 1958, Vol. 4, p. 197).

The organizational flaw was that the administration was arranged according to the appanage principles (Peter viewed courts as its integral part),[147] which produced divisions and subdivisions in arithmetical progression. Once the basic institutions were in place, only a complete dismantling of the system would get rid of red tape and corruption. Some Tsars realized that this would be too costly; others simply lacked the nerve or the vision. Among the two common systems of the day – corporate-aristocratic and bureaucratic – the latter took the upper hand in Russia pretty quickly.

Nikolai I expanded the federal administration even further, leaving local administration the same size. The size and the instability of this enormous bureaucratic structure inevitably led to inefficiency (ibid., pp. 253–5), which thwarted any reforms a Russian dictator might have tried to implement. The paperwork containing orders went from the capital into provinces. The amount was so huge that no one could hope to execute all the orders. This undermined the law and gave a lot of arbitrage to individual bureaucrats, whose main task now became to 'clear' the paper. In 1842, 33 million cases, written on at least 33 million sheets of paper, were still waiting to be cleared.[148]

The Tsars' personal traits and the ideas that influenced them were another factor that determined the direction of policies. Some were little educated, others were educated excessively, but the practical application of their knowledge often produced poor results.[149] Peter the Great, for instance, acquired skills in Europe but not social norms. He underestimated the importance of the evolution of civic institutions and misunderstood the nature of a functional law (ibid., p. 26). He thought that law and order in Europe was channelled through and supported by representative bodies of government.

His answer was to make similar bodies mandatory in Russia. For example, he ordered military garrisons stationed in towns to elect representatives to serve as local police. The resulting abuse of power was unprecedented (ibid., pp. 97–9). Although initially well-intentioned, his public policy ultimately failed. For instance, he still viewed the purpose of landed gentry as military and administrative servitors to the state, and simultaneously agricultural managers. The military function dominated in his view; therefore landowners were spread thin between the other two roles. Disarray of domestic agricultural production inevitably followed (ibid., pp. 75, 91).

Rulers with good intentions had to battle a host of problems, such as reconciliation of the interests of the gentry with the interests of the state, fighting high-end corruption, as well as impotence of the Russian legislature and 'self-government', and public neophobia.

Catherine II, for instance, was influenced by the French ideals of the time, wrote much about the wrongs of slavery, and probably recognized the economic benefits of free labour. However, she never thought that emancipation was feasible, and, in fact, she actively increased the number of serfs by presenting lands populated by the state peasants to her favourites (Kliuchevskii, 1958, Vol. 5, pp. 142–3).[150] Her Western European inclinations conflicted with the Eastern European reality of the country. Realizing that an effective legislative body was needed, Catherine ordered the establishment of the Emperor's Council. But soon she dissolved it, fearing that the powers of this legislative body would compete with her own (ibid., p. 71).

Local self-government and representative legislation was also a pure farce – the main task of governor-general was to block any local legislative initiative that went contrary to Catherine's own *Nakas* (ibid., p. 91).[151] Many laws were outdated and ineffective. The legislative body was simply a mockery: the committee, summoned in 1700 to update the old code, produced nothing for 20 years! Instead, drunken senators engaged in fist fights (Kliuchevskii, 1958, Vol. 4, p. 196).[152] The problem with the Senate was also that it carried a dual function: it was both a legislative and an executive body (ibid., p. 175). And as much as Russian autocrats reorganized this institution, for all practical purposes there was no separation of powers in Russia.

Up until the middle of the 19th century, if Russia had a progressive Tsar, he turned out to be more progressive then the public. As a result, the reforms were never finished and most of the time executed improperly. Just as the princes earlier lacked skilled masons, the Tsars lacked knowledgeable and skilled people to put reforms into action.[153]

Many times the next ruler actively tried to undo the policies of his predecessor. For instance, Empress Anna abolished many of Peter the Great's policies. Next, Peter's daughter restored them, Catherine II's husband reverted again, Catherine II restored, and her son changed the direction once more. Then in the 1840s and the 1850s Nikolai I, fearing political instability, resorted to some measures against industrialization and growth of the number of industrial workers (Owen, 1981, pp. 20–21).

Oscillating reforms send mixed signals to economic agents and ultimately generated apathy towards public policy. When the proper wealth-creating incentives were given, inertia among the population prevented a good or quick enough response to these incentives. Then, pressing needs of the treasury usually forced the state to step in and make into an obligation what had been presented as a choice before. Not only did Russians get limited assistance from the state in building economic infrastructure, they also faced severe limitations on their freedom should they desire to do it themselves.

In no small part did the hierarchical networks undermine the power of an all-compassing dictator. The Russian Tsar had to believe in people not in institutions. A weak Tsar depended on his supporters to stay in power; a strong Tsar depended on them to realize his ideas. Together with wars such dependency put a limit to the all-encompassing ability of the Tsar.

NOTES

1. While wars between other states, economic crises, natural disasters and even trends in philosophical thought that entered Russia from abroad, undoubtedly influenced foreign and domestic policy, the scope of this work prevents me, unfortunately, from discussing these external factors. One of the most detailed sources on this in Russian is Solov'ev (1959, 1960).
2. My main source in Russian on Russia's history before the 1917 revolution is Kliuchevskii (1956, 1957, 1958, 1959). I turn to Solov'ev (1959, 1960), Karamzin (1988–89) and others for additional details.
3. As much as it would be interesting to me, it is too large a topic to cover together with social network analysis. Statistical data alone do not tell very much about, for instance, the foreign entrepreneurial process (McKay, 1970, p. 39).
4. Pipes (1974, Chapter 2) also believes that the Slavs did not know any social and political form of organization at the time.
5. One has to remember though that the writer of the *Chronicle* was quite possibly biased. He wrote in the 11th century when the Viking dynasty had successfully integrated the Slavic tribes into one unity, and he probably overestimated the dynasty's positive influence of the last 100 years. Because of this bias, evidence from contemporary foreign travellers should be given more weight; and such evidence indicates that the second

theory is more accurate. Solov'ev (1959, Book I, Vol. 1, Chapter 4) though believes the *Chronicles*.

6. For details on the two theories and on the evidence, see Kliuchevskii (1956, Vol. 1, Lecture VII, pp. 102–13); and also Kliuchevskii (1959, Vol. 8, Lectures I–II, pp. 396–408).

7. A *veche* was a 'meeting of all free males, usually called by a prince or other townsmen, in a market place . . . to discuss and vote on such matters as the invitation or expulsion of prince, war . . . or the issuing of mutual agreements between the prince and the town' (D'yakonov, cited in Hamm, 1976a, p. 27). More details in Kliuchevskii (1959, Vol. 6, pp. 185–6).

8. Pipes (1974, p. 31) disagrees.

9. For more details on relationships among the princes, between the princes and the local population and on the systems of governing, see Kliuchevskii (1956, Vol. 1, Lectures XI and XII, pp. 169–206).

10. 'Rus'' or 'Russia' did not actually refer to the Slavic tribes. The Viking tribe that was summoned to rule Novgorod and later spread to Kiev and ruled it was called Rus' (Kliuchevskii, 1956, Vol. 1, p. 167).

11. This transition of administrative power was smooth. From Kliuchevskii's interpretation of historical documents, it appears that, besides the defence need, economic interest unified Slavic tribes under the rule of the suzerain prince in Kiev. It also appears that the princes and their armed retinue were not only the defenders of this economic interest but also its major promoters. Merchants often had to travel through hostile territory. They either had to have skills and armour to defend themselves or had to hire someone else to do it. Most Slavic merchants had military skills, but perhaps not as advanced as the more experienced Vikings. An armed retinue under the leadership of a prince was nothing more than a group of armed merchants. A prince collected tribute from the Slavic tribes in winter, and then his men traded it with the Byzantines and Greeks in summer (Kliuchevskii, 1956, Vol. 1, pp. 153–8; also Pipes, 1974, p. 31).

12. For a detailed definition, see Kliuchevskii (1959, Vol. 6, p. 145).

13. Solov'ev (1959, Book I, Vol. 1, p. 272) supports this as well. Pipes (1974) disagrees with this on p. 31, but supports it on pp. 32–3.

14. Solov'ev proposes an explanation as to why the Slavs did not generate their own leaders. At the time the Vikings were summoned, the Slavs had not yet organized into clans, that is, the leadership was *not* passed from father to son. Therefore, no one stock could advance ahead of the others. That is why Slavic princes disappeared after the Vikings' rule had started, and that is why there were not many Slavs among the Vikings' armed retinue and among the boyars (Solov'ev, 1959, Book I, Vol. 1, pp. 223–4).

15. Thus, upon the death of a father, his brother, not his son would govern. The son would get a remote town in the meantime, awaiting the death of his uncle.

16. Solov'ev (1960, Book II, Vol. 3, pp. 8–9) points out that we rarely observe the term 'suzerain prince' in the annals of Kiev Rus', but in the *Chronicle* of the north-east it is used very often.

17. For instance, Rostov and Susdal' *veche* (Kliuchevskii, 1956, Vol. 1, Lecture XIX).

18. For details on how rota (*ocherednoi poriadok*) was substituted by the appanage system (*udel'nyi poriadok*), see Kliuchevskii (1956, Vol. 1, Lectures XIX and XX). Pipes (1974, p. 32) believes this distinction is unfoundedly prompted by a Hegelian way of thinking dominant in the 19th century, and that in practice there was no working system of succession. For a good critique of the term 'appanage', see Pipes (1974, p. 42).

19. For details, see Kliuchevskii (1957, Vol. 2, Lecture XXI).

20. The rule of chance in these events is stunning. Ivan Kalita was an ingenious leader. Advantageously positioned for trade, Moscow was at the same time a remote principality given to those who had little chance of ruling a more prestigious town. That turned the efforts of Moscow rulers to building its commercial and political importance. Kalita used the Khan's army to fight off the other princes while the Horde was

still strong. Then, the Horde weakened just at the right time to leave all the power over the Russian principalities in the hands of the Moscow prince. It was also remarkable that Kalita and then his descendants for several generations happened to be strong and cunning leaders who met no comparable opposition, so that the struggle between principalities, especially between Moscow and Tver', was resolved favourably for Moscow. For more details, see Solov'ev (1960, Book II, Vol. 3, Chapters 5, 6, 7 and Vol. 4, Chapters 1 and 2).

21. For details, see Kliuchevskii (1957, Vol. 2, Lecture XXV) and Solov'ev (1960, Book II, Vol. 3, Chapters 5 and 6).

22. Whole villages along the southern border were turned into military garrisons. In the period from 1654 to 1679 at least 70,000 of the able work force were conscripted. Two military campaigns of 1654–55 cost as much as the yearly treasury income in 1680 (Kliuchevskii, 1957, Vol. 3, pp. 215–16).

23. Notes of a German ambassador to Russia (Kliuchevskii, 1957, Vol. 2, p. 137). When Ivan IV left Moscow to test his power, a decree was read to the Muscovites who gathered in the main square. The decree stated that the Tsar was not angry with the people but that he could not stand treason from the boyars and left the throne for good. Immediately all daily activities were stopped, shops and offices closed, all entertainment halted. In terror and desperation the Muscovites asked the *Mitropolit* (Patriarch, head of the Russian Orthodox Church) to beg the Tsar to come back. This, the Tsar, of course, did and followed up with the massacre of treacherous boyars (Kliuchevskii, 1957, Vol. 2, p. 174).

24. For a more detailed description of this class, see Kliuchevskii (1959, Vol. 6, pp. 145–7).

25. On *mestnichestvo*, see Kliuchevskii (1957, Vol. 2, pp. 146–56).

26. For details, see Kliuchevskii (1957, Vol. 2, Lecture XXVIII).

27. Until the late 19th century, government did little more than provide defence; more details in Hellie (1999, Chapter 22).

28. Kliuchevskii calls *sobor* a 'meeting of the government with its agents' (1957, Vol. 2, p. 382).

29. On the history of representative assemblies in Russia and their social composition, see Kliuchevskii (1959, Vol. 8, 'Sostav predstavitel'stva na zemskih soborah drevnei Rusi', pp. 5–112). *Sobor* gathered from 1550 for 150 years but at very irregular intervals. Kliuchevskii notes a very unrepresentative social composition of *sobor* (ibid., pp. 36–7). In fact, he draws a parallel between *sobor* and a prince's council with his armed retinue, as *sobor* overwhelmingly consisted of servitors (ibid., p. 72). *Sobor* was summoned by the Tsars' orders, except for once, and the number of representatives was extremely volatile (Kliuchevskii, 1957, Vol. 3, pp. 192–3, 195). Over half of the representatives were illiterate (ibid., p. 194).

30. In Western Europe by contrast, the equivalence of Russian *sobor* reconciled differences between classes, not fulfilled the administrative needs of the state.

31. A topic taken up by Baron (1978).

32. A leader of roving bandits in an anarchic environment who can hold a territory will find it advantageous to become a public-good-providing autocrat. He monopolizes theft, declares a constant theft-rate, provides a peaceful environment and public goods, which gives his subjects an incentive to produce and leaves him with more income than under competing theft interests (McGuire and Olson, 1996).

33. Eaton describes cadastres and censuses of the Muscovite state. They appear to be very detailed; bureaucratic scrupulousness is shown very well in the example of Tula (Eaton, 1967, pp. 54–69). Of course, there is no way to know how accurate the censuses are.

34. Currency debasement and, later on, the excessive use of the printing press. If deficits were incurred because of expenditures on infrastructure, first-rate public schooling and the like, some economists might find it warranted. But Russia's budget deficit was wasteful spending, such as bureaucratic expansion or concessions to the Tsars' favourites. Military expenditures in some cases covered territorial expansion; whether it brought long-term increase in productivity is arguable.

35. Interestingly, the word 'society' (*obshchestvo*) appeared only in the 18th century (Pipes, 1974, p. 71). This idea by Pipes is probably borrowed from Kliuchevskii. On the evolution of this word, see Kliuchevskii (1958, Vol. 5, p. 359).
36. Isolated cases of corporate bargaining perhaps were *mestnichestvo*, town residents' (*posadskie liudi*) exclusive right to trade in 1649 and serfdom as a concession to gentry. Even then, *mestnichestvo* was abolished, trade regulations were moot in the face of illegal economic activity and concession to gentry was rather a pre-emptive strike on the part of government.
37. For purposes of fiscal stability, for instance, it introduced commune in villages where it had not existed before the Emancipation Edict. There are some examples of how communal ownership among the peasants was encouraged by the state earlier (Mavor [1925] 1965, Vol. 1, pp. 275–6). In northern Russia in the 18th century the government essentially rewarded thriftless state peasants and punished the frugal ones by prohibiting sale and mortgage of land and imposing repartition (ibid., pp. 278–9). The state also encouraged thriftlessness among bonded peasants by requiring the landowners to support them during the years of inferior crop (ibid., p. 222).
38. Freeholders were originally given land as a pay for service and were the only category among the agrarian population to hold land (except in forests) in individual ownership and to practise inheritance laws. Under the system of Russian tax collection it was hard for this form of ownership to compete with peasant commune: by 1851 already half of freeholders adopted communal ownership (Mavor, [1925] 1965, Vol. 1, pp. 294–6).
39. The term originally defined a quarter populated by artisans and traders, a lot of times adjacent to the fortress (*kreml'*) and located outside the city walls. It also contained a market place. Later it came to mean urban residents obligated to pay taxes, loosely translated as townsmen.
40. For more details, see Kliuchevskii (1957, Vol. 2, pp. 300–308 and Lecture XXXVII Vol. 3, Lecture XLIX); for a complete history of Russian estates, see Kliuchevskii (1959, Vol. 6, Lectures I–XXII, pp. 276–463); also Pipes (1974, pp. 98–106).
41. Hellie believes that the middle service class drove the enserfment of peasants to a large degree. The middle service class was becoming obsolete in the face of gunpowder revolution and were anxious to elevate their social status by insisting on abasing the peasantry. For more details and an illuminating discussion of psychology behind this, see Hellie (1971, Chapter 14). Given how hard it would be for a large interest group to coordinate efforts in the 17th century, the force of the state was probably more important, although I acknowledge that both forces were at work.
42. Reforms of Peter the Great in the beginning of the 18th century made all landowners servitors.
43. This was started even earlier. Because appanage princes earned a lot more profit from taxing townsmen, they prohibited commendation (*zakladnichestvo*) among them already in the 14th and 15th centuries (Sakharov, 1959, p. 193).
44. On prohibition to settle on ecclesiastical land and engage in agriculture, see Kliuchevskii (1959, Vol. 6, p. 420).
45. Examples of petitions to this effect are in Miller (1976, p. 44).
46. In this relaxed caste system everyone sooner or later hit a ceiling of his sub-hierarchy. A townsman could become a merchant, and a merchant through his service could become gentry in rare instances, but there are no cases of a merchant becoming a boyar (Kliuchevskii, 1959, Vol. 6, pp. 442–3; and also Demidova, 1987, p. 55). Alexander Men'shikov, who jumped castes and will be discussed later, is one rare example I can think of; the nature of his relationship with Peter the Great would be a partial explanation.
47. Review of extensive literature on the conditions of townsmen and peasants does not warrant a conclusion that one group was significantly worse than the other.
48. In addition, Pipes (1974, pp. 147–8) believes that the system of rent (or *obrok*; the majority of peasants in northern and central provinces were on *obrok* by 1860) was relatively painless as opposed to corvée (*barshchina*). Mavor's position is different:

'The servitude of the peasant [on *obrok*] was not so obvious, yet it was servitude just the same. . . . It is clear that under *bartschina* custom determined the number of days which might be exacted, and the law determined the maximum; but law and custom alike had no control over the *obrok* payments, and thus these were frequently proportionately higher than *bartschina*. Moreover, arrears from *obrok* might pile up from year to year. . . . [I]n *bartschina* economy the landowner ran the risk of the season, while in *obrok* economy the peasant ran the risk of it' (Mavor, [1925] 1965, Vol. 1, pp. 419–20). *Obrok*, which forced a peasant to supplement their income elsewhere, also stalled the understanding of advantages of intensive agriculture on the part of both peasants and landowners (Kliuchevskii, 1958, Vol. 5, p. 155). Besides, in the 19th century the use of *barshchina* instead of *obrok* drastically increased (ibid., pp. 286–7).

49.   State peasants belonged to the crown.
50.   Worried about rural unrest, the government gathered reports on the eve of emancipation. One such report contains a conversation overheard on an estate:

> *First peasant*: They say that we will soon be free.
> *Second peasant*: Probably like the state peasants?
> *First peasant*: No, that's just it – completely free: They won't demand either recruits or taxes; and there won't be any kind of authorities. (Emmons, 1968, pp. 51–2)

Apparently serfs themselves did not think that the state peasants had that much more freedom.

51.   Church peasants, who were bonded as well, were secularized in 1764. They were no less discontent than those held privately. Overall after secularization they were better off than manorial serfs, but close in their status to state peasants (Mavor [1925] 1965, Vol. 1, pp. 233–45).
52.   From the point of view of official sources, a very comprehensive and scholarly study in English is presented by James Mavor ([1925] 1965, Vol. 1, Book II, Chapters I–IV). He examines the conditions of various categories of agricultural peasants in the 18th century, including: landowners' peasants, church peasants, peasants of the court, treasury and state peasants.
53.   Here are just some of the controversies. Kliuchevskii notes the atrocities of serfdom and its adverse economic and social effects. Pipes believes that a Russian peasant was not doing badly at all during the years of serfdom and was, in fact, better off than his counterpart in Ireland. He also thinks that there is a general misconception equating slavery in North America to Russian serfdom, which stems from Radischev's book *Journey from Moscow to St. Petersburg* (published in 1790) (Pipes, 1974, Chapter 6). To my knowledge, such misconception exists among neither general Soviet and contemporary Russian public nor historians. Kliuchevskii (1958, Vol. 5, p. 151) did draw a parallel to North American slavery, but it is a warranted comparison.

The general idea from Scott is that the state reforms in the beginning of the 20th century (Stolypin reforms), tried to reshuffle the communal ownership of land – interstripping – only to make it worse for everyone. The communal operation of land was in his view much superior to anything that could have emerged from the state's intervention (Scott, 1998, pp. 39–44). He blatantly ignores the fact that the 'intervention' did increase individual operation (as well as other facts, such as the adverse social influence of the peasant commune *mir*, which I will discuss in the next chapter). Volin (1960, p. 304), for instance, stresses that as a result of the reforms and anti*mir* policies on the eve of the revolution of 1917, small farmers owned about two-thirds of all land in European Russia, not included in the public domain; also on this see Pipes (1974, p. 169).

54.   For more details on tying peasants to land and their relationship with landed gentry before 1649, see Kliuchevskii (1957, Vol. 2, Lecture XXXVII and 1959, Vol. 6, Lecture XIX, pp. 429–36). For details on serfdom after Peter the Great, see Kliuchevskii (1958, Vol. 5, Lectures LXXX and LXXXI). Geographic mobility among the lower classes

was certainly much greater before the end of the 16th century. But while 'there was a considerable amount of vagabondage among the social elements that tended to become slaves', the peasants were 'not at all migratory and usually remained in the same place for generations' (Hellie, 1971, pp. 235–6; 1982, p. 407).

55. Agreements between princes to return runaways appear in the second half of the 15th century. Only in free towns, like Novgorod, we find peasants who worked the land that they owned. Even then, they owned and worked collectively, in communes organized with other free peasants (Kliuchevskii, 1957, Vol. 2, pp. 81–2; and Solov'ev, 1960, Book II, Vol. 4, p. 535). After Novgorod was crushed and its freedoms usurped, most of its land was repopulated by black peasants. People of Novgorod were resettled in Moscow principality where they were allotted land, but given no ownership. From the second half of the 16th century the state for financial and police reasons started assigning peasants permanent residence (Kliuchevskii, 1957, Vol. 2, p. 241). (Muscovite Russia solved the problem of runaways very differently from Western Russia – Western Ukraine, Belorussia and Poland – where equal privileges were shared by all landowners instead; see Solov'ev (1960, Book IV, Vol. 7, pp. 296–8).) Until then the peasant population for the most part roamed around, primarily due to the method of agriculture in the forest zone. This method, slash-burn, consisted of first making a clearing in the woods, burning the slugs and only then planting the seeds. It rendered soil unusable in a few years so peasants had to move on to another plot. This was the primary technique until the three-field system was introduced in the 16th century (Pipes, 1974, p. 27).

56. In 1649; for details see Kliuchevskii (1957, Vol. 3, pp. 144, 157).

57. For more details, see Kliuchevskii (1959, Vol. 6, pp. 422–8).

58. The number of runaways was large; so were the skirmishes between neighbouring landowners. Kliuchevskii thought that the conditions of peasants were much worse than Pipes would have us believe now – peasants were hunted with dogs, most of the time caught and severely beaten (Kliuchevskii, 1957, Vol. 3, pp. 188–9; 1958, Vol. 4, pp. 102–5, 325–9, 333–5 and 1958, Vol. 5, p. 144). If Pipes has advantage of reviewing additional materials in 1974 (unfortunately the format of his book prevents him from referencing them), Kliuchevskii has an advantage of being a contemporary of serfdom. Emmons (1968, pp. 47–9 and note on p. 48) describes increasing peasant unrest on the eve of emancipation although he cannot conclude with certainty that this was due to worsening of their conditions. For another example of controversy on the conditions of peasants, see Liashchenko (1949) and Blum (1961). A nice discussion of peasants and the law is provided by Wirtschafter (1997, pp. 118–23). But I would interpret the same facts in a less optimistic fashion. Russian legislature, however well-intentioned initially, is still best described by a famous Russian idiom – 'one step forward, two steps back'.

59. Factory peasants were not excluded from civic duties; for instance, they had to act as police or pay for a substitute or to build houses or to mow hay (Mavor [1925] 1965, Vol. 1, pp. 438 and 508).

60. For examples, see Zelnik (1968, pp. 169–73). Purchase though was restricted to those of non-noble origin. The gentry, who ran factories, used their own manorial serfs.

61. For this reason Brower calls Russian towns of the 19th and 20th centuries 'migrant cities' (1990, especailly pp. 76–7).

62. For more details and figures, see Wirtschafter (1997, pp. 140–61).

63. For a comprehensive analysis of industry under bondage and the conditions of factory peasants through the 18th century and the first half of the 19th, see Mavor ([1925] 1965, Vol. 1, Book III, Chapters I–III). Mavor's position is that the state peasants attached to factories were only nominally free; in reality they could not leave (ibid., p. 497). Kahan's investigation of Russia in the 18th century reveals the scarcity of data on spatial serf mobility. Even though there is evidence of serf movement other than illegal flight, most was done on the owners' orders or with their consent. The point being that labour market in Russia had significant restrictions (Kahan, 1985, pp. 72–7 and Hellie, 1999, p. 630).

64. For examples, see Wirtschafter (1997, p. 134).
65. For numbers, see Kliuchevskii (1958, Vol. 5, p. 156).
66. For a good short summary of the flaws of the Edict, see Wirtschafter (1997, pp. 111–14).
67. State peasants did not suffer such reductions (Volin, 1960, pp. 294–5, Note 6).
68. Note the proportion here, especially since the percentage of gentry was miniscule compared with that of peasants (Emmons, 1968, note on p. 46).
69. Abolished only in 1907.
70. Initially the Edict contained provisions allowing the consolidation of strips of land and separation from the commune, but these were subject to so many formalities that it was hard to take advantage of them; they were abolished in 1893 (Pipes, 1974, p. 166). Purchase became mandatory in 1883 (ibid., p. 165).
71. On restrictions of mobility, see Mavor (1925, Vol. 2, p. 362).
72. Among those were landless domestic serfs (Mavor 1925, Vol. 2, pp. 361–2).
73. 'A typical well-to-do household' at the turn of the last century was 'characterized by more members and larger numbers of mature male workers' (Shanin, 1972, p. 65). Taken simply as a fact (and not judged as a consequence or a cause), this confirms the logic behind the internal family pressure to keep members in or at least preserve their ties with the village.
74. More on this in Mavor (1925, Vol. 2, p. 394).
75. For details, see Kolle (1995).
76. Pipes says that 'nearly half of the serfs in the empire . . . were tenants on rent' (1974, p. 150). Therefore, they were allegedly free to go and earn money however they could; they were only obligated to pay tax, even though he acknowledges later, on p. 154, that Russian peasants essentially had no rights. At this point the relative freedom of peasants is pure speculation, as there is simply not enough evidence to support his point. There were quite a few limitations to this freedom, in my opinion. For example, the passport regime or regulation forbidding peasant trade in towns. Of course, they did it anyway, but this freedom in an illegal domain is very different from the sort of freedom that generates financially and socially stable society. Perhaps the question here is one of definitions.
    On the economic condition of peasantry and peasant unrest in 1905, see Mavor (1925, Vol. 2, Book V, Chapters VII and VIII). On labour-management problems post-1905, see McKay (1970, pp. 192–7); on the problem of labour faced by foreign entrepreneurs, see McKay (1970, Chapter 7).
77. And/or military – apparently the idea floating behind the emancipation was that recruits from the free population constitute a much better army (Emmons, 1968, p. 44).
78. To me it appears unintended for the simple reason that rulers setting policies in the 17th century could not have thought that such alienation might be beneficial for the police state in the 19th and 20th.
79. Apart from the fact that historians have different views on what actually defines a medieval town. On comparative approaches to urbanization, see Rozman (1976b).
80. For an excellent summary of comparison of Russian and Western European as well as Asian urbanization, see Blackwell (1976, pp. 291–319).
81. For example, the historians Karamzin (1988–89), Solov'ev (1959, 1960), Ditiatin (1875–77), Miliukov (1913), and Shchapov (2001) considered the cities as artificially established. Soviet historians, putting emphasis on Marxist periodization, often state that the city was evolving independently from the state; see, for example, Tikhomirov (1956). For a concise summary of Russian and Soviet scholarship, see Sakharov (1959, pp. 3–16). Sakharov (ibid., p. 201) himself notes backwardness. Western scholars recognize *some comparative* backwardness of Russian urbanization, for example Rozman (1976a). Jones (1977, p. 434) notes that the state undertook the building of roads, canals, schools and so on while the townsmen had little to do with it. Sakharov (1959) is an excellent source for details on towns in north-east Russia in the 14th–15th

centuries, aside from some reference to Marxist periodization, which was a must if the study were to be published at all in the USSR.

82. For example, Rostov in 1211 had 11 churches – a significant figure for a Russian town at the time (Sakharov, 1959, Note 23 on p. 31).

83. Most other towns were much smaller at the time. For more details and comparison with Western Europe, see Hamm (1976a, pp. 13–14).

84. For details in the 14th and 15th centuries, see Sakharov (1959, pp. 183–90).

85. A town according to different theories has different major characteristics. Russian towns do not satisfy the requirements of Weber's city (Weber, 1958a). But according to functional theory they were towns (Hittle, 1979, p. 19).

86. A lot were ordered outright by the government to be built; for details on these military outposts in the 16th century see Solov'ev (1960, Book III, Vol. 6, pp. 418–19).

87. Moscow as a prince's household (*usad'ba*) often pushed Moscow as a capital into the background (Bahrushin, 1954, 'Knyajeskoe hozyaistvo XV i pervoi poloviny XVI v.', in *Nauchnye trudy*, Vol. 2, Moscow, p. 14, quoted in Sakharov, 1959, p. 176). On how the appanage system reinforced patrimonial attitudes, see Kliuchevskii (1956, Vol. 1, pp. 345–50).

88. Novgorod of the 11th through the 15th century stands out as an exception here. There had been a set of laws before the Viking princes came; the trade and crafts were as advanced as in Western Europe at the time, and even though *veche* was not as numerous as some historians believed previously, Novgorod can be considered an independent republic. For details on excavations supporting these statements, see Yanin (1985, pp. 647–67). For details on Novgorod and its relationship with the princes, see Kliuchevskii (1957, Vol. 2, pp. 58–76).

89. *Veche* existed in Novgorod somewhat longer, but nevertheless failed to eliminate the princely power fully and later came under control of local elite. Solov'ev (1960, Book II, Vol. 4, p. 489) notes the absence of *veche* in the north-east in the 13th century and the absence of contracts between princes and towns. In pre-Muscovite Russia princes did not consult boyars any more (ibid., p. 505).

90. The post of chiliarch (*tysiatskii*), who was allegedly an independent executive official, was abolished while the princes' power was on the rise, but even before chiliarchs had been appointed by princes (Sakharov, 1959, p. 210).

91. A very distant approximation of craft guilds as we know them in the West.

92. Hellie (1999, p. 637) believes that guilds did not exist in Russia, with both positive and negative consequences.

93. Kliuchevskii believes that *tsehi* were *slobody* (plural). Of course, *sloboda* (singular) was not a Western European guild (Kliuchevskii, 1959, Vol. 6, pp. 248–9).

94. Also see Hittle (1979, pp. 126–9).

95. Most of it spent to finance army (Hittle, 1979, p. 27). A new government expense was readily covered by a new tax; for a list of these in the 16th century see Solov'ev (1960, Book IV, Vol. 7, pp. 29–34).

96. Details in the previous section.

97. Also see Hellie (1999, p. 536).

98. As Hittle (1979, p. 31) puts it, the identity of a townsman was derived based on principles extraneous to the urban context, therefore, we can not say that he was an urban citizen.

99. Neither did the autonomy of urban inhabitants, based on the law of the Hanseatic town of Magdeburg (Kliuchevskii, 1957, Vol. 3, pp. 96–7).

100. Also see Hittle (1979, Chapter 4).

101. The concept of service city and service state, where the status of a person was determined by his particular services to the state, is developed in Hittle (1979).

102. For details on Catherine II's reforms, see Hittle (1979, Chapters 9 and 10).

103. *Meshchane* were a less wealthy category than merchants, and were generally people of small trades and commerce. Later this category was infiltrated by peasants.

104.   For examples in the 16th century, see Solov'ev (1960, Book IV, Vol. 7, p. 43).
105.   For more examples, see Wirtschafter (1997, pp. 134–5).
106.   Sakharov (1959, p. 151) also could not establish any inter-regional trade connection between the towns of north-eastern Russia in the 14th and 15th centuries.
107.   Suzerain princes who lacked artisans, had to draw up a special contract to lure them from working for the church (Sakharov, 1959, pp. 135, 219). Even though Russia did not lack stonemasons in general, it lacked *highly skilled* masons (Hamm, 1976a, p. 23). In 1556 the Tsar ordered that captured foreigners who possessed craft skills must be sold in the Muscovite state or brought directly to Moscow (Solov'ev, 1960, Book IV, Vol. 7, pp. 49–50).
108.   Sakharov's conclusion (1959, p. 138). Solov'ev (1960, Book II, Vol. 4, pp. 555–6) believes that circumstances for the development of trade during and after the Tatar Yoke were mostly favourable. However, he provides no evidence that would disprove Sakharov.
109.   On competition from private suburbs, see Hittle (1979, p. 30).
110.   The tax payments were inappropriately high at times, because they were based on surveys of the male population that could never keep up with ongoing migration (Miller 1976, p. 37).
111.   It has to be noted that among townsmen there was little room left for those who were not officially affiliated with the state. In the 17th century, for instance, in the western part of Russia 71.2 per cent of city courts belonged to state servitors, in the southern part 85.3, and in the eastern part as much as 87.3 per cent (Hittle, 1979, p. 25).
112.   Also see Kliuchevskii (1957), Vol. 3, pp. 159–61. Even earlier, pointing out a very difficult situation for townsmen in the 14th and 15th centuries, Sakharov (1959, p. 224) wonders whether there existed exceptional incentives for people to move into the cities at all. Politically, fiscally and juridically, authorities evidently did not distinguish between the black town and rural population (Sakharov, 1959, pp. 217, 223; and also Hamm, 1976a, p. 24). On the obligations of townsmen, such as public works, and a long list of their dues and so on, see Sakharov (1959, pp. 191–201).
113.   In view of this, Rozman's numbers on urban growth are moot. The question here is also the legality of status and permanency of urban residence, which was hard to obtain.
114.   Of course, off-farm work did not always mean a move to a city.
115.   Hittle (1979, pp. 2, 123) says that the *posad* commune was a product of local initiatives. However it formed again for the sole purpose of collecting taxes. Town inhabitants had no consciousness of public service. They 'consider these [public] affairs to be something completely alien to them that do not affect their personal interests, a burdensome pastime that takes them away from their own affairs', cited in Brower (1990, p. 18).
116.   *Posad* communes also exhibited hostility to outsiders. For instance, 'freedmen' who were the result of individual cases of liberation at the end of Catherine II's reign, were met with hostility when they tried to join other social groups in towns (Mavor [1925] 1965, Vol. 1, p. 232).
117.   In the 16th century an administrative unit was given a right to be governed by locally elected elders for a certain sum of money (*otkupnaya*), but this opportunity was rarely used. Apparently, heavy responsibilities turned candidates away. An elder not only had to devote their time to governing and judging, but also had to deliver *otkupnaya* to Moscow; if late, they faced punishment whatever the mitigating circumstances, such as weather, might have been. Thus, many preferred a state appointee (Solov'ev, 1960, Book III, Vol. 6, p. 37).
118.   The governor also had a temporary suspensive veto (ibid., pp. 105–6).
119.   Details in Hanchett (1976). The statute disenfranchised most small property owners (third, and most of the second, curia), leaving the number of eligible voters at around 1 per cent of the urban population (Hamm, 1976b, p. 187). The elections were held in curias (divisions), into which all of the districts' population was divided. The first curia consisted of landowners who possessed 200 or more *desiatinas* of land (about 540 acres), or other real estate worth at least 15,000 rubles, or had a monthly income of at

least 6000 rubles. This curia consisted mostly of nobles and landlords, but members of other classes (merchants who bought nobles' land, rich peasants who acquired land, and the like) eventually grew more and more prominent. The second curia consisted of city dwellers who possessed merchant registration, or who owned trading and industrial companies with a yearly income of at least 6000 rubles, or held real estate worth at least 500 rubles (in small cities) or 2000 rubles (in large cities). The third curia consisted mainly of representatives of village societies and peasants who did not require a special posession permit.

120. For more details, see Hamm (1976b, pp. 186 and 190–91); and also Mavor (1925, Vol. 2, Book VI, Chapter III). On sanitation and local needs, see Brower (1990, pp. 125–35).

121. Hamm means World War I. As Kevin Brancato (pers. com., 2005) pointed out, these numbers appear to be slightly upward biased because Russia actively used forced labour for public works while Europe did not. Of course, forced labour was not financially compensated, so benefits from it did not factor in the calculations of expenditure per capita. The penal system including forced public works was detrimental to the rate of the population growth (Kahan, 1985, p. 11).

122. And that was in the capital!

123. For more details, see Brower (1990, pp. 66–7). Lack of private banks, of course, was a serious problem for small-scale commerce (ibid., pp. 67–8).

124. For example, in Barnaul (Siberia) the state prohibited all private production involving fire (*ognennoe deistvie*) and water wheel (*vodianye dvigateli*). Barnaul *kuptsy* (merchants) derived the majority of their income from fulfilling government's factory orders (*Kratkaya entsiklopedia*, Vol. 1, pp. 82–3).

125. For this purpose, monasteries built *dvory* (residences) in the *posad* part of towns (monasteries were usually situated outside the city borders). Large landowners, princes in pre-Muscovite Russia, also had *dvory* in *posad* because they carried on trade as well. For concrete examples, see Sakharov (1959, pp. 149, 150).

126. Of course, military conquest was a means in itself. It would provide access to economically important sea outlets and peace from the attacks of neighbouring nations, all of which in the end would allow Russia to take its rightful place among the most economically advanced nations of Europe. Peter the Great believed (at least in the beginning, it is likely that towards the end he realized his ambitions had failed) that this could happen, only if Russia was pushed hard enough.

127. Peter was, of course, influenced by mercantilism. As many economists, for instance de Soto in *The Other Path* (1990), point out, a very important path of mercantilist policy is distribution of monopoly rights by the government. For more on economic reform, see Kliuchevskii (1958, Vol. 4, Lecture LXIV).

128. For examples, see Kliuchevskii (1958, Vol. 4, pp. 118–20).

129. And there were many who took advantage of this (Kliuchevskii, 1958, Vol. 4, pp. 129–32).

130. Of course, nowadays many of these are incorporated in the sales tax, and most of us are used to it. As much as we do not like it, we can form an accurate expectation of how much to add to the tag price. But in the 18th century, Russia, apart from the uncertainty, simply the amount of taxes complicated economic transactions. Besides, the fact that any of your neighbours could be snooping around, looking to invent a tax on what you are doing, created an atmosphere of distrust.

131. In Russian *podushnaia podat'*. Soul tax was a fixed tax on a person regardless of income.

132. Even though both sides of budget equation went up, the proportions did not change for the better. Now expenditures for the army and fleet consumed 67 per cent of the budget (Kliuchevskii, 1958, Vol. 4, pp. 142–3).

133. But production had to remain small scale. Naturally, a large factory is hard to hide. Therefore, it would be a mistake to say that this sort of underground activity is a sign of economic development. Field studies have become fashionable where economists

together with anthropologists and sociologists document cases of indigenous (and ingenious) ways of dealing with trust and information problems. Social networks in Russian underground would qualify. But there is absolutely no indication that the cottage industry can produce industrialization on a European scale. After all, the Kula ring economy remained the Kula ring for a very long time.

134. Mavor thinks that this was due to the rise of skilled workers, not relaxation of government control (ibid.).

135. Mavor calls this absence of industrial capital; see Mavor ([1925] 1965, Vol. 1, p. 505).

136. More details on state policy towards industry in the 18th century in Kahan (1985, pp. 157–62).

137. Industrialization in Peter's time was superficial and the business know-how was not imported together with other items. The following is an illuminating example. Huge numbers of borrowed words from European languages entered Russian at the time. However, out of 3500 such words about one-fourth were shipping terms, one-fourth were terms related to government administration, one-fourth were military terms, one-fourth were miscellaneous terms mostly describing luxury items, and hardly two dozen could be stretched to fit the category of economic and business terminology (Gerschenkron, 1970, p. 81).

138. Those who favour government involvement in the economy generally believe that the most important cause was the protective tariff. Those whose sympathy lies with laissez-faire, believe that free trade policy in the 1860s and the 1870s stimulated the growth of Russian industry. With the competition of foreign producers the prices on iron were kept down, which was good for the railroad construction. And the railroad in turn had an immensely positive effect on industrialization. Although a protective tariff does stimulate domestic production in the short run, it impedes technological improvement in the long run. For a full representation of this argument, made by Tugan-Baranovsky, see Mavor (1925, Vol. 2, pp. 380–88).

      Although the growth trend of Russian economy in the second half of the 19th century was overall positive, the economy experienced quite a few slumps. For example, the immediate effect of emancipation was return of possessional workers back to their villages. Industry in the outlying regions, especially the iron industry, suffered the most (ibid., pp. 368–9). The railroad construction itself produced a disturbance because a large amount of capital was quickly transformed into an inconvertible form. By the 1870s Russia was well drawn into international markets and international crises contributed to its economic downturns. Deficient harvests were also a contributing factor. For more details, see Mavor (1925, Vol. 2, pp. 370–75). On foreign capital, see McKay (1970) and discussion in Chapter 5 of this volume.

139. Apparently, household or cottage industry in villages took a different turn partially in response to stimulation from the protective tariff. In many regions, but especially in the Moscow region, in production of iron ware, cardboard, leather, woodwork, artisans managed not only to compete with large factories but to direct the trade wholly into their hands (Mavor, 1925, Vol. 2, p. 367).

140. Prior to the 1860 reforms, Russia had only state banks. Some details on the problems of Russian banking are provided in Brower (1990, pp. 67–9).

141. For details, see Owen (1981, pp. 54–8).

142. In addition, because many towns' economic livelihood depended on the existence of a rail line, the railroad itself became the object of bribery. Both local municipalities and private producers were prepaid to either make concessions or to bribe directly those who were in charge of railroad planning. For examples, see Brower (1990, p. 45).

143. For more details, see Owen (1981, pp. 59–64). Of course, the other side, free-traders, most notably liberal economists Bezobrasov and Vernadski, also sought to establish their supremacy through personal connections, referred to as 'economic dinners' (ibid., p. 64), but they failed.

144. The Slavs of Kiev Rus' also faced this problem but in the context of a less autocratic regime.

145. In fact, Peter's recruiting activities decreased taxable population by one-fifth over 30 years, which of course depleted the treasury in return (Kliuchevskii, 1958, Vol. 4, p. 128). Also see Kahan (1985, Tables 1.4 and 1.5 on p. 9 and Table 1.6 on p. 10).

146. Kliuchevskii (1958, Vol. 4, p. 213) believed that Peter the Great neither interrupted the old foundation nor built a new one, only rearranged pieces.

147. For details, see Kliuchevskii (1958, Vol. 4, p. 186).

148. On the growth of bureaucracy during this period, see Kliuchevskii (1958, Vol. 5, pp. 270–71). One case was ordered to be sent to Moscow. It took several dozen horse carriages to accommodate the paperwork (ibid.)!

149. Of course, this is also the problem of a central planner, who can never possess full knowledge of the economy to implement his programme correctly.

150. After Peter the Great's death, large landowners, who were also military officers by the nature of their obligations to the state, were closely involved in every coup d'état in the course of the following 30 years. As a result they formed an elite interest group of favourites at the court.

151. *Nakas* contained thoughts on legislature, norms and so on written by Catherine II, though mostly consisting of borrowed ideas.

152. One further example shows how non-autonomous the Senate really was. Peter the Great left the Ladoga canal unfinished. Whether the job should be completed led to a heated and long discussion in the Senate. However, when a messenger declared that regardless of the Senate's decision the will of the Empress would prevail, the Senators were only disappointed that they wasted their time, not that their decision did not matter (Kliuchevskii, 1958, Vol. 4, p. 271).

153. For details on Peter's Collegiate reforms, see Kliuchevskii (1958, Vol. 4, pp. 168–9). On the pitiful state of public and private education, see ibid., Lecture LXIX.

4. Social norms

Some components of the cultural make-up of Russians stalled free markets and advanced hierarchies: networks of civic engagement did not develop but strong ties did. Establishing these aspects of Russian culture and their causes are the subject of this chapter.

Geographical composition of a country, such as its size, the presence or absence of waterways, the abundance or lack of natural resources, external forces, such as invasions and religious beliefs, all determine how people of a particular society relate to each other. From repeated previous experience they form an expectation of how a stranger might act and adjust their behaviour accordingly.

It appears that a combination of forces produced a culture of a very retrospective people, who carry a tint of negligence in practically everything they do, who generally prefer a collective way of life, yet through their collective activities have not generated norms that ensure the anonymous trust in the society as a whole. Russians rarely act in large organized groups, and when they do, success is seldom. In fact, it seems that Russians would readily participate as a society in only two extreme cases – drinking at holidays or funerals, and war – cases both *polar* and of *immediate* danger or satisfaction. When they need to work side by side for a purpose of *incremental* wealth building, then differentiation by gender, ethnicity, skill, education, social status or generation takes precedence over a common future interest.

As noted in the preceding chapter, after the 1800s Russia was catching up with modernized Western European societies and exhibited a pattern of development that was similar to those societies on the macro level. But macro by definition does not exist without micro. Russia's unique social norms that dominated the behaviour of economic agents on the micro level, failed to limit autocratic power, failed to produce long-term sustainable economic growth and made Russia susceptible to political instability of the kind that resulted in the 1917 revolution.

GEOGRAPHY AND A WEAK PROPENSITY TO SELF-GOVERN

The previous chapter demonstrated that the state significantly weakened the institutions of urban self-government. This section shows that rural organs of self-government met a similar fate and investigates how social norms made that a likely outcome.

The state successfully shaped and moulded social institutions to its own liking because their foundation was weak to begin with. The lack of self-reliance among the general population is noted by historians early on.[1] It appears that the geography of the territory had a profound impact on the Russian character, the best description of which is given by Kliuchevskii (translated by Hogarth):

> The physical features of the country likewise influenced the racial character of the Great Russian. Everywhere the swamps and forests of Great Russia of the thirteenth, fourteenth, and fifteenth centuries confronted the settler with thousands of unforeseen risks, difficulties, and hardships. Consequently he learnt to watch nature very closely . . . to scan and probe the ground on which he walked, and never to attempt a passage of a strange river where there was not a ford. All this bred in him resourcefulness in the face of minor perils and difficulties, and inured him to patient wrestling with hardship and misfortune. (Hogarth, 1911, Vol. 1, p. 218)[2]

The unpredictability of northern Russia's climate made 'sport of the best-laid agricultural plans' (ibid., pp. 219–20).[3] The Great Russian peasant became accustomed to disappointment in the work that was most important and life-sustaining to him. He would often find pleasure in taking the off chance of beating the odds. *Avos'* – loosely translated as 'perhaps' – summarizes this characteristic trait in the psychology of a Russian. The short summers demanded highly intense labour, and, indeed, no people in Europe are able to accomplish so much in such a short period of time. However, he is hopelessly incapable of '*long-sustained, systematic toil*' (ibid.; original emphasis):[4]

> We have seen that the natural features of the country influenced the distribution of Russian settlement, and led to the adoption of small, isolated hamlets. Naturally, this lack of social intercourse did not teach the Great Russian to act in large unions or compact masses. The scene of his labours lay, not in the open field, in the sight of all men, as did that of the inhabitant of Southern Rus, but in the depths of the primeval forest, where, axe in hand, he waged a strenuous war with nature. It was a silent, secluded struggle in which he was engaged – a struggle with the elemental forces, with the forest and the wild morass – a struggle which left him no time to think of the community, nor yet of his feelings towards

his fellow men. This made him self-centred and retiring, cautious and reserved, diffident in public, and non-communicative of speech. (ibid., p. 219)[5]

Kliuchevskii stresses the role of uncertainty further:

[T]he impossibility of seeing far ahead of him, of formulating any definite plan of action against unforeseen perils or invariably taking the nearest road to a desired point, is strongly reflected in his psychology and models of thought. The changes and chances of life early taught him to look back whence he had come rather than forward whither he was going. Sudden blizzards or thaws, unexpected August frosts or January mildness, have made him observant rather than provident, attentive to consequences rather than to their prevention, careful of sums-total rather than of their constituent amounts. By some observers he is accused of lack of straightforwardness and sincerity. That is a mistake. True, he often takes two views of a question, but this seeming double-mindedness arises from the fact that, though his mental process leads him to make straight for his goal (ill-considered though the goal often be), he does so by looking to either side of him as he goes, even as his ancestors scanned the surrounding fastnesses which they were forced to traverse. (Ibid., I, pp. 219–20)[6]

No matter how profound the economic and institutional developments of Kiev Rus' may seem, it was only a short period in the history of the Russian people.[7] The institutions of Kiev Rus' were not prevalent and deep-rooted enough to be preserved in a different, more unfriendly, environment. These institutions did not have a firm foundation as the foundation that Greco-Roman traditions gave to Germanic tribes who settled in Western Europe.[8] Even though the first Russian law code (*Russkaya Pravda*) was a Scandinavian-based law, the influence of Germanic law on social norms was very limited (Solov'ev, 1959, Book I, Vol. 1, p. 273).[9] Poland acted as a barrier rather than transmitter of this influence, partially because it was Catholic (ibid., pp. 270–71);[10] Novgorod was also too alien to north-eastern Russia.

The majority of the Slavs moved to the north-east a few centuries after they had spread eastward from the Carpathians. Around the 13th century they colonized the Oka basin, met and assimilated Finnish tribes – Chud', the native population that was alien in origin and inferior in its development (Kliuchevskii, 1956, Vol. 1, Lecture XII). Here a peasant way of life took precedence over the commercial way of life that the Eastern Slavs knew in Kiev Rus', and presumably here the prototype of the peasant commune *mir* was born.

The landscape of north-eastern Russia was different; there were more marshes and forests and fewer rivers and plains than in the south. In the south, the open plain made people settle in large numbers in order to be able to defend themselves better. In the south the Slavs, even those who engaged exclusively in agriculture, organized around commercial centres.

In the north-east, Slavs spread throughout the plain not so much because they grew in numbers, but because migrating was the most practical response to the environment (ibid., p. 31). As pointed out in the previous chapter, the method of slash-burn soil cultivation forced the settlers to move to a new location every few years. Marshes made it hard to find dry land suitable for building houses and growing food (ibid., p. 29).

The vastness of the territory precluded the population from concentrating in a few particular areas (ibid., pp. 28–9), which would have given an advance to social cooperation, exchange of skills and ultimately a higher economic and social development. In the north-east during this period the settlements consisted of two- or three-house villages. Peasant settlements along the upper Volga resembled (especially to a Western observer) temporary nomad camps. This was a consequence of a continuous life on the move and chronic fires – circumstances that over generations bred scornful indifference to domestic improvement and to everyday conveniences (ibid., p. 71).

The vastness of territory played in favour of the strong state. As Solov'ev (1960, Book IV, Vol. 7, pp. 300–301) notes, instead of concentrating in towns and forming opposition groups, the discontent migrated to remote corners of the country, leaving the state to do as it pleased.[11]

Remoteness from trading centres gave no incentive to produce more than was needed to sustain a family (Kliuchevskii, 1956, Vol. 1, pp. 308–9). The decline in interest rates shows that capital was not needed in north-eastern Russia in the 13th–15th centuries as much as it had been in Kiev Rus'. Prince Monomakh's decree allowed interest on a multi-year loan up to 40 per cent, while in the north-east it was 12–14 per cent (ibid., p. 366). Merchants, as well as venues for foreign and domestic commerce were sparse; peasants led a self-sustained existence, and, therefore demand for capital declined.

Hardships associated with climate were matched by difficult neighbours. The Slavic territory was always on the routes of Asiatic nomads going to Europe and back. The steppes in the south were the home of the Cossacks, which in Russian means a homeless, unproductive, free-roaming looter (ibid., p. 68). Because of lack of defences against the nomads, the Slavs from the start got accustomed to paying a tribute. Though not overly burdensome, it was nevertheless a tribute that the Dnepr Slavs paid to the Chozars[12] in the 8th and the first half of the 9th century in order to be permitted to trade with Asia. Slave and commodity raids by the Tatars and other nomads continued well into the 17th century. Not only were ransoms paid to release Russians and goods from captivity, but also tributes to persuade the nomads to curtail their raids.[13]

Mir

The institution of *mir*, or the peasant commune, is most likely indigenous in origin. Still, the derivation is uncertain. Some scholars view *mir* as an organic entity, where the organization of the commune itself reinforced its practices; others believe it was a product of the state's policy. Kaufman's view stands out: he turned his attention to the processes governing the creation of communes in Siberia at the time of its colonization by Russians. Apparently there land redivision came first and the institutionalization of the commune second. Once there was a critical mass of families participating in the commune, the rest in their settlement joined under pressure. It was only natural then to delegate certain governing functions to *mir* because the state was far away and disinterested at the time.[14]

My informed conjecture is that over a period of time in the northeast, as well as later on in Siberia, a hostile environment – be it nature or unfriendly neighbours – determined centripetal tendencies exhibited by peasant households. Perhaps for some, repartition of land created an illusion of hedging against the unpredictability of the environment. Perhaps for others, who were interested in staying put for longer than the current methods of soil cultivation permitted, it was insurance that, with growing population and decrease in land available for cultivation, they would always get a share.

Mavor cites another, physical, cause operating in the north. A shifting of the rivers in the swampy plains resulted in the movement of the soil from one bank and the deposition of it on the other. Unless there was a frequent repartition of land, peasants on the one bank would be getting richer and richer, while the others poorer and poorer (Mavor [1925] 1965, Vol. 1, p. 272). Either way, once some form of communal ownership was in place, egalitarian ideology was how it held together. The importance of the communally owned land persisted through the centuries and at the turn of the last century was as shown in Table 4.1.

The table also demonstrates that the importance of communally held land declined in the direction from the north, north-west to the south, south-east. The numbers of households per commune increased in the same direction across the European Russia (Shanin, 1986). The commune varied structurally among different regions. In the north, land repartitions were less frequent and individual households had relatively more power than in the central and southern region of Russia.

Despite some variation of the communal land repartition[15] among localities, the basic principle behind *mir* was that the right to use land belonged to individuals but the right of disposition of property belonged to the community as a whole.[16] *Mir* supported the less thrifty,[17] the aged

Table 4.1   Communally owned land as a percentage of total peasant land

Region	Per cent
Eastern steppe	98.4
Far north	98
Western Great Russia (densely populated)	97.1
Western Great Russia (sparsely populated)	96.5
Great Russia	95.8
Perm border	93
New Russia	88.9
Large-village Ukraine	80.4
Bessarabia	77
White Russia	39
Left-bank Ukraine	33
Right-bank Ukraine	13.9
Lithuania	0
Baltic	0

Source: Watters (1968, p. 146).

and the orphans out of common reserves. These reserves were also used to lease additional land from the state and to pay taxes, and later on to cover the official and unofficial expenses of the local branch of the federal government.

By the 16th century, *mir* was the landlord's agent for implementing directives and collecting taxes. In the following centuries its role and functions were reinforced by the state: communal pooling of resources was partially influenced by how the taxes were levied.[18] Uniformity of taxation promoted the desire for uniformity of condition. The landowners enjoyed the advantages of communal operation as well – it was communal responsibility to support the poorer members and tax collection was delegated to an elder (*starosta*) although with some supervision by a landowner.

Individual ownership of land distributed through the custom of inheritance was incompatible with levying of soul tax because the amount of land had no correspondence to the size of the family. 'From the Western European point of view . . . this condition was piously regarded as a dispensation of Providence; from the Russian point of view it was an injustice which might and should be rectified by the Government' (Mavor [1925] 1965, Vol. 1, p. 294). After the emancipation in 1861 the collective responsibility was still actively encouraged among the villages, and only the Stolypin reforms in the beginning of the 20th century changed the direction of this policy.[19]

The heads of all landholding households formed the communal assembly (*skhod*). Decisions made were usually unanimous, but this was not a near perfect society. Simply, apathy and conformism among the majority of peasants ensured that the most influential ones had it their way.[20] In other words, unanimity was supplemented by tyranny from within and from outside (Mavor, 1925, Vol. 2, p. 273). An elder exercised executive power, collected taxes, oversaw the selection of recruits and so on. Peasants did not welcome the commune offices, which were often a heavy burden, but the appointment was treated as compulsory and refusal to accept office was punishable under the pre-revolutionary law. It is not surprising then that the appointment was shunned by all means:

> Whom shall we choose [for *starosta*]?
> As soon as the question is asked, several peasants look down to the ground or try in some other way to avoid attracting attention, lest their names should be suggested. When the silence has continued a minute or two, the graybeard says, 'There is Alexei Ivanoff; he has not served yet!'
> 'Yes, yes' . . . shout a dozen voices, belonging probably to peasants who fear they may be elected.
> Alexei protests in the strongest terms. He cannot say that he is ill . . . but he finds a dozen other reasons why he should not be chosen. (Koslow, 1972, p. 15)

In the sphere of social and economic relations the commune practised traditionalism, conformism,[21] and egalitarianism. Though clearly many peasants gained from economic egalitarianism in the short run, in the long run such practice prevented their enrichment (Mavor [1925] 1965, Vol. 1, p. 219).[22] *Mir* reinforced social inertia among the peasants.[23]

The fact that peasant-workers resisted their new status, and constantly petitioned to be returned to their traditional social role is not perhaps so remarkable for a pre-industrial society. It is remarkable that this desire for a traditional way of life persisted over several generations among various social groups (Zelnik, 1968, pp. 172–3). Social attitudes among the peasants to mass production stalled division of labour. Peasants regarded it wasteful, virtually immoral, to buy things manufactured away from home. Purchasing commercially produced cloth, for instance, symbolized to them disregard of their local tradition of costume and imitation of the hated gentry (Mavor [1925] 1965, Vol. 1, pp. 518–19).

Socially, *mir* promoted small clusters of strong hierarchical ties and extreme hostility to outsiders, which raised entry and exit costs. Within *mir*, interaction occurred outside any market mechanism. This was detrimental for exchange.

Despite the fact that to an outsider *mir* looked like a closely knit cohesive community, it was very much subject to internal tensions at least in the last century of imperial Russia. Households and factions clashed in dispute over the distribution of tax, military and administrative obligations, and over the distribution of land. Even though wealthier peasants bought their way out of recruit duty, and bribed estate clerks for extra access to forest resources (Wirtschafter, 1997, pp. 106–7), egalitarian tendencies of the commune as a whole as well as the general state of economic opportunities outside *mir* put a check on the growth of their wealth. Other branches of provincial self-government, such as *zemstvo*, did not fare any better than *mir*.[24] Provincial gentry's organizations, though existing as early as the 16th century, were formed because of military requirements and were also based on the mutual responsibility principle (Kliuchevskii, 1957, Vol. 2, pp. 235–7).

RELIGIOUS DOCTRINE IN ECONOMIC DEVELOPMENT

The Russian Orthodox Church prided itself in conserving the purity of the Christian doctrine. It believed that Western religions, like Catholicism, thoughtlessly let themselves be blended with classical civilization, which assigned too much of a role to analytical reason and led to the sin of arrogance (Pipes, 1974, p. 222). In practical matters the Russian Church found it advantageous to ally itself with the state, although such political involvement went against its underlying religious principles.[25] This behaviour supported the duality of Russian life. But as much as the Church played puppet in the hands of the government, the basics of the Orthodox creed, such as abomination of worldly life, praise of silent suffering and conformism, did exert an important influence on the general population. As far as reasserting the state's power over individuals, the Orthodox creed was exactly what the state needed. However, it is impossible to tell with certainty whether the religious doctrine was 'corrected' by either side for future benefit.

Russia accepted the Eastern branch of Christianity. In a few centuries after the fall of Byzantium, Russia was left without a paternalistic overseer. The stronger the assaults from Catholicism, the more Russia withdrew away from its Western neighbours, isolating itself from European civilization (Pipes, 1974, p. 223). Even though foreigners had always lived in Russia, their religious and cultural influence was limited. In the times of Ivan IV, Germans, for example, were permitted to settle only in the German quarter in Moscow. In the first few decades of the Romanov dynasty they started spreading to other parts of Moscow, but once again were exiled to their quarter. In the middle of the 17th century the patriarch asked that the Tsar prohibit Germans from building churches all around

Moscow and from buying real estate from Russians, thus not completely eliminating but limiting the interaction with and the influence of German culture (Kliuchevskii, 1957, Vol. 3, pp. 269–70).

The influence of the Orient and Islam was much greater. Many of the nomadic tribes with whom Russians often came into contact practised Islam. The culmination of the Church's economic power occurred during the Tatar Yoke (see Chapter 3). Tatars exempted the Church from dues; princes generously paid for its support of their power, so it accumulated money and land. Monastic landholdings expanded to compete only with those of princes. By some accounts monasteries had about one-third of all land property in the Muscovite state in the 16th century (Kliuchevskii, 1957, Vol. 2, p. 278 and Solov'ev, 1960, Book II, Vol. 4, pp. 601–4).

The Church exerted significant economic influence for a period of time because of its close involvement in secular affairs. The majority of monasteries were built in or near towns on the donations of princes or boyars and remained active participants in the commercial life. In the Middle Ages, monasteries regulated trade and commerce,[26] and despite the official Church doctrine were dynamic players in the lending market.[27] The Church's influence on the economic development was twofold.

First, as *an institution*[28] it acted initially in concord with the state and later as a part of the state. Second, intellectual efforts of the Church's outstanding clerical minds were very limited, and the general public was influenced primarily through the everyday practices of provincial priests. In the early centuries there was little attempt to enlighten the masses; later the illiteracy of the population as well as of the priests was an obstacle. In the 19th century the writings of the clergy were censored, and priests were forbidden to interfere in civil affairs (Freeze, 1989). Provincial Russian priests were much like the peasants. They had to support their families and work the soil in addition to their clerical duties. A typical Russian priest delivered two or three different sermons a year, while his English counterpart did that much every week (ibid., p. 365).

From the 14th century, hermits began organizing monastic communities in rural north-eastern Russia, thus heading the colonization parallel to the peasants who often joined the monks' settlement and shared in their efforts (Kliuchevskii, 1957, Vol. 2, Lecture XXXIV). Interested in advancing the colonization, the state granted monasteries and all the incomers not only land but also privileges, such as exemption from dues.

For years, monks and peasants built, harvested and worshipped side by side. It is not clear how exactly, but it was then that Russian clergy amended and popularized, and by some accounts invented, a peculiar redemption doctrine. This doctrine could have shaped the practice of hierarchical gift-giving. It professed that for those who did not have time for good works during the earthly life, salvation could be secured through monks' prayers upon their death. These prayers were locked by material contributions to the monasteries, such as money, candles, cattle, land, alcohol and so on. This habit became so widespread that gradually a standard will came to include contributions to monasteries. The so-called 'soul contributions' – personal donations to the Church – became yet another source of the Church's enrichment.

The practice inevitably led to moral degradation. It was customary to provide so-called 'feedings' for the monks twice a year by the relatives of those who had passed on. But many petty princes, boyars and peasants wanted to solicit prayers for their own health and success in the earthly life. For that they were also supposed to provide feedings, which turned into expensive feasts and which were quite contrary to the principle of ascetics in the first place. The moral degradation of the clergy adversely affected the morals of the general population.[29]

The Church's possession of land was decentralized – land belonged to various patriarchs, monasteries and parishes. Thus, in their capacity as landlords monks and bishops were subject to the state and were politically impotent (Pipes, 1974, pp. 226–7). By the end of the 15th century when the state established its claim to power and no longer needed the Church's support, the latter was easily subdued to the secular authority.[30] Four important postulates of the official ideological doctrine were then worked out: that the Romes of Peter and Constantine fell as heresies and Moscow was the only pure Christian state; that Moscow rulers' line goes back to Emperor Augustus;[31] that Russian Tsars possess the divine authority, which effectively abandoned the principle of duality of temporal and spiritual authority; and that the rulers of Russia were automatically sovereigns of all the Orthodox (ibid., pp. 232–3).

Thus, in spite of a short episode of economic grandeur, Eastern Orthodoxy, from the beginning, was tied closely to the state both politically and financially, and its decentralized structure[32] prevented it from standing up to it later (Pipes, 1974, p. 224 and Kliuchevskii, 1956, Vol. 1, pp. 251–2). After Byzantium fell, the Russian Church became ever more dependent on the state for financial and physical support, while the papacy in the West grew not only richer but more independent (Pipes, 1974, p. 224). The inherent conservatism of the Russian Orthodoxy, which manifested itself in strict adherence to rituals, made it necessary for a strong secular authority to be at its side (ibid., pp. 225–6). Under Peter the Great, the Russian Church as an institution formally merged with the state, a merger that met no resistance whatsoever.[33]

Needless to say, the priests led an everyday way of life, dictated by economic hardships and guided by survival techniques, which was not usually an example of a life full of higher aspirations. The Church preached the 'provident nature of the existing order' (Freeze, 1989, p. 366) sometimes justifying it, not unlike Thomas Carlyle, by reference to the inherent inequality between the social classes. At the same time the Church taught that the poor and 'dispossessed enjoyed a certain spiritual privilege . . . over the wealthy', and that the wealth of the wealthy was 'an emanation of divine grace' (ibid., p. 368) and not a product of their labour.[34] These teachings laid the foundation of the anti-'capitalistic spirit' in Weber's (1958b) terminology and the anti-bourgeois mentality of the general population. Both the state policy and religious doctrine punished financial success.

SOCIETY OUTSIDE THE LAW: LAW, CONTRACT AND PRIVATE PROPERTY IN RUSSIA

No class in Russian society lived by or understood the rule of law. The nomadic way of life in Russia in the early centuries, as opposed to a settled way of life in Europe, sparked a major difference between the appanage and feudalism. In the West a person was guaranteed his rights through hereditary order; relations between superiors and subordinates became permanent social institutions. In Western Europe, where most people stayed put, 'vassalage produced a whole network of human dependencies. Its by-product was a strong social bond linking society with government' (Pipes, 1974, p. 50). Hence, the independent courts, the rule of law and the idea that anyone, including the rulers, could be bound by contract.[35]

In Russia, landownership was not connected with personal service[36] on a permanent basis. It remained temporary, more like fortuitous rewards for personal service. Free persons in Russia, including princes' armed retinue and farmers, constantly moved around. Therefore, those seeking to serve the prince had to back the fulfilment of the terms of agreement by some sort of personal bond (Kliuchevskii, 1956, Vol. 1, pp. 361–2 and 1959, Vol. 6, pp. 340–41), which in the 13th and 14th centuries was often temporary (one could serve prince A, but live on the land in the region governed by prince B). The continuity of a contractual form of relationship between prince and his retinue as well as between retinue and farmers was almost always broken. Therefore, it was hard for any form of common law to take root. The ad hoc nature of the law in effect made relationships between superiors and subordinates tangential on personal connections.

The circumstances of the transition from the rota to the appanage system also inhibited the development of proper contractual relationships. The struggle for possessions and power created severe hostility among close relatives; and the Tatar khans posed a grave danger as well. In the fight for self-preservation all means came in handy – treason, cheating and breaking agreements (Solov'ev, 1960, Book II, Vol. 4, pp. 616–17). Moreover, in the 16th century the basic understanding of what a contract meant was tainted. As mentioned in the previous chapter, the state prohibited termination of contracts before the expiration date, even if the faulty side provided adequate compensation and *both* sides were in favour of contract termination (Kliuchevskii, 1959, Vol. 6, p. 422).

Russia knew no distinction between political authority and outright ownership, and the extent of freedom of free persons in Russia is questionable.[37] Because Russia was often at war, legislative efforts were concentrated on how to distribute military obligations between social groups. The state was not concerned with how to secure rights to justice for each group, much less what those rights were.[38] *Social* status was never equated 'with specific occupations and service functions' (Wirtschafter, 1997, p. 132). But *economic* status was tied to government service from the time of the Muscovite state (Kliuchevskii, 1959, Vol. 6, p. 374). Since there were no juridically defined social boundaries, individuals with a potential common interest had no foundation to come together as a group and fight for their right to promote such interest.[39]

Even though successful law-making needs some flexibility for the formal requirements and informal practices to better fit together, Russian legislative efforts resembled an unproductive locomotion – one step forward, two steps back – which resulted in a very ambiguous and disjoint collection of laws. Isolated within small communities without common law and isolated as a nation,[40] Russians related to the world through closely knit social clusters, such as family units, close friends, *mir* and *posad* communes. Since demands as social groups were uncommon, Russians positioned themselves in the hierarchical networks individually; success based on the potency of their personal connections (Figure 4.1). A very important positioning game was played between bureaucrats and the citizens.

Had the bribes been limited to contributions for services and conducted as an everyday economic exchange, it could have been just a simple case of corruption. But endemic to Russian culture the practice of self-interested gift-giving (Kelly, 2000, p. 66) was the most logical method of building personal bonds outside the family unit. It is quite reasonable to assume that the practice of gift-giving was learnt from the interaction with Tatars,[41] and reinforced by the clergy. A Russian believed that if he showered a bureaucrat with gifts and attention not for a specific service but on other, unrelated to service, occasions, such as holidays and birthdays, he would make a bureaucrat go an extra mile, should the gift-giver need assistance in resolving a problem with the authorities or evading taxes.[42] After all, even salvation could be secured through gifts to the monks. Curiously,

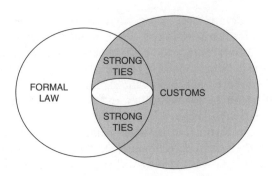

Figure 4.1   Interaction of formal law and customs

many clerks were sons of the clergy (Demidova, 1987, p. 58), hence, it was not surprising that they carried the gift-accepting practices into the new profession.

Federal and provincial administrations were probably equally bad. By some accounts, already in the time of Ivan IV clerks pocketed up to one-half of the treasury's income (Kliuchevskii, 1957, Vol. 3, p. 131). Because Russian bureaucracy grew out of the administration of a prince's household of the appanage period, its agents assumed personal rather than functional relationships. Bribery was widely acceptable already in the 16th-century local administration.[43] Voivodes (*voevoda* in Russian)[44] in the 17th century sustained this practice: they continued to 'feed' off the population. Unrelated to service, contributions 'in honour' of a voivode were common, and he accepted as much as 'a hand can give'. Voivodes were not only administrators, but also judges. The law provided no clear limits on their power, opening a door to arbitrage.

Localities were supposed to support a voivode and his administrative retinue out of dues gathered from either urban or peasant communes. The expenditure books of local elders describe that they regularly provided voivodes with meat, fish, pies, candles, paper and ink. On holidays and name-days they brought gifts, sweets or money wrapped in paper for the voivode himself, his wife, and his children, his clerks, servants, even for the 'God's Fool'[45] who lived at his house (Kliuchevskii, 1957, Vol. 3, pp. 149–51),[46] much like the princes showered Tatar khans and their families with gifts a few centuries earlier. In the late 18th century, Catherine II was still getting complaints about voivodes, who often took bribes to compensate for their lack of government salary.

The rising Muscovite state needed educated clerks to fill in the ranks of administration. But learned gentry, much less gentry who felt a longing for education and hence professional dedication, were rare. Forcible schooling by the state produced not only poor results, but formed an army of clerks who in a primitive utilitarian way viewed education as a sure way into the ranks of bureaucracy and to bribes (ibid., pp. 11–12). Especially vicious extortionists and thieves were the clerks and scribes in local offices who collected dues. A scribe who started with one shabby outfit in about four to five years was able to build a stone house for himself.[47] Graft was acceptable not only customarily but also officially. Clerks themselves acknowledge bribes as a supplementary income. Petitioning for a higher pay they complained that their work yielded no under-the-table income because it concerned papers for the government, not private ones (Kliuchevskii, 1958, Vol. 5, p. 235).[48]

The miserably low pay and the opportunity to use law enforcement power for extortion produced incentives for corruption among police as well. Police used 'requests for travel permits, navigation permits to boats on rivers and canals, the right to open taverns . . . as occasions for accepting bribes' (Brower, 1990, pp. 15–16). There is evidence that in the 18th century, Moscow administrators took hefty bribes from foreign entrepreneurs.[49] Even access to the official publishing press of the Church (the synodal typography) in the 19th century required 'good connections', which were available for high-ranking clergy but not to provincial priests (Freeze, 1989, p. 12).

Often, the government anti-corruption measures only made it worse. Trying to stop theft from the treasury, Peter the Great instituted positions of financial inspectors to discover the embezzlers. If a thief was discovered, the inspectors were entitled to keep half of the monetary penalty for themselves, but it was prohibited to complain about or appeal the inspectors' accusation. While these measures were necessary to give inspectors the incentives to perform well, the arbitrage of their power inevitably led to huge bribes (Kliuchevskii, 1958, Vol. 4, pp. 165–6).

Corruption and theft permeated all levels of society, from peasants to the court's nobles.[50] Theft among the higher ranks of bureaucracy and among the nobles was hushed up through personal connections (ibid., p. 154). Enthroned at very young ages, the first three Tsars of the Romanov dynasty were unsure of their policies and promised not to prosecute or punish by death any noble for corruption (Kliuchevskii, 1957, Vol. 3, p. 131), which of course encouraged bad behaviour. In the 18th century the Senate farmed out *all* customs duties for 2 million rubles. When Catherine II brought them back under the state's supervision, it turned out that St Petersburg customs duties *alone* brought more than 3 million rubles of income.

Similarly, factories were farmed out by the Senate to the court's favourites (the Shuvalovs, the Vorontsovs, the Chernyshevs) together with millions of rubles in financial assistance (Kliuchevskii, 1958, Vol. 5, p. 67).[51]

Local elites controlled the municipalities by the beginning of the 20th century (Hamm, 1976b, p. 189), perhaps even earlier. The lower ranks of the nobility did not fall too far behind. During Peter the Great's reign, when military service became obligatory for all landowners, many avoided military duty by obtaining a bureaucratic post through personal connections (bureaucrats were exempt from military service) or bribed an official to relieve them of service altogether (Kliuchevskii, 1958, Vol. 4, pp. 76, 78).[52]

The peasants confused law with custom and private property with usage or possession (Pipes, 1974, pp. 157–8). For many centuries *mir* was literally a peasant's world, where his life was organized as a member of a relatively small group, where his life brought him in contact with raw facts of nature and where his interaction with the outside world occurred through hands-on experiences. Therefore, abstract concepts, such as 'state', 'society', and 'law' were incomprehensible to him because they could not be filled with or related to real things and people that he knew.[53]

Attitudes to justice,[54] often expressed in the decisions of peasant magistrates, were determined by an overriding concern for communal cohesion: the maintenance of good neighbourly relations was valued more highly than impartiality. A peasant did not understand due process, nor did he seek it, being best suited to autocracy. As a result of lawlessness of the land the peasants resorted to disobedience, theft,[55] rowdyism, which in the absence of constitutional rights became functional (Wirtschafter, 1997, p. 123).[56]

Private Property

Many scholars point out that Russians have no history of private property. One of the reasons is that the Great Russian plain was populated by colonization; people were scarce and the land abundant. Russians seldom learnt to value the land as a resource.[57] To peasants land had little value; for a prince's armed retinue the land without peasants (and therefore no collectible income) had no value as well (Solov'ev, 1959, Vol. 1, p. 227).

Before the rise of the Muscovite state, land belonged to the commune, not to the individuals. The Muscovite state encouraged colonization by individuals, families and communes, but it was interested in keeping it in the status of black, taxable, land. Therefore, even though individuals had the land for their private use, passed it on to their heirs, sold it and rented it, they had never officially bought it from the government and did not hold a property title. Neither Russians, nor the Tsars equated such possession with full private property rights (Solov'ev, 1960, Book II, Vol. 4, pp. 538–9). Petty princes were prohibited from selling their land without the Tsar's approval (Solov'ev, 1960, Book IV, Vol. 7, p. 92).

Under the pressing needs of national defence the Muscovite state tied land ownership to an obligation of service (Kliuchevskii, 1959, Vol. 6, p. 396). In essence, land rights could be revoked from a landowner at any time if he or his heirs stopped serving.[58] The informal individual communities were respected neither by central or local government nor by the courts. The government exercised quite a number of takings of land and administrative restructuring without the consent of those residing there, and thus ignoring rights to ownership based on heredity. When appealed to, the courts produced contradicting decisions creating juridical ambiguity.[59] In fact, until the 18th century the word for private property (*sobstvennost'*) did not exist in Russian (Hittle, 1979, p. 33).

Private property laws were most problematic for the least educated and the most traditional members of the society. Post-1861, there were a lot of disputes about land boundaries in the countryside because peasants refused to recognize the formal definition of property rights. They continued to use meadows and forests, which officially belonged to the landlords, not the commune. The market in land expanded tremendously in the years following the emancipation. Though willing participants in the sale, post-transaction the peasants did not recognize formal rights of the buyers, because those were often outsiders to the commune and were more likely to restrict peasants' access and raise fees for use (Wirtschafter, 1997, pp. 126–7).

IN CONCLUSION: SOCIAL DIFFERENTIATION AND STRONG TIES

Russia had no rule of law, no one uniform system of due process, if any at all. Individuals were united in communities by their obligations to the state not by their rights. Therefore, the venue of uniting their efforts for corporate rights bargaining was not suggested to them by the circumstances of their environment and was not immediately available or easy to pursue, even if they decided to do so. Instead, personal connections and bribes as ways to avoid obligations and to find ways around the law were more obvious, available and immediately effective methods. 'The failure to overcome pervasive social and institutional fragmentation resulted . . . from the strength and durability of countless, practically invisible microcommunities' (Wirtschafter, 1997, p. 140) – clusters of strong ties based on kin or illegal transactions.

The strength of such ties resulted from the failure of local communities to provide a social and legal safety net for Russians. When individuals turned to the state for that, they encountered patrimonial attitudes.[60] In Western Europe many achievements were made by the efforts of individuals and

private civil organizations without government knowledge and intervention. In Russia there were no networks of civic engagement, therefore the
state was expected to fulfil the gap. Western estate representation formed
in order to limit the autocratic power; in Russia it formed to support it
(Kliuchevskii, 1957, Vol. 3, p. 211).

Perhaps the most crucial factor in the proliferation of strong ties and
social differentiation was the concept of 'otherness'. Individuals and
groups in Russian society defined their own status by differentiating
themselves from other individuals and groups that lacked certain characteristics that they themselves possessed – they acquired positive identity by
negative definition.[61] Outsiders were not only foreigners: a peasant was an
outsider in an urban environment; a merchant was an outsider at a village
flea market; and a peasant belonging to a commune near Moscow was an
outsider to a commune in Siberia.[62]

Trust relationships usually did not transcend narrow geographical and
social boundaries. Many villagers found employment in towns through
personal connections with their fellow citizens (Wirtschafter, 1997, pp.
147–8 and Brower, 1990, p. 88), but the workers' collectives were still
torn apart from within because of differentiation.[63] Because of 'otherness'
the Russian pre-revolutionary society made poor progress in establishing
general trust and social cohesion on the national level. In Mironov's words,
Russian *Gemeinschaft*, a commune where social links are based mostly on
emotions and friendly dispositions, did not transcend into *Gesellschaft*, a
society or a large community where they are based on 'rational exchange of
goods and services' and therefore can include exchanges between enemies
(Mironov, 2000, p. 286). The economic logic of benefit never overtook the
social logic of clan loyalty.

The circumstances that made Russians a people that they are,
complemented each other remarkably well. The unpredictability of the
law but malleability of its executors fitted well with the Russian *avos'*
('perhaps'): in gambling against nature a Russian had no way of increasing
his odds, gambling against the law presented a better opportunity because
of personal connections. Patrimonial role and strength of the state, which
dictated the circumstances of life for a Russian, mimicked the way a Russian
had to succumb to the forces of nature. And the Orthodox religious doctrine
succeeded in convincing Russians that the world is fair this way.

NOTES

1. According to the most accepted version of the origination of the Rurik family in
    Russia, the weak propensity to self-govern drove the people of Novgorod to invite

the Ruriks, who were from a Viking tribe Rus', to rule their land. The Novgorodians asked for assistance because although their 'land was large and plentiful, it had no order' (*Novgorodskaia pervaia letopis'* (*The First Chronicle of Novgorod*), 1950, p. 106). Kliuchevskii does not believe that the Slavic tribes summoned the Vikings because they could not govern themselves. He believes that Rus' were hired to defend the Slavs from other Viking tribes and other invaders. In time the Vikings took power into their hands (see Kliuchevskii (1956, Vol. 1, Lecture IX)). Vikings were called Varyagi in Russian, which means a peddler or a small-scale merchant, and this is precisely what they were in Russia at the time. They settled in quite substantial numbers in commercial towns and blended with local merchants, because they shared trading goals and because they had military skills to defend themselves from invaders. The population around large towns was probably quite accustomed to their presence and was aware of their military potential. Perhaps this explains why the transfer of power happened without a fight (ibid., pp. 134–5).

2. Translation from Russian. For the original Russian text, see Kliuchevskii (1956, Vol. 1, pp. 310–11).
3. Translation from Russian. For the original Russian text, see Kliuchevskii (1956, Vol. 1, pp. 313–14).
4. For the original Russian text, see Kliuchevskii (1956, Vol. 1, pp. 313–14).
5. Translation from Russian. For the original Russian text, see Kliuchevskii (1956, Vol. 1, p. 314).
6. Translation from Russian. For the original Russian text, see Kliuchevskii (1956, Vol. 1, p. 315). For description of the Russian national character, see also Losskii (1991, pp. 238–360).
7. Some scholars point out that the Great Russian plain has a very complex river system (Kliuchevskii, 1956, Vol. 1, pp. 56–60). A people, who had such a great support system as rivers, did not have to work hard to invent anything else, such as a more complex social interaction. Limited access to the shoreline made Russia more similar to Asia than to Europe (Kliuchevskii, 1956, Vol. 1, pp. 46–7).
8. They settled among the ruins, but these were the ruins of the great civilization.
9. Also at the time Western Europe was occupied with its inner war conflicts, thus, its cultural influence could not be spread through conquest of the Slavic territory. Instead, the Slavs had very close contacts with nomads on the eastern and south-eastern borders, such as Polovtsy, whom the Slavs called 'our own infidels' (Solov'ev, 1959, Book I, Vol. 1, pp. 669–70).
10. In the early 16th century Rome moved to reinstate its dominance in Poland because of threats of Protestantism. The Orthodox population had to acknowledge Rome's authority; however, many refused to do so and looked to the east for support. The religious division caused hostility between the Poles and the Russians (Pipes, 1974, pp. 38–9).
11. In the Muscovite state the armed retinue succumbed to the suzerain prince's power, while in Poland it became a formidable opposition (Solov'ev, 1960, Book IV, Vol. 7, p. 27).
12. The Chozars (also known as Khazars) were a Turkic people who appeared in Transcaucasia in the 2nd century AD and later settled in the region of the lower Volga. At the height of its power, in the 8th to the 10th centuries, the Chozar empire extended from the northern shores of the Black Sea and the Caspian Sea to the Urals and as far westward as Kiev.
13. And the prices were rising at the rate of about 7 per cent a year (Hellie, 1999, pp. 519–20).
14. For more discussion of the origins of *mir* and Kaufman's work, see Shanin (1986). Kliuchevskii notes that even though the commune acquired some new characteristics in the 16th century, land repartition and mutual collective responsibility had existed before and bred social norms that quite comfortably accommodated changes in that century. For a comprehensive description of *mir*, see Kliuchevskii (1957, Vol. 2, pp. 295–308).

15. Land repartition itself was of three basic types. In the first type, a whole new redivision of plots occurred each time. In the second and third types, the sizes and number of plots remained the same; for more details see Watters (1968, pp. 142–4). There existed the so-called non-repartitional communes, where arable lands were held in permanent possession by individuals and which in 1905 accounted for 19 per cent of the peasant lands of European Russia. Geographically, however, these communes were located in the western and north-western regions – in the areas that had previously been under Polish or Baltic-German rule. But even these in practice were close to repartitional ones. They often used meadows and forests in common and exhibited the same hostility to outsiders, that is, land was rarely sold to someone who was not a member of the commune. Curiously, the same centripetal tendencies were reported in Belorussia, where there was no communal land redivision (Shanin, 1972, p. 80). Perhaps the social structure of the peasant household together with external dangers or their perception on the part of peasants reinforced these tendencies. Kolle documents that married sons living together with their parents in one large household in the 19th century was common in Russia (virilocal residence) but not in Europe (neolocal principles). Also, Russian peasants exhibited early mean and practically universal marriage, while the Europeans married later and many remained unmarried (Kolle, 1995, p. 61).

16. A short summary of characteristics of the commune is provided by Watters (1968, pp. 134–5).

17. Later on, *obshchina* (peasant commune, *mir*) often got rid of some burdensome members by sending them off as recruits.

18. On the differences between *mir* on *obrok* and *mir* on *barshchina*, see Mavor ([1925] 1965, Vol. 1, pp. 217–18). Partially it was influenced by kin relationships and mutual aid obligations in the village (Kelly, 2000, pp. 69–70, 71). See Note 48, Chapter 3 in this volume for definitions of *obrok* and *barshchina*.

19. For more details on the evolution of *mir*, see Watters (1968, pp. 137–41). There were projects recommending individual peasant ownership, for example Elagin's project in the end of the 18th century. An investigation, however, showed that such projects were alien not only to the peasant but also to the official mind and were abandoned (Mavor [1925] 1965, Vol. 1, pp. 255–7).

20. Land repartition was insisted upon by the poorer peasants with smaller plots of land (Mavor [1925] 1965, Vol. 1, pp. 250–51).

21. This, of course, does not mean that the commune worked to prevent any change. It incorporated quite successfully new social and economic experiences *to fit into existing customs* (Wirtschafter, 1997, p. 116). Perhaps too successfully, otherwise it might have been forced to abandon the old, unproductive, ways.

22. Wirtschafter (1997, pp. 112–17) holds a very different, positive, view of *obshchina*. She is, of course, partially right: many of the climatic and economic difficulties were better overcome collectively. Wealth stratification within the commune was not great; for details see Hartley (1999, pp. 45–6).

23. But among the peasants, townsmen and the gentry alike, social (and eventually economic) inertia also stemmed from the lack of proper education. 'The access of peasants to books was hindered to the utmost by the authorities; lectures and talks in the village . . . met actually almost insurmountable obstacles', cited in Volin (1960, p. 297). Both higher and lower ranks of nobility were poorly educated. The first wave of schooling came with the French Enlightenment, but the French teachers did not encourage independent thinking. Jesuits, who came later, taught independent thinking and critical analysis, but their influence was rather limited (Kliuchevskii, 1958, Vol. 5, p. 246). For more on education during Catherine II's reign, see ibid. (Lecture LXXXI); on compulsory education and its disastrous results during Peter the Great's time, see Kliuchevskii (1958, Vol. 4, pp. 78–80 and ibid., pp. 236–55). Education in economics was non-existent in the 17th and 18th centuries (ibid., p. 82). The leading scholar of social sciences at the time and one of the few learned people in Russia, Tatishchev, considered both Locke's and Hobbes's writings harmful (ibid., p. 269).

24. For more details on self-government, both rural and urban, post-1861, see Vucinich (1960, pp. 191–206).
25. For example, the Church supported the state and autocracy during the struggle between Vasilii and Shemyaka in the Middle Ages; see Solov'ev (1960, Book II, Vol. 4, pp. 413–15 and also pp. 583–4).
26. Zaozerskaya finds that monasteries were important for industrial development, cited in Bushkovitch (1980, p. 127).
27. For more details, see Kliuchevskii (1957, Vol. 2, Lecture XXXV).
28. Freeze (1989) tries to trump a popular assumption, held among others by Pipes, that the Russian Church was an instrument of the state. He investigates the micro activity of the clerics on the issue of social injustice and concludes that although the majority of priests were simply silent on the issue, some indeed were not. As soon as we accept Pipes's criteria of looking at the Church as an institution, it becomes unequivocally clear that the efforts of a few did not produce any sizeable effect either on micro or on macro level. In fact, my reading of Freeze's evidence only supports the theory that the Church was reinforcing the existing social order.
29. And also sparked the debate about the rights and wrongs of the Church's material possessions.
30. In a complicated ideological battle within the ranks of clergy one side was against keeping the Church's properties and the other side for it. The pro-property clergy saw no other way but to turn for help to the state, which was already dissatisfied with the extent of monastic landownership. They won and for the time being saved the property of the Church but at a price of losing whatever remained of their independence; for details see Pipes (1974, pp. 229–32); and also Kliuchevskii (1957, Vol. 2, pp. 279–86); and also Solov'ev (1960, Book III, Vol. 5, pp. 196–7). On how schism further degraded the Church by depriving its ranks from the most dedicated, see ibid. (pp. 236–9). On the history of schism, see Kliuchevskii (1957, Vol. 3, Lectures LIV and LV). It cannot be denied though that schism opened the door to Western influence among the elite, however limited it was.
31. In order to be able to establish this claim, a Russian Tsar married Sophia Paleolog, the niece of the last Emperor of Byzantium.
32. For example, regional parishes were permitted to use local languages, and there was no more or less rigid unifying organization.
33. For details, see Pipes (1974, pp. 239–44).
34. Of course it was not directly the product of labour for most nobles, but it was through personal efforts that many peasant entrepreneurs succeeded.
35. More on this in Pipes (1974, pp. 50–52).
36. Land tenure was introduced when boyars were not vassals anymore (Pipes, 1974, pp. 52–3). Presumably Pipes here retells the work of Pavlov-Sil'vanskii. N.P. Pavlov-Sil'vanskii (1869–1908) belonged to the 'new' generation of historians who in the early 1900s put forward a theory that many of Russia's institutions were similar to European institutions of feudalism: see Pavlov-Sil'vanskii (1988). For more details on Pavlov-Sil'vanskii's work, see Gerschenkron (1970, pp. 5–6).
37. Quite illuminating in this regard is the origination of the word 'freedom' in Russian, *svoboda*. According to one source *svoboda* was a synonym to a privilege or a particular given right. It came from the word *sloboda*, which was a settlement founded by a prince or a landowner. The settlers were granted certain rights or privileges, but not freedom to do as they please (Kliuchevskii, 1959, Vol. 6, pp. 247–8). To indicate freedom to do as one wishes Russians used the concept of *volia* or having one's way. Pipes (1974, p. 157) cites Belinskii on the interpretation of this word: 'Our people understand freedom as volia, and volia for it means to make mischief. The liberated Russian nation would not head for the parliament but it would run for the tavern to drink liquor, smash glasses, and hang the dvoryane who shave their beards'. According to another source *svoboda* came from Indo-European root *sue-* meaning one's own and suffix *-obod* (Chernyh, 2002). Either way, Russian etymology of the word is different from Greek, German and English etymology.

38. As applied the Russian law practised that it is better to punish an innocent person than let the guilty one go (Kliuchevskii, 1958, Vol. 4, p. 179).
39. Vucinich rightly defines estates (*soslovia*) as 'neither social classes nor castes. They were social strata that were more dynamic – and more susceptible to vertical mobility – than castes; yet they were more rigid and subject to appreciably less mobility than social classes' (1960, p. 199).
40. Isolation of Russians was further reinforced by the state law: the Muscovite state had certain prohibitions on travel abroad (Kliuchevskii 1957, Vol. 3, p. 44). In addition, the 16th-century Baltic countries deliberately prevented migration of educated people to Russia (Solov'ev, 1960, Book III, Vol. 6, pp. 498–9). Until Peter the Great, centuries later and quite unsuccessfully, tried to encourage travel and education abroad.
41. It is worth noting that the proper gifts and timely gift-giving rituals preserved many commoners the well-being of their families, and many princes their lives. So it is reasonable to assume that this practice left more than a trivial trace in Russians' social memory.
42. This, of course, implies that any law could be bent. Indeed, this was and still is true.
43. Local administration shared the extorted income with their superiors in the capital (Solov'ev, 1960, Book IV, Vol. 7, pp. 284–5).
44. Equivalent to governor of province in Poland. Voivodes in the 17th century were sons and grandsons of governor-generals a century earlier in the same provinces (Kliuchevskii, 1957, Vol. 3, p. 148). Presumably they were granted their posts either to simplify the selection process or by way of personal connections.
45. A person usually with mental disability, an invalid, whose only means of survival is through charity. Wealthy people or people of power often gave those invalids a place to live and fed them because it was believed to be good works.
46. At the *sobor* (see Note 29, Chapter 3 in this volume) of 1642 a complaint was submitted describing exceptional riches of the Moscow clerks (Kliuchevskii, 1957, Vol. 3, p. 203). High ranks of Moscow administration, including members of the Tsar's family and a few wealthy merchants, profited from debasing copper coins for quite a while before being discovered (ibid., pp. 223–4).
47. In the 18th century it was a significant upward jump in the standard of living, and it did not come out of official salary, but from bribes and theft. Both accounts of foreigners and contemporary Russians note the corruption. By some estimates out of 100 rubles in collected taxes only 30 went to the treasury, and the rest was divided between the clerks (Kliuchevskii, 1958, Vol. 4, p. 144). For examples of bribery among the officials at the mountain works in the 18th century, see Mavor ([1925] 1965, Vol. 1, p. 456).
48. Law also acknowledged some 'extra' fees as legal (Potter, 2000, p. 27 and Kelly, 2000, p. 74). In any event, even though taking or extorting payments was most of the time officially renounced, giving bribes was not. Official salaries were negatively related to the amount of illegal income in the forms of bribes and gifts; for examples in the 17th century see Demidova (1987, pp. 137–45). Hellie found evidence that before the end of the Times of Troubles (ca. 1598–1613) bureaucrats were paid well and in full, but not so afterwards. Peter the Great would often refuse to pay the officials because he had no funds (Hellie, 1999, pp. 519, 530).
49. Account of Ivan Pososhkov who wrote in the 18th century, cited in Kliuchevskii (1958, Vol. 4, p. 113).
50. Including the Tsars. For instance, Alexander II received millions for railroad concessions (Solov'eva, 1975, pp. 104–5).
51. Nobles even collaborated with the wealthy peasants (*kulaki*) in the mountain works region. *Kulaki* manipulated village elections and imposition of taxes, proceeds of which they shared with factory authorities (Mavor [1925] 1965, Vol. 1, pp. 477–8).
52. For more details on bureaucracy and examples of bribery and gift-giving practices, see Lovell, Ledeneva and Rogachevskii (2000, pp. 1–140).
53. Pipes (1974, pp. 157–8) cites anthropologists referring to a Russian peasant having a 'primitive mind', which resulted in inability to think abstractly. This should not be taken to its extreme meaning, however, as peasants proved to be very resourceful and

intelligent, although again when it came to practical decisions in everyday circumstances (Mavor, 1925, Vol. 2, pp. 253–5).

54. Justice was understood in a perverted way. Often a confession, obtained through torture, was the only evidence by which the accused was found guilty (Pipes, 1974, p. 158).

55. Amongst other criminal offences, theft was common in a Russian village. To steal from one's neighbour was quite acceptable (Mavor, 1925, Vol. 2, p. 261). Theft of goods under five rubles was not a criminal offence (Hartley, 1999, p. 86). Even though five rubles was a small sum, the fact itself is enlightening.

56. 'Flight, evasion, and the assumption of false legal identities' were common practice; for examples see Wirtschafter (1997, pp. 123–4).

57. Soul tax was not tied to land but directly to a person.

58. Curiously, the idea among the gentry was still that the serfs, much like the land, were the Tsar's property granted to them temporarily (Kluchevskii, 1957, Vol. 3, p. 183). The same idea prevailed among the peasants as well (Kluchevskii, 1958, Vol. 4, p. 103).

59. For examples, see Wirtschafter (1997, pp. 139–40).

60. Although patrimonial attitudes, characteristic of the state actions, did not go astray from the population's general beliefs (Hittle, 1979, p. 3). When asked about something they did not know, Muscovites answered that it is only known to God and to the Tsar of Russia (Kliuchevskii, 1957, Vol. 2, p. 137).

61. For a full discussion of otherness and foreigness, see Wirtschafter (1997, pp. 163–8).

62. Russians are known for their hospitality to strangers. But this should not confuse the real picture: as long as the stranger remains a guest they will be treated well. As soon as they make a move to enter a local community, to bring their business in, or to participate in everyday life in any other capacity than that of a guest, they will be scorned and inhibited.

63. For examples, see Wirtschafter (1997, pp. 144–5, 157).

5. Status of merchants

The peculiar social and political status of merchants affected their economic power and predisposed their reliance on connections rather than on market mechanisms. The development of the informal institutions of private enterprise was at least very integrated with and, perhaps, subservient to the development of the institutions of state power.

FIGURES, CIVIL AND TAX DUTIES

The number of merchants was low throughout the pre-revolutionary period and civil and tax duties levied on them were quite burdensome.[1] The size of the merchant class remained small because it was more advantageous for the wealthy merchants to enter a higher stratum[2] and because official entry into the merchant profession was very limited for those from other classes. Moscow *kuptsy* – merchants – of the 14th and 15th centuries tried to buy up as much land as they could to enter the ranks of boyars.[3]

Trade was carried out under the auspices of the princes; consequently, the major source of material wealth for merchants did not rest on being a merchant, but on owning *votchinal* (patrimonial) land (Sakharov, 1959, p. 163).[4] The Russian bourgeois class lacked exclusive characteristics from the start: in general, merchants differed insignificantly from boyars and the types of privileges given to landowners and to merchants were very similar. Politically, merchants behaved the same as the high-ranking boyars: they used the right to leave the service of one prince for another (ibid., p. 164), although they did not have corporate rights and did not form guilds.[5]

Towards the end of the 16th century, the Moscow merchants were officially ranked according to their wealth and obligations to the state. Those who were especially wealthy – called *gosti* – were few, perhaps 20 or 30 in the 17th century.[6] *Gosti* were most numerous in Moscow.[7] The state employed these wealthiest merchants to collect taxes from the state monopolies and later to manage state enterprises. For that (and only for that) they received the status *gosti*, which gave them certain privileges,[8] although initially few asked for them, and many were simply dragooned into service.

Moderately wealthy Moscow merchants formed two so-called 'hundreds' (*sotni* – plural): *gostinnaia* and *sukonnaia sotni*. Their obligations to the state were less than those of *gosti*, but still quite onerous.[9] State service required a certain amount of wealth as a back-up guarantee,[10] and service often took merchants away from their families and business for years at a time. Their numbers were scarce relative to the demand for state tax collectors, therefore many were forced to serve every other year (Kliuchevskii, 1959, Vol. 6, p. 164).[11]

Besides 'tax farming', merchants supervised fulfilment of state obligations performed in kind, such as the repair of bridges, town fortifications and managed state factories and works, such as salt-mining (ibid., p. 413). Petty traders and artisans formed several 'black hundreds' (Kliuchevskii, 1957, Vol. 2, p. 380 and 1959, Vol. 6, pp. 165–6).[12]

Many *gosti* ended up serving in the government as trade councillors – *kommertsii sovetniki* (Kliuchevskii, 1959, Vol. 6, p. 165). In the 18th century, wealthy entrepreneurs, including traders and bankers, were referred to as the 1st guild, and petty traders and artisans were included in the 2nd guild (Kliuchevskii, 1958, Vol. 4, p. 187). The 18th-century *posad* (urban resident) tax rolls show that 'over 40 per cent of Russia's so-called merchants were hired laborers, unemployed and impoverished persons' (Hittle, 1976, p. 56).[13]

Sources dated 1854 show that 'only 42 per cent of Moscow townspeople possessed a demonstrable trade' (Wirtschafter, 1997, p. 134). The 1897 Census shows that merchants constituted no more than 0.2 per cent of the total population of Russia. This percentage declined afterwards. The true numbers, in fact, may have been even lower because some individuals bought titles to a trade for other reasons than merchandizing (Bokhanov, 1994, pp. 20–21).[14]

The composition of the merchant class was relatively diverse in terms of ethnicity because there were many trading foreigners (Rieber, 1982, Tables 2.3, 3.2, 6.3, 7.1), and religion (ibid., Tables 2.1 and 2.4), but less in terms of origin. The Church schism[15] redefined the religious composition of Russia's trade capital – Moscow – in favour of Old Believers.[16] Old Believers' frugality by some accounts helped the original accumulation of capital in Russia (Semenova et al., 2000, pp. 437–9).[17] After the war of 1812, when most Moscow merchants' estates had not survived the fire, merchants of the old faith from remote regions moved in and later constituted a significant part of the merchant class.

The implications of Church schism and its connection to the business culture of Old Believers are interesting. As an ostracized religious minority, Old Believers turned their efforts to economic success. Their community acutely showed the attributes of the 'capitalistic spirit' at work. However, the migration to Moscow among other factors attenuated previous differences with the political regime, and already by the 20th century, merchants of the old faith did not express a strong opposition to government actions. Their economic success was limited to individual families and had no political consequences.

Profit margins were high only for a few court favourites, but for them they were very high. According to the 1902 Moscow Census, owners of industrial enterprise, of commercial and credit establishments and those who derived income from renting land and capital, with annual incomes exceeding 50,000 rubles (which was very high for that time) constituted only 1.4 per cent (little over 300 people) of the total Moscow population. St Petersburg had 236 such people. In Moscow their combined annual income was 74.6 million, and in St Petersburg 71.6 million (Petrov, 2001, pp. 48–9), to compare with approximately 25 million Petersburg city income in 1907 and 43.5 million in 1912 (Beliaev, 2001, p. 42, Table 3.3).[18]

For the majority, profit margins were very low for several reasons. First, merchandizing was heavily taxed. In addition to regular dues, there were emergency taxes – those introduced without proper notice. In the 17th century[19] a 20 per cent income tax was introduced as an emergency tax. Because of unclear formulation, it was often confused with taxing the value of possessions, profit and capital turnover.

But taxes 'in extreme circumstances' became a frequent occurrence. The 20 per cent tax was collected in 1614, 1615, twice during the Polish war in 1633 and 1634; in the period between 1654–80 a 5 and a 6.66 per cent tax were collected, as well a 10 per cent five times and a 20 per cent twice (Kliuchevskii, 1957, Vol. 3, pp. 233–5). Given that money was scarce in Russia at that time (Pipes, 1974, pp. 203, 206–7)[20] and the law determined 20 per cent as the upper limit for lenders (Kliuchevskii, 1957, Vol. 3, p. 234),[21] the amount and the unpredictability of taxes easily created havoc in the business environment. Hellie found some 280 different taxes in the 17th century (1999, Chapter 23 and Table 23.1 on pp. 537–40), which rose substantially throughout the century without a corresponding rise in prices or productivity (ibid., pp. 568–70).[22] In the 18th century only among customs dues were there 17 different ones (Kliuchevskii, 1958, Vol. 4, p. 308).[23]

It is illustrative to describe a sample of dues that a 17th-century merchant had to pay. First, there was a 2.5 per cent levy on any cash carried by a merchant paid at every custom station. Sold merchandise was taxed between 2.5 and 5 per cent, and probably unsold merchandise as well, plus other fees for registration, storage, weighing, boat or cart tax and so on:

> At home, that merchant had to pay a tax on his house (median, 65 kopeks), the various taxes to support the cossacks (4.5 kopeks) and musketeers (1 ruble),

the irregular fifth taxes (2 rubles), the fortifications tax (20 kopeks), the tax to ransom captives from the Tatars (5 kopeks), probably post taxes (10 kopeks) and road taxes (22 kopeks), a tax on his shop (1 ruble). (Hellie, 1999, p. 570)

Excluding the fifth tax, this came to 3.25 rubles minimum. Any document that needed to be written, signed or sealed came with government fees. Given that the median wage was four kopeks a day, one can see they had to put in a considerable number of hours to support the state (ibid.).[24]

Already under Ivan IV internal customs were widely spread. To avoid paying customs dues, merchants organized fairs in other, remote, locations where there were no customs yet.[25] This is possibly one of the reasons why seasonal fairs dominated over regular town markets.[26] Also, as Langer points out, although the Tatar Yoke did not extinguish trade in general, by destroying the urban infrastructure it prevented Russian merchants from giving up long-distance trade for sedentary business with 'bookkeeping, credit, bills of exchange' (Langer, 1976, p. 31).

A fair is an organism independent of the territory on which it is held while a 'market is a part of a superior organism on which it is dependent' (Rozman, 1976a, p. 126). A fair is also independent of the institutions and social networks of the locality.[27] Fairs clearly dominated markets in 18th-century Russia[28] and by taking over the inter-regional trade, they infringed on trade in stores and markets. Markets, in fact, met only periodically.[29] Most businesses were not stationary; merchants had to undertake the role of both retailers and wholesalers simultaneously. As a result of the dominance of fairs over the city markets, market participants in Russia had less chance to shape the formal networks and institutions in the cities. They had to resort to infiltrating the informal sphere. Only around the 1900s did city markets start gaining importance as hubs of trade and production (Brower, 1990, pp. 62–3).

Second, after the taxes, the self-sustained existence of most Russians and the privileges solicited by interest groups limited the scope of private entrepreneurship. And, third, local authorities gave a lot of leeway to foreign merchants, who were richer on average and gave larger bribes (Kliuchevskii, 1958, Vol. 4, pp. 112–13).

Fourth, the religious doctrine, which scorned wealth, reinforced negative social attitudes towards merchants, breaking the already shaky bridge of trust between businesspeople and their customers. The general public thought of people of trade as street-smarts and cheaters (Kliuchevskii, 1958, Vol. 4, p. 112),[30] which many of them were, though not completely by their own doing.[31] Fairy tales never portray the rich (except princes) as virtuous (Bokhanov, 1994, pp. 8–9). Towards the 19th century we already see very little of a positive image of a merchant in literature. It depicts

merchants as greedy and cunning,[32] dominant traits that were the unfortunate result of the process of 'natural selection' due to the 'hazards' of their
profession. Wealth from trade and works (*promysly*) was always associated with high risk, but there was money to be made if the circumstances
were right. Those who deliberately undertook this risk already possessed
ruthlessness and dishonesty that came in handy when manipulating connections, cutting corners and cheating on law enforcement and customers.
Others developed these traits through adaptation behaviour.

Fifth, backwardness of the institutional organization of merchants left
them helpless against the growth of tax-exempt entities, like monasteries.[33]
Pre-Petrine Russia knew only a few forms of trade association. One was
the *torgovyi dom* (trading house), which consisted of close relatives. They
had neither joint capital investment nor joint management decisions – all
decisions were made by the eldest family member. Another form was an
association for retail, where one travelling merchant distributed goods of
several others for a fee. The law of 1699 *ordered* entrepreneurs to form
trading associations, but volunteers were scarce because no one knew how
this was supposed to work. As usual, Peter the Great resorted to luring
entrepreneurs with privileges and, if that did not work, he simply coerced
them (Kliuchevskii, 1958, Vol. 4, pp. 114–17).[34]

Sixth, Russian merchants were technologically backward. Councillor
of state Sievers wrote to Catherine II about the merchants of Novgorod:
'They carry on trade without any order, seldom with written documents,
without books and almost without numbers' (Jones, 1977, p. 433, Note
33). The pitiful state of education in Russia has already been mentioned
above.[35] McKay (1970) cites foreign reports that assess extreme technological backwardness before the large wave of foreign business in the late 19th
century.[36] Most ventures, in fact, were organized and led by foreigners.[37]

And finally, peasants and other categories of population successfully
competed with merchants for a share of domestic market, although many
illegally:[38]

> By the beginning of the nineteenth century . . . there were more than two thou-
> sand peasants selling goods in St. Petersburg basements and small shops daily,
> using the identities of the petty bourgeois. Foreign employees were selling
> 'secretly' under the protection of their employers right out of their homes,
> 'foreign and Russian couriers, the commanders and the entire crews of packet
> steamships, boatmen of all nations trading in Russia' were also engaged in
> illegal trade. (Lebedev, 2001, p. 23)

Foreign merchants broke the prohibitions on retail trade (ibid.).[39]
Landowners too, but as an interest group, secured a large share of the
more profitable industries in the 18th century.[40]

Commercial and civil law in Russia was only weakly distinct; for the most part state officials settled disputes involving merchants.[41] This raised the bankruptcy rate among merchants. Nobility and state officials bought large amounts of goods from merchants on credit, but never paid back. The courts did not honour merchants' complaints; in fact, many promissory notes written by the nobles were simply 'lost' in the process. At the same time, merchants borrowed predominantly from foreign bankers (operating within Russia), which were not so forgiving of defaults on payments: often a merchant continued paying interest on the interest, when the capital had already been lost (Lebedev, 2001, p. 24).[42]

MERCHANTS' POLITICAL PARTICIPATION

Not only were merchants resented by the general public, but merchants themselves appear to have resented serving the public through the local government (*zemstvo*). This public servant position took a merchant away from his business, and offered him very little potential for independent action (Owen, 1981, pp. 16–17).[43] At least before the reform of 1862, merchants had a very minor role in city administration (Hamm, 1976a, p. 24). In the 1870s merchants did acquire the quantitative majority in the city council – *duma* – of Moscow,[44] but their influence remained limited. To merchants, public office was a burden, a token of status recognition,[45] a way to keep the property taxes down, in other words, anything but a way to influence the structure of government, the political order or even economic infrastructure.

Two generations of merchants are commonly distinguished in the last century before the revolution.[46] The older-generation merchants (the 1850s to the 1890s) stayed away from politics, which was not surprising since active political participation outside of assigned office was directly punished[47] and generally unfruitful. The leading merchant figures of this period directed their non-commercial efforts not to public affairs but to cultural patronage.[48] And as private philanthropists they were indeed successful, but when their participation was required in areas of public life where the state presence was far greater, they succumbed to the bureaucracy.[49]

It is illustrative that the Russian merchants had difficulty distinguishing between serving the state as representatives of the town population and serving the community as participants of the municipal organs, such as the city council.[50] They were completely incapable of generating effective decisions through a democratic process. The only way they acted together was to lobby the government for concessions in trade and industry.[51] Among many mayors of Moscow that came from the ranks of merchants, only one was successful in providing for the community, but he acted as an autocrat (Ruckman, 1984, pp. 115–17).

The younger generation (the 1890s to the 1910s) did not show any more political vigour until 1904.[52] Even then it is believed, and not unreasonably, that such vigour was brought on by the revolutionary movement (ibid., p. 175). Greater political participation came out of fear of a nationwide labour strike on the one hand and dissatisfaction with too much government intervention in business–labour relations, as well as in other areas, on the other.[53] But the fact that in the beginning of the 20th century merchants supported liberal policies[54] does not mean that their political orientation changed from reactionary to favouring free market – they had no reason to associate continuous prosperity of business enterprise with laissez-faire – liberalism simply promised most profit *at the time*.

MERCHANTS AND INTELLIGENTSIA

Merchants traditionally had a poor relationship with the intelligentsia.[55] But the latter, through greater political power, influenced merchant culture and business practices. Somewhat coincidental circumstances determined a greater influence of the Slavophile ideology over the other ones. This dominance was significant in two respects. First, this ideology reinforced the closed-minded outlook of the merchants and their resentment of Western business norms; and second, Slavophiles possessed superior ideological and/or political group positions in hierarchical networks.

Slavophiles and merchants were first united through *duma* participation.[56] Merchants were very much influenced by Slavophiles' nationalistic (and at times chauvinistic) ideology, at first simply because the intelligentsia were the only role model in the arena of public affairs. Later, pragmatic interests led them to befriend Slavophiles as the latter had connections to the court. These connections offered protection and privileges to business and trade. Slavophiles believed that free trade made peasants poor, which could lead to social unrest. Merchants therefore should participate in setting tariffs[57] and, ultimately, industry must be subsidized (Owen, 1981, pp. 29–45). This apparently fell on fruitful ground, since, as discussed below, most Russian merchants at that time favoured mercantilism.

Slavophiles also exhibited hostility to Western constitutionalism and 'legalism' (Haimson, 1960, p. 114), which resonated with merchants' beliefs as well. All property in the country was potentially subject to confiscation. Had merchants held their wealth in perpetual ownership, they would have bargained for transparent laws. As it were, an obscure legislature presented more options to retain their possessions.

MERCHANTS, CENTRAL GOVERNMENT AND REGIONAL BUREAUCRACY

The links between merchants and the government were extensive. However much hostility there might have been between business and government, the economic logic would tell *kuptsy* to cooperate, and so most did. Various factors – the small number of merchants, their inferiority to the Western merchants, their unwillingness to form trading companies or to cooperate in any other way in large numbers, their political passiveness, the risk and uncertainty in business venture, the high rate of defection on loans and business agreements and the role of government as 'first merchant'[58] – pushed the merchant class to accommodate the state rather than to oppose it.

Because Russia was behind Europe in skill and capital accumulation, the merchant class, though having abundant resources at its disposal, did not have a competitive advantage in international markets. Recognizing their inferiority, Russian merchants preferred mercantilism (Baron, 1978).

Initially, direct connection to the Tsar or to the court was important. Once *gosti* were dragooned into government service, they competed with each other not for goods and customers, but for royal favours (Pipes, 1974, p. 197). Pipes (ibid.) pretty harshly describes a Russian *gost'* as 'an enemy of free trade' and one who 'fawned on authority'. An oligarch of the pre-revolutionary period was already quite a different animal from a Western bourgeois.

As the territory of the Empire, power and the numbers of regional bureaucracy grew, the connections to local government became no less essential. Sources directly describing the nature of relationship between government and merchants or, on a lower level, the relationship between citizens and bureaucracy in this period are not abundant. However, some evidence on government foreign trade and tax policy, and on how merchant titles were retained, suggests[59] that cooperation between business and government was mutually advantageous and exploited whenever possible.

Foreign trade was one of the more important and also one of the first areas where merchants and the state were connected. The relationship is not crystal clear (Bushkovitch, 1980, p. 152), although mostly because of unrecorded transactions. In the 17th century, for instance, state exports amounted at most to 10 per cent of total exports, which would be equivalent to what two to four middle-income merchants of Moscow sold. On the one hand, this suggests that the state was not a serious competitor to merchants; on the other hand, since the state granted the monopoly right to trade a certain good, one can reasonably expect that rent seeking took place, the amount of which of course was unrecorded.

The second basis for cooperation was tax farming. Although merchants were often abused by the local administration, they nevertheless took part in forming the administrative system of taxation on a countrywide scale. Tax farming (from the 17th century) was the single largest source of state income at the time. Predominantly Moscow merchants were hired as tax collectors. They had some discretion as to how much to tax based on local circumstances (ibid., pp. 159–67 and Mavor [1925] 1965, Vol. 1, p. 436). In fact, social conflicts sometimes put the state and the merchants in one camp, and perhaps at times the merchants 'squeezed the state dry' (Bushkovitch, 1980, p. 166), but *kuptsy* were certainly the best available category for performing administrative duties for the government.

There were many other areas where cooperation for profit took place. The government played a role not only as a formidable power and regulatory authority, but as a potential sponsor and, importantly, as a large business partner. Government's needs for iron, weapons, ships, cloth for uniforms, sails and so on (Baron, 1978, especially pp. 8–10) required contracting the merchants. For example, there is evidence of bread supplies (*khebnye podriady*) for the army being undertaken by Sitnikov as early as 1582 (Solov'ev, 1960, Book IV, Vol. 7, p. 21); later taken up by Peter the Great's favourite Men'shikov. The Kalmykovs and the Ushakovs 'made their fortune principally by way of contracts to supply the government with fish, grain, liquor and beer' (Baron, 1978, p. 23).[60] Even though profits for such endeavours were limited to 10 per cent, the majority did better by false reporting (Hittle, 1979, p. 103).

Some families had a long history of relationship with the Tsars. For helping out the suzerain prince, the Stroganovs were granted land and monopoly privileges on salt production in 1696 (Platonova, 1995, pp. 59–60), as well as the right to search for and mine ore (ibid., p. 68).[61] A large number of mountain works were transferred for a pittance to Counts Shuvalov, Vorontsov, Chernyshev and others (Mavor [1925] 1965, Vol. 1, p. 442). Yet others were suddenly elevated into higher strata by whims of fortune. For example, a favourite of the court, Potemkin, granted someone named Sobakin the right to sell food to the army, which was a source of huge income at the time (Platonova, 1995, p. 115).

Others, like Astashev, combined professionalism and insider knowledge of how to dodge the law. Using his old connections among Petersburg and Tomsk bureaucrats, Astashev annexed the basin of the River Kondystyula for his own operations. Since another merchant, Ryazanov, had earlier discovered and claimed gold in that region, he sued Astashev, but the courts found in favour of the latter (Rezun and Tereshkov, 1994–98, Vol. 1, pp. 43–4). Connections were exploited through marriage of convenience as well. Merchant Bazanov's daughter was married to the chamberlain (*kamerger*) of the court, Councillor of State (*Deistvuiushchii Statskii Sovetnik*) Sievers. Such connections gave Bazanov a lot of influence in the administration of Irkutsk *guberniia*[62] (ibid., pp. 55–6).

Banking was another area of close business–government cooperation. Large banking institutions, which emerged in the capital in the 18th century, were of state origin. Even though some were labelled private, they operated under the auspices of the state, or were headed by people who had formerly occupied prominent positions in the government (sometimes they occupied those positions simultaneously with appointments at 'private' banks). The state performed the largest transactions in the country, and these were conducted on its behalf by the court bankers. In the beginning of the 19th century a large group of private bankers became connected with government circles (Anan'ich and Beliaev, 2001, pp. 9–10).

One example is the Stieglitz family.[63] The majority of commercial banks leaders were the former officials from the finance ministry or from the trade and industry ministry.[64] Another category of bankers, former St Petersburg or provincial merchants (ibid., p. 18),[65] closely cooperated either with the current government or solicited favours through the former government officials. The credit office distributed the sums, which were held overseas, for an extremely low interest among the branches of private banks. For this kind of service, directors of the administration were guaranteed high-paid positions at private banks in the future (Anan'ich and Beliaev, 2001, p. 18).

Through the lobby for the tariff protection in the middle of the 19th century, merchants established personal relations with the finance ministry and with various highly placed bureaucratic figures. The economic effects of specific government programmes often counterbalanced each other because the state's fiscal needs were always a priority. However, merchants discovered that they could influence government policies through personal connections, which they worked hard to maintain (Ruckman, 1984, pp. 141–2). This said, it must be noted that the main (if not exclusive) beneficiaries of strong ties were large merchants and industrialists. The overall effect on the small business was negative,[66] at least until the 19th century.

Cooperation for profit occurred among the large merchants, but small businesses cooperated often to avoid abuse and to protect their legal income. Pipes cites foreign accounts of the 17th century describing how, except for 20 or 30 *gosti* and the *sotni*, Moscow merchants were defenceless against the service class, which not only had the power to regulate them but also bullied them. They hid their possessions in monasteries and in the woods as if in fear of foreign invasion (Pipes, 1974, p. 206).

Ruckman says that bureaucrats (like most intelligentsia) not only despised *kuptsy* but also used their power to extract as much as possible in bribes (Ruckman, 1984, pp. 40, 112–13, 131). This power was enormous before the 1862 reform, but even afterwards the bureaucratic grasp was quite strong. Already in the 17th century, arbitrary abuse by the local administration became so obvious that the government had to acknowledge the existence in the country of an extensive system of pickets (*zastav*) for purposes of extraction from trading persons. In most cases this led to a private agreement between the extortionists and the abused (Semenova, 2000, pp. 119–22).[67]

By the end of the 19th century, and especially in the period preceding World War I, the alliance between large merchants and bureaucrats took on a more organized form. Bureaucrats began using their positions in government to assist merchants and to secure high-paying positions in private business or simply grafts in return. The law of 1884, which prohibited civil servants from involvement in private enterprise, did not damage the alliance (Bokhanov, 1994, pp. 26–32).

One stunning example is the shipbuilding industry. The Shipbuilding Council, which consisted of large industrialists, acquired the right to determine the distribution of government military orders among national companies, the amounts of compensation and project deadlines.[68] So did many other 'councils' of this sort.[69] As a trust they eliminated competitors, but without competitive, as well as legal and popular pressure, these trusts did not advance the industry technologically.

Why did merchants avoid efforts to overcome institutional and technological backwardness? Why did they cooperate with the bureaucracy and not with each other against the state? Such undertaking would have required long-term planning, but political uncertainty and insecurity of private property always gave more weight to short-term gain.[70]

FOREIGN DIRECT INVESTMENT

From 1890 to 1914 foreign businesspeople made their largest contribution to the Russian economy by direct investment. Many of the partnerships established during this period had leading Western parent firms behind them (McKay, 1970, pp. 40–52).[71] Foreigners brought advanced technology and management to Russia, which was their main source of profit. Without question, technology was incorporated into the economy as the decade before World War I shows more and more Russian industrialists squeezing foreigners out of active participation. Western-style management and business norms however, are a different story.[72]

Partnerships were founded because on Russian terrain foreign industrialists faced very alien social norms and a shady legal system. Foreign ventures demonstrated a clear trend toward Russification of management as firms established more or less normal operations (ibid., pp. 182–200, 377).[73]

McKay's diligent study of foreign entrepreneurs between 1885 and 1914 documents a whole host of bureaucratic and legal problems that businesspeople faced in Russia. Their only possible effective response was adaptation because they were politically impotent (ibid., pp. 276, 385). As mentioned above, all joint-stock companies had to seek permission from the state to make any changes in their structure. These difficulties amounted to an effective state regulation and control of private enterprise (ibid., pp. 276–7).[74]

The most important part of this adaptation strategy was securing government contracts through connections with bureaucrats. Sometimes the hierarchical connection was established through an individual promoter (ibid., pp. 52–62), sometimes by employing a connected Russian in the management (ibid., p. 186). McKay notes 'that relations between government and private enterprise were close and continuous in Russia' (ibid., p. 268). Therefore, this relationship had much more far-reaching consequences for an individual enterprise in Russia than in Europe (ibid.). Space here does not permit me to list all the relevant examples, which are plentiful. When it came to state-demanded goods, bureaucratic decision, which incidentally was not guided by cost or quality considerations, guided the choice of the favoured supplier.

Partnership really meant that foreign businesspeople supplied technology and managerial skills, while Russian bureaucrats supplied markets through long-term contracts (ibid., p. 269). Metallurgical, railway equipment, munitions and shipbuilding industries all followed this pattern. Streetcar producers and electric companies were completely dependent on the municipal authorities for orders.[75] As much as the bureaucrats were interested in the success of their protégés and progress of industry in general, such activity was not exactly welfare enhancing. Unwarranted subsidies, such as subsidization of the Russo-Belgian Company's pig-iron production, were yet another instance (ibid., p. 272).

By the early 1900s, however, foreigners' active participation was already on the wane (ibid., pp. 236–41 and Chapter 12), but the Russian economy received a much-needed boost. We cannot solve the historical would-have-beens – 1917 effectively stopped Russia's integration into Western capitalism. Although Russian businesspeople picked up and continued the progressive changes in industrial development, there is no evidence they were less dependent on the vertical networks. Technology was finally there, but so was opportunism, asset specificity and bounded rationality; the effective legal system and market institutions were not.

IN CONCLUSION: RUSSIA AT THE TURN OF CENTURY

Russia was one of the world's larger economies by World War I.[76] There were signs that the Russian bourgeoisie was becoming more and more aware of its economic and political role. However, there is no indication that the bourgeoisie would go about establishing its corporate rights through the pursuit of legalism, liberalism and individualism.[77] Merchandizing was not as well developed in Russia as in the West, and it was not supported by an effective commercial code. Merchants had a long-standing history of cooperation with the state and did not form an independent faction vouching for free market.[78] Russian consumers disliked merchants for their fraudulent business practices; dislike that was reinforced by the doctrine that condemned wealth. Russian entrepreneurs, though certainly closer to self-sufficiency by 1914, still lacked managerial techniques and capital (McKay, 1970, p. 368). They were able to see economic opportunities and mobilize capital when needed, but the 'anti-foreign' attitude prevented them from reaping the full benefit from partnership with the West.

As the only force that not only had an interest in supporting free market but also bargaining potential with the government, merchants failed to realize this capacity because of their conservatism and an immense investment in vertical networks.

NOTES

1. I use the term 'merchant' because the fusion of merchant and industrial capital did not happen on a large scale until the 19th century. Even then, though many industrialists came out of merchant ranks and many merchants cooperated with industrial oligarchs, there was tension between the two groups (Rieber, 1982, pp. 360–63).
2. Once ennobled, these ex-merchants constituted severe competition to their former counterparts; their capital, however, no longer belonged to the middle class.
3. Examples of Ermoliny and Hovriny in Tikhomirov (1957), *Srednevekovaya Moskva*, Moscow, pp. 152–6, quoted in Sakharov (1959, p. 163).
4. However, only the richest ones could afford to do that, simply because middle-income merchants did not have resources to engage in both business and cultivation of land. The state, on the other hand, did not like the fact that merchants were buying up land. Landowners were expected to perform military duties and merchants to pay taxes, but it would be difficult for any landowner to satisfy both the taxpayer and servitor functions (Solov'ev, 1960, Book II, Vol. 4, pp. 536–7).
5. A few argued otherwise (ibid., pp. 165–9). Sakharov thinks that the rise of princely power adversely affected the power of merchants as a class.
6. *Sobor* (representative assemblies) of 1598 called for *gosti* by name to participate as part of the popular assembly and they amounted only to 21 (Kliuchevskii, 1957, Vol. 2, p. 380). For more on *gosti*, see Baron (1973), 'Who Were the *Gosti*?', *California Slavic Studies*, 7, (1973), pp. 1–40, reprinted in Baron (1980), and 'The Fate of the *Gosti* in the Reign of Peter the Great', in Baron (1980).

7. St Petersburg was not as attractive to Russian merchants. Moscow and Tula had the largest percentage of *gosti* among merchants; for more details see Hittle (1979, pp. 98–9).
8. *Gosti* were permitted to make spirits for domestic consumption without paying fees, they were allowed to buy and accept *votchinal* lands as loan guarantees, they were also on the government payroll for their services (Kliuchevskii, 1959, Vol. 6, pp. 161–3). Pipes (1974, p. 196) calls *gosti* 'state-employed businessmen'.
9. Their privileges were similar to those of *gosti*, except that they could not own land (Kliuchevskii, 1959, Vol. 6, pp. 163–5).
10. For details on back-up guarantees, see Kliuchevskii (1959, Vol. 6, p. 414) and also (1959, Vol. 8, pp. 98–100). Tsars preferred to appoint wealthy merchants, so that if they failed to collect an estimated amount, all or part of their wealth could be expropriated. The government thus punished economic success.
11. Merchants from 'black hundreds' and from wealthy peasantry were appointed against their will to perform state service (Kliuchevskii, 1959, Vol. 6, p. 417).
12. As noted before in Chapter 3, 'black' referred to taxable.
13. Also see Owen (1981, pp. 1–2).
14. Over 20 per cent of 'merchants' in the end of the 19th century were trading peasants. In 1898 there were 6500 1st guild merchants and 138,000 2nd guild merchants. But in the following year the numbers fell to 4000 for the 1st guild and to 38,000 for the 2nd (Brower, 1990, pp. 55–6).
15. In the years following the separation from Byzantium, half-literate Russian monks corrupted the texts of the Church, which also corrupted certain rituals. Eventually, the move was made to correct those. Some clergy and many parishioners refused to follow the changes; they were called Schismatics or Old Believers. They continued to make a sign of cross with two fingers instead of three. But Russian schism must not be likened to Western Reformation. There was no fundamental disagreement about the Orthodox doctrine itself (Gerschenkron, 1970, pp. 11–17).
16. Old Believers, though formally opposing such trivial reform as a new ritual of the sign of the cross, were also against further centralization of the Church, blending it with the state and subordinating the population to one homogeneous doctrine. For a short but informative summary on Old Believers, see Brumfield, Anan'ich and Petrov (2001, pp. 79–88) and also Gerschenkron (1970, Lectures 1, 2).
17. Many turned to industry and commerce after Peter the Great levied a double soul tax on them. They had a reputation of being the most honest businesspeople in Russia (Pipes, 1974, p. 238).
18. Interestingly, McKay made the same assessment of foreign entrepreneurship at the turn of the 20th century. 'A few did very well; the rest struggled along' (McKay, 1970, p. 140).
19. Burdensome taxes were noted even earlier (Solov'ev, 1960, Book IV, Vol. 7, p. 288).
20. Trade was carried out by barter, and capital was in the form of merchandise.
21. From other sources, such as Hellie's work, I got the impression that this cap at 20 per cent was not respected.
22. Hellie conjectures that perhaps the rising taxes were not paid and the arrears mounted. The peasants were the easiest category to force to pay more, so the government tried to compensate by curtailing peasants' consumption (Hellie, 1999, p. 570). The state was not shy of using the mint or the printing press (toward the end of the 18th century) to cover the deficits.
23. The state generally preferred indirect taxes over direct taxes (Kliuchevskii, 1957, Vol. 3, pp. 221–2). Multiplicity of big and small dues was in the interest of numerous government bureaus, whereas tax payments would have been much simpler with just an income and a sales tax. For more details on taxation in the 18th century, see Kahan (1985, pp. 322–49).
24. In addition to heavy dues, poorly formulated policies and thieves often put businesses at risk. One particular instance occurred in the 17th century with the debasing of silver

coins. Since recent wars had depleted the treasury, various court nobles, *gosti* and money-makers (*denezhnye mastera*), not without the knowledge of the Tsar, debased the coins with copper and put them out in circulation. The scam did not last long, but in the end the treasury had to replenish its silver reserves. In order to accomplish that, it bought exportable goods, such as furs, from the Russian merchants for copper money, and resold them to the foreign merchants for silver. At the same time, the Russian merchants were allowed to buy goods from foreigners only for silver; thus, the silver they spent did not return to them, and eventually they lacked currency for foreign goods. The treasury, which borrowed money from the merchants, declared bankruptcy and paid back between one and five kopeks for a ruble (Kliuchevskii, 1957, Vol. 3, pp. 223–6). One ruble = 100 kopeks.

25. But the state officials discovered a new fair relatively quickly (Solov'ev, 1960, Book IV, Vol. 7, p. 56).

26. Of course, the nature of merchandise had a seasonal impact too. For example, one-third of Makar'evskaya fair turnover was in foodstuffs (Hittle, 1979, p. 101).

27. For more details on and description of fairs, see Rozman (1976a, pp. 119–29) and also Brower (1990, pp. 58–9). For a very detailed description of small wholesale markets in the end of the 18th century, see Demkin (1999).

28. For example, marketing settlements in Kovrov *uezd* (an administrative territorial unit, a subdivision of *guberniia*) attracted 300–700 people regularly, fairs in the *uezd* brought up to 1000 people. At Moshki 100–500 people attended market on Mondays, while the fair in June attracted up to 2000 people; for more examples see Rozman (1976a, pp. 126–7). In the 1780s, only 23 out of approximately 80 settlements in the study had both fairs and a periodic market; 47 had only fairs and no market (ibid., p. 123). For more on fairs and state prohibitions on exchange, see Kahan (1985, pp. 50–51).

29. Another cause could be the geography and climate: it was hard to travel in the spring and autumn, and long distances required time for goods to be delivered. Small numbers of merchants was, of course, another reason.

30. Another etymological excursus is quite illuminating. *Put'* in Muscovite Russia meant a state tax (Kliuchevskii, 1959, Vol. 8, p. 78). *Putevyi* is a derivative of *put'*. Over the centuries the phrase *putevyi chelovek* came to mean a person who knows how to make a living, often describing an ideal marriage candidate.

31. The Russian market was Asian-oriented. With Asia merchants traded directly; with Europe Russians traded through foreign intermediaries because the market was more sophisticated. Therefore, a lot of business etiquette came from the Orient and the Middle East. Many foreigners marvelled at the art of defrauding customers in Russia (Pipes, 1974, pp. 204–6 and Brower, 1990, pp. 60–61).

32. Examples of this can be found in selected works of Ostrovskii, Chekhov and Gor'kii. This turns out to be a persistent belief, although the history of merchants in Siberia, for example, shows they were quite charitable (Rezun and Tereshkov, 1994–98, Vol. 1, p. 8). This may be because a lot of them were of the old faith. For merchants' own attitudes, see Kupriianov (1996, pp. 91–2). As far as attitudes towards the Old Believers, interesting are the peasant accounts offered by Mavor. Apparently, peasants complained that Jews stole by cheating in money and in weight; Greek Orthodox stole timber, but the Old Believers stole anything. The reason for that is believed to be that sectarians were free peasants, without land allotments, and were forced to steal to support themselves. Also, a sectarian priest would reprimand a thief who took from the poorest family, but it was not considered a crime to steal from abundance (Mavor, 1925, Vol. 2, Book V, pp. 261–3).

33. Ivanskoe *sto* (hundred) in Novgorod, *gosti-surozhane* and *gosti-sukonniki* in Moscow are a few exceptions. The so-called *bratchina* (brotherhood), was a group of monastic servitors, but did not represent separate crafts (Hamm, 1976a, p. 25).

34. One example colours the situation. Displeased with high cost of woollen manufacture operations and low quality of wool, Peter the Great decided to transfer the management into private hands. 'Knowing how unventuresome Russian traders were, he appointed

members of the Company by picking names from lists of the Empire's leading merchants. This done, he sent soldiers to fetch the victims and bring them to Moscow on "temporary exile" . . . "whether they wished it or not." They were given by the treasury some capital without interest, and told that they had to deliver to the state, at cost, whatever woollen cloth it required; the remainder they could sell for their own profit free of sales tax. As long as they operated the enterprise satisfactorily, the manufacture was their "hereditary property" (!); should they fail, the state would claim it back and punish them to boot' (Pipes, 1974, p. 210). This was a well-founded threat: there were real cases of property confiscations (Mavor [1925] 1965, Vol. 1, pp. 506–7 and Hellie, 1999, p. 636).

35. Only towards the second half of the 19th century did the taxable population take the majority of seats in the secondary schools, which were formerly held by the nobility (Pipes, 1974, Table on p. 262). Even then the quality of education remains questionable.

36. Cites throughout the book, for instance, pp. 106–7.

37. For example, 'the foundries . . . from which developed the Russian iron industry, were the creation of Dutch and German mining experts'. One of these experts also 'laid the foundations of Russia's copper industry. Paper and glass manufactures were founded by Swedes. The Dutch erected in Moscow the first woollen mill' (Pipes, 1974, p. 196). 'The modern coal and steel industries were founded by the English and financed by a combination of English, French, and Belgian capital. The Caucasian oilfields were developed by English and Swedish interests. Germans and Belgians launched Russia's electrical and chemical industries' (ibid., p. 218). For details in Russian, see Kliuchevskii (1957, Vol. 3, pp. 265–6). For shares of foreign capital by nationality and possible explanation of such distribution, see McKay (1970, pp. 32–6).

38. For instance, it was extremely difficult for a peasant to become a merchant legally. To start out, they had to obtain a release letter (*uvol'nitel'noe pis'mo*) from their landlord or the commune, then petition to the *posad* commune. The guild and town and regional administration would not favour the request unless bribes were paid. And then they would succeed only to pay dues! (Jones, 1977, p. 429). It was much more sensible to trade illegally.

39. Examples also in Pipes (1974, pp. 212–13).

40. Even though this privilege suffered some regress later, the consequences for the merchant entrepreneurs were severe. Alcohol distilling became the nobles' monopoly; in the beginning of the 19th century the nobles 'owned 64 per cent of the mines, 78 per cent of the woollen mills, 60 per cent of the paper and glass and crystal manufactures, and 80 per cent of the potash works' (Pipes, 1974, p. 212). The foundations of the textile industry were laid not by merchants but by rich peasant entrepreneurs with the technical help of a German, Ludwig Knoop (ibid., pp. 214–15). A good discussion of competition posed by the nobles, foreigners, merchants of other ethnicities in the newly conquered areas and trading peasants can be found in Rieber (1982, Chapter 2). In the 18th century a number of state-owned ironworks were transferred or sold below market price to the nobility. These were pure subsidies, as is shown by the reselling price of the works a few years later, given that production was not expanded or improved by the nobles and prices for final products did not change significantly (Kahan, 1985, pp. 134–36, especially Table 3.57 on p. 134).

41. Novgorod *veche* (see Chapter 3, Note 7) acted sometimes as a court, but there is absolutely no evidence that other ones in north-east Russia did (Hamm, 1976a, p. 28). On the weak distinction between the jurisdiction of commercial and civil codes, see Rieber (1982, p. 83).

42. Abuses of due process occurred because the curators deciding the fate of a debtor had personal interest in confiscating the debtor's property; for more details see Lebedev (2001, pp. 24–5). On banks and credit, see also Brower (1990, pp. 67–9). Moscow bankers were more independent from the government than those from St Petersburg.

43. Public service was also shunned before the middle of the 19th century because at the time many businesses were not yet solidly established, and they required the owner's constant involvement (Ruckman, 1984, p. 113).
44. Partially, through intentional efforts, partially because the state changed the income requirement. Previously, a certain number of representatives from each estate were guaranteed a seat. The new law raised the required income for potential *duma* representatives, and that excluded many, leaving merchants with the majority of seats; for details see Ruckman (1984, p. 115). The periphery presented a somewhat different picture; more details in Rieber (1982, Table 3.3); on merchants and local government, ibid. (pp. 92–103). In fact, merchants were very much hostile to rural self-government after its creation in 1864 (Owen, 1981, pp. 95–101).
45. On viewing office as a mark of honour, see Ruckman (1984, pp. 122–3).
46. For the political attitudes and culture of the old generation, see Owen (1981, pp. 9–28); on the new generation see ibid. (Chapter 6).
47. For details on two cases, on Kokorev's banquet organized in sympathy with emancipation and in defence of Chicherin's liberal views, see Ruckman (1984, pp. 136–7).
48. For examples, see Pipes (1974, p. 218).
49. 'Elected officials were . . . faced with the prospect of being taken to court after their term of service was completed if the bureaucrats to whom they were responsible found their performance in any way unsatisfactory. Under such conditions, it is not surprising that most *kuptsy* considered it a great misfortune if they were unable to argue or buy their way out of election to public office' (Ruckman, 1984, p. 112).
50. On the failure of Moscow merchants in municipal government, see Ruckman (1984, pp. 109–12).
51. In fact, many point out that their interests never transcended beyond business and local events, such as weddings and deaths in the neighbourhood. Interests in politics were limited to casual discussions of foreign policy (Ruckman, 1984, pp. 133–5). Boycotts were *very* few. On merchants as the most submissive estate in Russian society, see Rieber (1982, p. 23).
52. Extreme apathy of most *duma* members and among the general electorate as well was still the dominant characteristic of Russian political life (Ruckman, 1984, p. 121).
53. For details on the labour question, see Ruckman (1984, pp. 187–93, 204–8).
54. On the changed views of the new generation in the beginning of the 20th century, see Ruckman (1984, Chapter 6).
55. In fact, dispute over the use of bondage labour brought to the forefront the hostility between these two classes. The nobility acquired a significant advantage when the use of bondage labour by factory owners was prohibited by Peter the Great's successors. This measure in itself significantly reduced the size of the bourgeoisie class in Russia (Mavor, [1925] 1965, Vol. 1, p. 490).
56. In *duma*, they had to take the lead from the intelligentsia, many of whom were Slavophiles, simply because they were inexperienced in public affairs (Ruckman, 1984, pp. 114, 118, 125–6).
57. Chapter 3 discusses how merchants became active participants in protectionism.
58. Traders and artisans were excluded from the most profitable commercial ventures. Whenever private initiative demonstrated that profits were to be made, the state claimed it as government monopoly. For example, in the case of madder leather, see Pipes (1974, pp. 194–95).
59. With some objections, for example Bushkovitch (1980, pp. 157–58).
60. For the documentation of ties between government and higher strata of merchant class, see Baron (1978, pp. 28–30).
61. The Stroganovs paid ransom for the suzerain prince, Vasilii Vasil'evich, who was taken captive. They were granted permission to populate and build settlements in Siberia because of their wealth. They financed small military units, which protected the settlers from hostile local tribes. The state gave them permission to set up fairs, where goods were sold tax-free; for more details on the Stroganovs see Solov'ev (1960, Book III, Vol. 6, pp. 688–701).

62. A *guberniia* was an administrative territorial unit or region. Russia was divided into 50 *guberniias* in the 19th century.
63. The Stieglitz brothers started with a trading house. They became commercially successful during the Napoleonic War and were requested to purchase gold on behalf of the finance ministry. Shortly after that they started carrying out financial operations outside Russia's borders, such as paying off and organizing foreign loans for Russia, and overseeing all the expenditures abroad. In 1857, A. Stieglitz became one of the founders of the Main Society of Railroads of Russia; for more details see Anan'ich and Beliaev (2001, pp. 10–13).
64. For a page-long list of examples, see Anan'ich and Beliaev (2001, pp. 17–18).
65. On the St Petersburg financial oligarchy and its ties with government, see Rieber (1982, pp. 364–71).
66. Merchandizers were obligated to sell the most profitable goods to the state for the government-determined price, which was below the market value (Kliuchevskii, 1957, Vol. 3, p. 235). Small-scale businesses had no connections to the court to bargain their way out of it.
67. Direct physical abuse was not shunned either. For example, in 1758 a special representative was sent to force the richest merchant of Irkutsk along with his partners to refuse their privilege of monopoly production of spirits in favour of Glebov, a member of Senate. The merchants had been severely tortured (including the rack), and after this they complied (Rezun and Tereshkov, 1994–98, Vol. 1, p. 122). Nikolai Brechalov was investigated for illegal profiteering in the production of spirits as well, although the original complaint came about his unsanctioned barter of fur for Chinese fabrics. After he had been tortured, he gave Glebov a bribe in the amount of 23,000 rubles (almost five times more than his illegal income) to dismiss charges against him (ibid., p. 149).
68. Starting in 1908, already in a few years the union between the Council and the naval ministry was solidified through personal connections. Many ministers served both in the government and in private industry supplying for the navy. Naturally, they received high compensation for their private 'jobs'. Newly retired admirals were offered 'consulting' positions in private industry often the next day after retirement not for their technical expertise (many simply did not possess it) but for their connections with the ministry. For multiple examples, see Shatsillo (1968, pp. 288–310).
69. The leader of the Southern Industrial Group (primarily involved in coal mining) Avdakov, 'served on every government commission and conference dealing with problems of southern railroads, coal mining, and commercial tariffs. On critical issues he favored close cooperation with the bureaucracy and was less disposed than his Polish colleagues to take the initiative in launching purely industrial solutions to economic problems' (Rieber, 1982, pp. 229–30); and more details on southern engineer-capitalists, ibid. (pp. 227–43). For details on the activity of the Russian Technological Society in St Petersburg (later succeeded by the Society for the Assistance, Improvement, and Development of Factory Industry), see ibid. (pp. 251–5).
70. For Baron's thoughts on this, see Baron (1983, pp. 53–8); and for Hellie's, see Hellie (1999, pp. 638–9).
71. On benefits of foreign business, see McKay (1970, pp. 135–8).
72. As late as 1909 the head of the French Cousulate in Russia remarked that a Russian director was a waster and that his administration was ruinous to companies. Part of a foreign manager's job was to make sure that the Russian ones did not steal (McKay, 1970, pp. 109, 187, 198).
73. Aside from bribes, there were nagging problems such as legal conflicts with previous owners and customers (McKay, 1970, pp. 177–8). Peasants often did not understand that a sale was irreversible, unless parties had been fraudulent under the law.
74. Nor did the state fear foreign entrepreneurs when they combined forces (ibid., pp. 278–9). Some foreign capitalists felt at the turn of the century that their investment was being slowly expropriated by the Russian government (ibid., p. 281).

75. For concrete examples, see McKay (1970, pp. 184–5, 270–80). In 1902 the state gave railway orders only to six producers, excluding others who were just as adequate; ibid. (p. 272).
76. An in-depth quantative account of the Russian economy in late 19th and early 20th centuries may be found in Gregory (1994, Chapters 2–4).
77. 'Liberalism of the moderate, constitutional variety was never very strong in Russia' (Kline, 1960, p. 607). Collectivism was not surpassed by individualism, even with the rise of intellectuals' efforts in the 19th century. The tragedy was that the defence of individualism fell to the radicals (ibid., p. 606). For further details, see this essay.
78. Differentiation among the merchants (as well as among the 19th-century intelligentsia who understood the need for democratic reforms), created a situation where gentry and not bourgeoisie was one prevailing player on the political scene. Of course, gentry were not interested in curbing the state's power. On social fragmentation among the merchants in the 20th century, see Rieber (1982, Chapter 9).

PART III

The Soviet Period: 1917–85

6. The dominant role of the Soviet state in governing economic and political affairs

Part III of this volume examines the impact of cultural, political and economic environment on the governing structure of market and hierarchical exchanges in the Soviet period.[1] The state's anti-market policy raised the cost of market-governed exchanges. The legacy of pre-revolutionary networking lowered the cost of hierarchical exchanges. Combined together they resulted in the dominance of hierarchical networks in almost every sphere of life and in a much wider use of horizontal networks for purposes of the exchange.

This chapter draws on specific cases of networks that were built because of economic incentives, but in the absence of officially supported (or supported by law) market mechanisms. Soviet networks originated in the atmosphere of economic shortages and government monopoly, and matured during growing centralization and regulation of economic activity. Created by the ruling elite and bureaucracy, the system of privileges – a hierarchical network system – assigned an economic value to each position of control over the allocation of goods and services and was fundamental in building the scheme of perk distribution among the population.

The 1917 October Revolution constituted a major change of political regime in Russia. Even though the continuity of some policies, such as government monopoly in some markets, is traced from the Tsarist into the Soviet period, the attempt to abolish market relations and currency and to create forced labour was a new and devastating shock to the economy. A concise list of the events is as follows.[2]

After the 1917 February Revolution, the Provisional Government coexisted with the Soviet, itself comprised of socialists. This period was called the period of *dvoevlastie* (dual power) and was not a period of power struggle but rather a period of political confusion.[3] In October 1917 the Bolsheviks took over not only the Provisional Government but also the Soviet itself, where they started as a minority.[4] World War I involved Russia from 1914. In March 1918 the Bolsheviks signed a peace treaty in Brest-Litovsk by which Russia lost significant territories in the West.

The Civil War started after the 1917 October Revolution and was mostly over by 1920.[5] As Boettke (1988, pp. 136–7) points out, the nationalization attempts began as early as spring of 1918. Immediately after the revolution, a government monopoly on foreign trade was declared, consumer coop-eratives were placed under the jurisdiction of the Soviets and private trade was forbidden, the banks were nationalized and the Supreme Economic Council of National Economy was formed.

There is some disagreement in the literature about the continuity of government policies in Russia from the pre-revolutionary period into the Soviet, and between policies of War Communism and the New Economic Policy (NEP). To resolve the first issue an estimate of how well pre-revolutionary Russia was doing economically and politically is needed. Some of the issues were discussed in previous chapters, and to present all the background research here is not possible due to space limitations.

Pipes believes that Soviet policies, though more inhuman by an order of magnitude, were a natural extension of the Tsarist ones (Pipes, 1995, Chapter XVI). Peter Boettke (pers. com., 2005) points out that there was cause for an optimistic assessment of Russia's economic and political progress on the eve of World War I. Gregory believes that Russia was still relatively backward in 1914 but had good potential for develop-ment (Gregory and Stuart, 1986, pp. 44–6). Shanin (1972) argues that though not stagnant at the turn of the 20th century, Russian society was developmentally backward:

> [A]s soon as related to the size of the population and compared with the per-formances of other European countries, the huge absolute figures reveal poverty and backwardness. The income *per capita* in Russia in 1900 was 3 times lower than that in Germany, 4.2 times below that in the U.K., even 1.5 times below that in the Balkans.[6]

When the per capita growth rate of gross industrial output was high, agri-culture was largely stagnant, growing only slightly ahead of population growth, and industrial success was achieved because of heavy government and late 19th-century foreign investments both in industry and the rail-road. The rise in grain production in the first decade of the 20th century was achieved by ploughing the grazing fields, thereby diminishing the livestock. Russia's success depended on various, unsustainable factors – favourable terms of trade, foreign investment, foreign debts by the govern-ment, strength of the Tsarist regime and its continuing intervention in the investment and mobilization of resources.[7]

Hence, even though Russia was progressing industrially, the economy was predominantly rural; the majority of large businesses were connected with the government – this connection being the source of their enrichment

– and even though Russia acquired a multi-party representative system[8] and a constitution, the bureaucracy and the monarchy remained beyond the scope of the parliamentary or constitutional power. Just how disrespectfully the State Duma was treated is evidenced in the account by Gippius. Nikolai II sent deputies home at will (Gippius, 1990, p. 238). Once, for several days, the newspapers simply appeared with blank sheets because Duma minutes and speeches were removed from the public press by censorship (ibid., p. 249).

To establish continuity between policies of War Communism and the NEP, one has to consider the accounts of contemporaries and the writings of the Soviet leaders. My own interpretation of this is very much in agreement with Boettke's (1988) analysis. The Bolsheviks solidified their power by declaring a political monopoly.[9] Their economic goals were quite consistent as well, starting from 1917.[10] Based on the evidence from the Soviet archives, the interconnection between Leninism and Stalinism is much greater than was conventionally believed (Gregory, 2001, p. 40).

WORLD WAR I AND CIVIL WAR

World War I and the Civil War constituted a transition period from Tsarist to Soviet Russia, although the economic problem of the agents remained the same – namely, how to satisfy demand in spite of economic shortages produced by the war and by government policies. The economic problem of the state also remained the same – how to satisfy the demands of the army in spite of an empty treasury – although the new political task of building communism added further complications. The turmoil of World War I created food shortages in urban centres.[11] Ultimately, the war economy reinforced exchange through the networking system and away from markets.

In March 1915, the Tsarist government limited trade in bread by private agents. In 1917, the Bolshevik government monopolized trade in grain and in grain products, whereby it reserved the right to confiscate all grain and bread from peasants leaving only the part perceived as necessary for private consumption.[12] Peasants immediately responded by smuggling grain in burlap sacks into the urban areas, which suffered most from the restrictions on bread sales. This phenomenon was called *meshochnichestvo* or small bread speculation.[13]

When guards were put around the towns to prevent illegal trade, peasants bribed them in order to get through. The profits were so high[14] and alternative income earnings were so limited that even the fact that this was a life-endangering operation did not stop the trade. Gradually the urban population joined *meshochnichestvo*, and under the Bolshevik regime, and especially during the period of War Communism, bread speculation grew at an astronomical speed. Two major features of a *meshochnik* were physical strength – to be able to carry heavy sacks – and, not surprisingly, an outgoing personality – to be able to make a connection with a guard, bureaucrat or anyone standing in the way of supply meeting demand.

As a result, during War Communism the Soviets were collecting only one-third of all produced bread, grain and bread products. The illegal burlap sack market generated auxiliary markets, for example a market for illegal credit, a market for bags with false bottoms and semi-legal flea markets (Latov, 2001, Chapter 6).[15]

CENTRALIZATION AND NATIONALIZATION OF THE ECONOMY, AND THE NEW ECONOMIC POLICY (NEP)

The key elements of the Soviet reforms – centralization and nationalization of the economy – had elimination of free markets as their goal.[16] *Meshochnichestvo* and low pay for workers in urban centres gave a jumpstart to industrial illegal markets in the cities. In order to pay for expensive bread (and other food and necessity goods, such as firewood in winter) urban dwellers either stole and traded industrial goods[17] or started small enterprises on the side (Latov, 2001).

Open illegal trade was subject to more severe repercussions than disposing of goods through an informal network.[18] Of the private traders and private manufacturers the Bolsheviks hated the former far more (Ball, 1987, pp. 3–4, 127–8). But nationalization and state price regulations not only failed to destroy the black market but, ironically, fuelled it, as it was the only source of food, even for the communists (ibid., pp. 6–7). 'In summer of 1919, for example, the urban population obtained approximately 70 per cent of its grain products through private channels. . . . Nor was grain the only product involved. Throughout the War Communism private entrepreneurs accounted for the lion's share – between one half and two thirds – of all retail trade' (ibid., p. 7). Because the currency collapsed, by 1920 90 per cent of wages had to be provided in kind, so many joined the ranks of *meshochniki* in order to barter for food (ibid., p. 8).[19]

The New Economic Policy was instituted by a series of decrees in 1921. Private trade was legalized, state enterprises were permitted to sell their products through private dealers, private persons were permitted to establish small-scale manufacturing, restrictions on freight shipments were lifted, private businesspeople received the right to set up credit, loan and savings associations, inheritance was permitted as well as ownership of foreign currency and precious stones and metals.[20]

Small-scale commerce and cottage industry, which had existed illegally before, in the 1920s became preferred economic activities. These small-scale enterprises allowed individuals to hide profits better and allowed for sufficient mobility of capital, which was crucial given some legal aspects of regulation and given the uncertainty of the regime and economic policy (Ball 1987, p. 7 and Banerji, 1997).[21] Yet, as much as this economic activity might seem impressive, it must not be overestimated – both industrial and agricultural output shrank dramatically in comparison to before the revolution (Ball, 1987, p. 8).

The volume of trade was also only a fraction of what it was before the revolution (ibid., pp. 93–4). 'It was not a time of abundance, but rather a period of relative prosperity' (Osokina, 2001, p. 3 and Chapter 1). An émigré secretly visiting Russia in 1925 remarked in his memoirs that everything bore close resemblance to the way things were before the revolution, except the quality – there were shops, there were hotels, restaurants, there were private horse carriages and abundance of goods in comparison to the time of War Communism, but everything was still a grade (perhaps several grades) inferior to Tsarist Russia, not speaking of Western Europe (Shul'gin, 1991, pp. 161–238).[22]

Trade was the predominant occupation of the 'Nepmen',[23] who operated mostly in foodstuffs, with remaining private sales in textile products and handicraft items for home use.[24] They also served as intermediaries between state industrial enterprises and the countryside, purchasing food and raw materials to be consequently distributed through the state channels (Ball, 1987, pp. 151–4). Small retails shops designed for a customer to enter had as much capital invested in them as all other enterprises (ibid., p. 93). Yet over 70 per cent of all private traders did not operate from permanent stores designed for a customer to enter. Instead, the majority traded in the streets, bazaars and open stalls (ibid., pp. 92–3) – meaning that there was not enough capital and/or incentive to set up stationary stores.

Although official tax rates were low, except on luxury goods,[25] the ambiguity of the law necessarily left room for arbitrary measures on the part of local bureaucrats. The laws on speculation did not draw a clear line between permissible profit and illegal speculation, which allowed the state to attack a business whenever it wished.[26] One store would be unexpectedly and heavily taxed, forcing it to close down, while other stores in the neighbourhood would remain untouched (ibid., p. 33). Many local Bolshevik officials were hostile to the NEP and implemented restrictions on trade and performed arrests and property confiscations on their own authority. And others were simply confused by the mixed signals from Moscow (ibid., pp. 34–7).[27]

Even though the system of collecting these taxes was poorly developed, and many businesses eluded them, preserving income, uncertainty remained.[28] Consequently, small-scale producers and petty traders could not accumulate enough financial capital to outweigh the importance of social capital. I would go even further to argue that any amount of financial capital accumulated outside the official law cannot outweigh the importance of social capital. In fact, the very accumulation and sustenance of illegal riches depends on connections. The Russian oligarchs of our time are the living proof.

During the NEP, social networks continued to play an important role because of the uncertainty that agents faced:

> Throughout the period this [government intervention and contradictory expectations of government policy] had the undesirable effect, from an economic point of view, of reducing the amount of private trading activity that was going on and limiting that private trading that did go on to arbitrage activity and short-term speculation, rather than long-term entrepreneurial ventures. (Boettke, 1988, pp. 289–90)

Arbitrage, which involved 'marketing large quantities of state's own goods for sizable profits' (Ball, 1987, p. 18) suggests a strong link between business and state representatives and that networking played at least some role in distributing the goods. Indeed, it was rather difficult to obtain goods for sale. A lot of purchasing went on legally, but the illegal distribution of state property during the NEP was also pronounced. Many state enterprises had to hire people with experience in private trade:

> These people were then in the position to divert state supplies into the private sector, because they were often more aware of what materials were on hand than were nominal managers. It was not unheard of at the beginning of NEP for a private trader to have a second 'full-time' job in a state enterprise. In 1922, for instance, the state trading agency Gostorg had a number of employees who simultaneously operated private businesses that were well stocked with Gostorg's wares. Occasionally a private contractor or supplier for a state agency who was also an official in that agency could buy and sell goods to and from himself – on rather unattractive terms for the state, one might suspect. (Ibid., p. 114)[29]

Cosy relationships between private business and state officials were a source for many goods to reach the consumer. The state tried to outlaw these informal channels but was unsuccessful; since record-keeping was particularly poor, the state goods that were stolen or privately sold by a state official to a Nepman, did not exist on paper.[30]

Who were these traders? The pre-revolutionary merchants either emigrated or perished during the War Communism and the Civil War. There were only a few notable exceptions.[31] However, most of the Nepmen among those who owned stores and engaged in wholesale trade had been nothing more than small-scale businesspeople or shop employees before the revolution (ibid., pp. 91–2).

'BEHIND THE FAÇADE OF ABUNDANCE': A NOTE ON THE RELIABILITY OF SOVIET STATISTICS

Aggregate figures are very elusive. Therefore, it is worth taking a moment to discuss the reliability of Soviet statistics. We know relatively more about the 1920s than about the later period. It is hardly necessary to mention that the official statistics in the USSR were unreliable. As Nutter (1962, pp. 13–18) discusses, the pressure for accuracy was there, but it came top-down – from the state, which needed accuracy to get a clear picture and proceed with planning, and was counterbalanced by self-interests of lower-level statisticians, bureaucrats and managers, who misreported often to avoid penalty for not fulfilling the plan or simply because of negligence.

However, if approached with care and understanding of these underlying processes, Soviet statistics can be analysed to provide a realistic picture of the trends and growth of industry.[32] The materials from now open Soviet archives confirm that the Western scholars, though often working in the dark did draw an overall correct picture of Soviet economic development (Gregory, 2001).

POST-NEP POLICIES AND SHORTAGES

With the end of the NEP, there came an end of legal small to medium-scale production and trade and the beginning of illegal redistribution of goods on a countrywide scale. While the Nepmen were rapidly driven out of business, even more quickly than the authorities themselves had anticipated, the state system did not come in to replace the private shops as rapidly.[33] Due to food and consumer goods shortage, speculation soared and *meshochnichestvo* revived again, although this time on a smaller scale.[34]

Rations covered only a portion of the population; the elite in the 1930s was rather small.[35] Even with the relative luxury that the elite enjoyed over the industrial workers and the industrial workers over the other urban dwellers, it was still a 'hierarchy of poverty' in Osokina's words (2001, Chapter 6).[36] Again, the state had to allow a small amount of private trade in flea markets, which bartered goods for food, simply to help the starving population get by.[37] Peasant markets and individual agricultural plots were even encouraged. Between 50 and 80 per cent of food for the urban population during the famine was provided by peasant markets (ibid., p. 112),[38] which were not prohibited by law.[39]

In the mid-1930s Stalin proclaimed that a new era – an era of 'free trade' – had come. But it was merely rhetoric, as it meant neither expansion of private trade nor free enterprise.[40] The rationing system was sought to be abolished only to show the inadequacy of government policies, as the supplies were immediately bought up and hoarded by citizens in the anticipation of change in state's policy. The shortages continued to persist:

> [I]n 1937 the state produced two watches for every hundred people; four gramo-phones, three sewing machines, three bicycles, two cameras, and one radio for every thousand; and six motorcycles per hundred thousand people. The state food industry produced only thirteen kilograms of sugar, eight to nine kilograms of meat and fish, about forty kilograms of dairy products, five kilograms of veg-etable oil, seven cans of canned food, five kilograms of confectionary products, and four kilograms of soap per person in 1940. (Osokina, 2001, p. 145)

Poor transportation and storage capacities permitted even fewer goods to reach the market; yet another share went to supply state institutions.[41] The 1930s ended with rationing, initiated by local authorities to simply combat the shortages, and with the revival of closed distributor stores and canteens for the party elite and those involved in the defence industry (ibid., pp. 171–3). The new agricultural policy handed a severe blow to the domestic economy. Peasant plots were inspected for size and curtailed back to legal limits (many were larger); exports of raw materials and food to Germany, which had hardly started in 1939, were curtailed as well. Milk was sold by the cup and potatoes, individually, as no one could afford to buy by litres or kilograms (ibid., pp. 167–8).[42]

Rapid industrialization, with an emphasis on heavy industry started in the late 1920s. Quick results were achieved, but it was not a modern Western-type enterprise that emerged from it, but a unique Soviet version of a factory created under the pressure of central planning and with the private initiative of Soviet managers, supervisors and workers looking out for their own interests. The traditional managerial techniques used to run small firms and artisan workshops were used in large Soviet factories as well, making them 'a patchwork of factories within factories' (Shearer, 1993, p. 194).[43]

In the 1930s regional umbrella organizations were substituted by central agencies in Moscow, each corresponding to all factories in a particular line of production (for example, turbine) no matter where in the country they were located. This kind of central planning provided quotas and sent quota monitors, but failed to organize an adequate supply of raw materials. In addition, the accounting practices were so poor, or even non-existent, that the majority of factories did not provide good feedback to the centre. Therefore, shop administrators and supervisors began contracting with other shops and factories on their own.[44]

In the industrial sector, the central plan demands were often inconsistent with the capacity of an enterprise, but more importantly, inconsistent with the capacity of the system to supply sufficient inputs or supply them in time; as Boettke puts it, there were 'discrepancies between the *de jure* system of planning, and the *de facto* existence of internal and external markets which attempt to coordinate production plans on the one hand, and satisfy consumption demands on the other' (2001, p. 69).[45]

The networks filled in the gap. *Snabzhentsy*[46] acted as intermediaries between state enterprises. They were a more sophisticated, and a more connected sort of intermediary who grew out of the tradition of *meshochniki* and of the Nepmen, on whom at the beginning of the NEP the state enterprises relied heavily to deliver raw supplies due to the inherent inefficiencies of the socialist sector.[47] 'He [*snabzhenets*] is a nervous, energetic man, a master of high-pressure techniques, able to talk his way into enterprises and quickly establish a working friendship with the relevant officials. He is lavish with gifts and entertainment and "knows how to drink" with all people' (Berliner, 1962, p. 424).

Snabzhentsy could hold an official job as supply expediters with an enterprise, but often were unofficially employed by several firms and resided in Moscow or in other large cities (ibid.; Rutland, 1993, p. 77 and Note 24). A good *snabzhenets* was very costly. Not only had a manager to pay his salary and living expenses, but to offer him an incentive to compete with other *snabzhentsy* and include a risk premium (Gregory, 2001, pp. 139–40).[48]

Soviet industrial networks were by no means limited to suppliers' networks. Similarly to the Tsarist Russia's *krugovaia poruka* (collective responsibility [Chapter 3], often translated as mutual support when referred to the Soviet period), where the community as a whole was responsible for each member, individuals in the Soviet Union were forced to collude inside professional communities, and across social and political strata. Inherent inefficiencies of central planning left many important decisions regarding firms to be made not based on objective parameters but 'on the basis of personal influence and cloakroom bargaining' (Berliner, 1962, p. 429 and Gregory, 1990, Chapter 5). For instance, Soviet supply planning protocol required enterprises to submit their input requests six months to a year ahead of receiving their output plans. Enterprises then ended up with materials they did not need and that were not easy to return (Gregory, 1990, p. 95). Therefore, it is not surprising that managers relied on informal redistribution of supplies. Material exchanges between ministries and local party officials were governed by their own, unofficial, structure and rules (ibid., p. 51).

A lot of effort on behalf of managers went into influencing – to reduce – production quotas and input allocation orders given by the State Planning Commission (Berliner, 1962, pp. 423, 429). The state's demands would be impossible to satisfy without breaking the law. Not only was everyone bound to cheat but anyone was bound to make honest mistakes. Both, however, could lead to severe punishment if discovered.[49] Ministry officials and managers integrated themselves 'excessively both vertically and horizontally' to break the dependence on outside supplies (Gregory, 1990, p. 49). Mutual support networks were built on cover-ups and lies, and trust was based on self-deception. The People's Commissariats were quite extensively involved in this web throughout the 1930s.

Thus, political networks blended with industrial networks rather early on in the evolution of the system.[50] Government policy was responsible for the alliance though, because it staged political secretaries at the factories, often promoted party officials to manage enterprises and encouraged managers to become involved in politics. This created occupational fluidity among them (Berliner, 1962, p. 426).

A manager's success depended on networking both outside their own enterprise and within. To the extent that everyone, the manager, the workers and the local party officials, were interested in plan fulfilment, the 'loyalty network' was 'to some extent automatic, not requiring material incentives' (Gregory, 2001, p. 151). Loyalty network expansion was also self-perpetuating – the more people were involved, necessarily including high-ranking officials, the less was the probability of detection. Berliner (1957) calls this collusion on misreporting a 'web of mutual involvement'.[51]

Superficial specialization gave a boost to networking:

> The collapse of systematic engineering and managerial control accentuated the local character of production and work organization. Despite the pretense to planning, organization of work in most factories came to depend largely on the local labor market and the technological and production structure in the individual shop. Jerry-rigging and cannibalizing machines and their fixtures became commonplace. This resulted in a process of technological evolution that defied standardized operating procedures. A skilled worker entering a shop for the first time required training on machinery in that shop even if that worker had operated similar equipment in another shop or factory. Shops and factories guarded their production secrets jealously, and that accentuated the ad hoc character of work organization.
>
> Because of the often unique character of work organization that evolved in shops, work experience in one locale became as valuable to the maintenance of production lines as either formal skill or engineering knowledge. Successful production strategy became contingent not on the maintenance of formalized

managerial structures and standardized engineering techniques but on knowledge of local conditions and on the combined skills and experience of *all* groups
in the factory. (Shearer, 1993, p. 214, my emphasis)

While successful managers enjoyed higher incomes, commerce offered
even more materially lucrative positions. Position in any branch of commerce, no matter how low, gave an advantage of being at the hub of redistribution.[52] Some directors of stores had unofficial incomes much larger
than political leaders got from bribes.[53] Trade employees enjoyed patronage of leaders of Soviet, party and judicial agencies, who received payment
in scarce commodities (Osokina, 2001, p. 186).

Industry continuously suffered from mismanagement. The Soviet Union
grew extensively into the 1960s because the imbalances could be corrected
by more investment, but when the limits of expansion were reached and
growth started depending on intensive factors, the imbalances became
more obvious and more ominous.[54]

Consumer shortages persisted throughout the Soviet era. In fact, even
though living standards increased through the 1960s, they grew much
slower than nominal money income. Thus, the population had large sums
of cash hoarded because they could not make use of it.[55] The goals for
increased consumption levels were never a priority, in fact, consumption as
a share of total production remained rather low.[56] The defence industry ate
up a large share of investment starting from the 1930s (Harrison, 2001)[57]
and through the end of the Cold War. Attempts to improve the consumption situation ended up in fiasco because the state had no credibility and
could not stop the population from buying up anything that appeared in
the stores, which echoed the situation at the end of the 1930s.

Even though, after World War II, there was a trend in relative
improvement of living standards,[58] the leadership had to face trouble-
some facts in both industry and agriculture. Any attempts of reform in
the post-Stalin period until 1985 were essentially administrative measures and did not touch on economic issues.[59] Khruschev attempted to
reform the system by abolishing the industrial ministries and replacing
them with regional councils. The reforms 'did nothing to convey to state
enterprise managers, agricultural workers, or urban citizens that economic activity would be insulated from political manipulation' (Boettke,
2001, p. 163).[60]

Both managers and private citizens relied heavily on the networks at
work and for everyday necessities because the state's policy was anything
but credible or economically efficient. 'The only stable political economy
rule in effect was that the planning bureaucracy could arbitrarily change
the rules any time it desired' (ibid., p. 165).[61]

SOVIET SYSTEM OF PRIVILEGES

The economic aspects of stratification of Soviet society had an important effect on the hierarchical networks, in particular the Soviet system of privileges. Even though we observe economic stratification in the Western economies, it is based substantially on one's labour productivity and accumulated wealth. In the Soviet Union a pattern was established where returns on social capital were much greater than returns on financial and human capital. Lack of markets prevented competition on the basis of innovation and quality improvement; competition on the basis of network advantage was least costly and most beneficial. Network connections were often a prerequisite to the accumulation of wealth.

As early as in the 1920s many unofficially exploited their party membership to achieve higher incomes. Brovkin cites a number of cases where communists befriended *kulaki* (wealthy peasants), Nepmen and other small bourgeoisie elements. They shared in the spoils from illegal trade or redistribution (Brovkin, 1998). Graft and favouritism in administrative positions compensated for the small paycheque (Harper, 1937, pp. 112–13). Even though the benefits and salaries for the higher-level officials were made substantial specifically to prevent corruption, these measures failed to deliver the projected results (Gregory, 2001).[62]

As the ranks of the party expanded as well as its administrative apparatus, there appeared a greater number of party officials holding jobs exclusively in bureaucratic matters (as opposed to party officials staged at the factories) and thus completely disconnected from the masses. Most were located in Moscow.[63] The party's own white-collar class enumerated more than 15,000 by 1922 (Pipes, 1995, pp. 365–6).

As the Central Committee proceeded with the centralization of political life in Soviet Russia, the local leaders were no longer chosen by their peers, but appointed from above. Such authority, together with virtual immunity from legal prosecution, inevitably led to the corruption of party cadres. Top officials, in addition, enjoyed economic privileges, such as extra food rations, special housing, medical care and clothing allowances (ibid., p. 367).[64] They were 'entitled to lengthy stays at foreign sanatoria at government expense. The Party's leaders qualified for dachas'.[65] In 1919 Sovnarkom (the Council of People's Commissars) cafeteria, though it did not sparkle with cleanliness, served excellent food for the party members at ridiculously low prices. This was at the time when the famine that would shortly claim millions had already begun its toll in Moscow (Solomon, 1991, p. 281).[66]

Stalinist policies in the end of the 1920s and in the 1930s created a highly stratified system of supply and anchored the distribution of privileges to a position in the hierarchy. The Red Army and the industrial workers received the highest rations because the state's priorities were military and heavy industry.[67] But proximity to power gave an even higher standard of living. The fact that so many of the Soviet leaders enjoyed special privileges so early raises the question about the truthfulness of their ideological beliefs.

Although it is undoubted that many were ideologically driven in their policies in 1918,[68] by the end of 1920s there came a new generation of communists who were more interested in their own well-being and merely learnt the rhetoric. Category A rations (the best in the country) went to 'party secretaries, presidents, and deputies of state planning, people's commissars, and their assistants and families. The Soviet diplomatic corps and veterans of the revolution living in Moscow also received A rations' (Osokina, 2001, p. 71). B rations went to managers of central state and party departments, chairs of departments, groups, sectors, and their deputies, heads of central newspapers, professional specialists who worked in central departments, such as economists, accountants and engineers (ibid.).

One of the first steps towards official inequality[69] in Soviet society was the creation of *nomenklatura*.[70] Stalin's daughter, Svetlana Allilueva, writes that by 1937–38 the party leaders as well as their 'staff' had already fully enjoyed *nomenklatura* privileges. The staff included cooking, cleaning, teaching and supervising personnel for children, personal drivers, bodyguards and so on. All personnel were members of MGB (Ministry of State Security) with salaries drawn out of state budget. The number of personnel grew at an increasing rate, especially in the households of the members of the Politburo (Allilueva [1967] 1968, pp. 116–34).

During the crisis in 1939–40, the local leaderships took advantage of closed distributors, often consuming over 90 per cent of supplies from funds intended for the general population (Osokina, 2001, pp. 173, 175).

By the 1980s the staff of a candidate for Politburo membership (not actually a member yet) included three cooks, three waitresses, one cleaning maid, a gardener with staff for summer cottages and a personal airplane (TY-134). The head of personal security would fulfil any wish his master might have – a new suit, a gift for the wife, holiday in a Black Sea resort (Yeltsin, 1990, pp. 70–76). The privileged status of the staff provided them with income and access to shortage goods and connections, which they used to pay for the services obtained elsewhere; so virtually the whole population to a various extent was milking off the Politburo leftovers. For example, 40,000 people just in Moscow received the Kremlin food ration (Yeltsin, 1990, pp. 70–76). Many enjoyed the services of special sections in state department stores (for instance, in Moscow GUM) or special shops, which sometimes used their own currency called *bonny*.

Since the ration cost only half of what it would be in regular stores and included food unavailable to an ordinary person, a profit opportunity from selling the Kremlin ration begged to be exploited. People at the top of the hierarchy had all privileges but did not own them – the system did (Boettke, 1993, p. 150).[71] The intermediate strata of population who had some privileges, but used cash from selling the shortage goods to pay for other things they did not have, were the ones who kept the exchange churning.[72] Naturally, goods and services, as well as membership in Politburo and staff were not sold in the street – connections were crucial. Because embezzlement on the job was criminally prosecuted, the internal (to the official economy) illegal activity[73] required trust networks not only to obtain shortage items for the purpose of reselling them at a mark-up but also to avoid prosecution.

NETWORKS AND BUREAUCRACY

Under the Soviets both the size of the bureaucratic apparatus and economic shortages in legal markets skyrocketed. The bureaucracy started growing together with 'the dictatorship of the proletariat'. The attempts to reform the bureaucracy had been undertaken after the revolution by reorganizing the Office of State Control (Goskontrol') but had virtually failed by 1922.[74] To rationalize planning during War Communism the government had to employ huge staffs. For example, one bureaucratic organization, the Benzene Trust, employed 50 officials to supervise a plant with a workforce of 150 (Pipes, 1995, p. 198). As a result of the expansion of the Commissariat of Enlightenment, in 1919 it employed ten times as many officials as had the corresponding Tsarist ministry (ibid., p. 367).

Because being on the government payroll gave access to goods ordinarily unavailable, citizens enrolled en masse:

> [T]he ratio of white- to blue-collar workers was one-third higher [in 1918] than in 1913. Although railroad traffic declined fivefold and the number of railroad workers remained stationary, the bureaucratic personnel managing transport increased by 75 per cent. Overall, between 1917 and the middle of 1921, the number of government employees grew nearly five times. (Pipes, 1995, pp. 367–8)

In the beginning of the 1940s there were some 40 ministries. 'In 1953, there were less than ten thousand centrally set indexes; by the mid-1980s, there were fifty thousand' (Gregory, 2004, p. 247).[75]

Transregime continuity can be attributed to both people and situational and historical factors (Ryavec, 2003, p. 61). The Soviets lacked their own

ideologically cleansed cadre to fill in the bureaucratic positions immediately following the revolution, so most of them were not filled by the
Bolsheviks. In 1919 as much as 70 per cent of staff was carried over from
the Tsar's apparatus (Adams, 1977, p. 23). Pipes (1995, p. 368) refers to a
Russian source as well, estimating that 'more than one-half of the officials
in the central offices of the commissariats, and perhaps 90 per cent of the
officials in the upper echelons of the state bureaucracy, had held administrative position before October 1917'.[76]

Ryavec (2003, p. 61) cites several authorities concluding that the Soviet
civil service sector was dominated by people originating in the petty-
bourgeois group. In 1918 'holdovers' constituted 57 per cent of specialists
in one commissariat's central apparatus; by 1923 this percentage increased.
In the People's Commissariat of Health holdovers made up 60.9 per
cent of employees in 1918, and even in Cheka (state security organization) they had 16.1 per cent. 'Holdovers included former White Army
officers; gentry; priests and their children; functionaries from the former
zemstva [provincial self-government organizations] . . . and members of
the revolutionary parties opposed to the Bolsheviks' (ibid.). Ryavec (pp.
60–61) also cites Rigby (1999) on the mechanisms of transformation of
the Tsarist bureaucracy into a Soviet one. Many of the officials got their
jobs back after the initial dismissal (immediately following the revolution).
In addition, the Bolsheviks did not have their own concrete blueprints of
government, so they found models of the pre-revolutionary governance
quite suitable.

Bureaucratic extortion was also not a new phenomenon in Russia. So
the methods of dealing with it were not novel either. Ironically, economic
shortages, from which all in the system suffered, gave a certain advantage
to an ordinary person without high-level connections (although with social
capital concentrated in lower-level *blat*[77]) in compensating bureaucrats
for their services. Not all bureaucratic positions, and certainly not low-
level ones, yielded a great amount of privileges. If one petitioner had a
connection in a food store, another could get car parts or a nice bottle of
cognac, then a bureaucrat, who received these as gifts, saved time on standing in a queue for these goods or trying to establish connections himself.
Bureaucracy therefore stimulated development of social networks outside
of its ranks. These included horizontal exchange networks.

No less important was the stimulation of both hierarchical and horizontal networks within bureaucracy itself. Corrupt client–patron relationships
between higher- and lower-level bureaucrats are prone to be found in any
highly centralized bureaucratic structure. While the lower-level officials
obtain otherwise scarce government resources to 'fulfil the plan' from
the higher-level bureaucrats, the higher-level officials besides material

compensation (bribes) receive 'power rewards' from the leader, which enhance their influence 'through resources supplied by their clients'.[78]

Top officials on the other hand organize into privileged cliques. They 'seek to organize relationships in such a way that every member of the clique has an opportunity to take advantage of the resources controlled by other members. . . . This leads . . . to the virtual reprivatisation of the state economy, but without the obligations and responsibilities normally involved in private ownership'.[79]

NETWORKS AND POLITICS: SOVIET STATE AND PERSONAL NETWORKS, COMPETING OR COOPERATING FORCES?

The use of networks was not a novelty for the Bolsheviks. The dissemination of revolutionary propaganda (revolutionary *kruzhki* before 1917) and carrying out party orders was ensured through a system of personal networks. The incentive here was originally ideological. But the socialist ideology, in spite of vigorous propaganda, was understood by the populace only to a somewhat limited extent. As a result the ideological basis for networks gradually dissipated, even though the structure remained.

Easter (2000) analyses the state building and personal networks in the example of provincial *komitetchiki*.[80] Informal contacts held the party together. The more intense was the required paperwork, the more repetitive and meaningless it became, and the more party officials relied on informal contacts (Rutland, 1993, p. 39). The networks were the basis of state building and state running in the USSR, and although a force in creating the state (especially in territorial administration) they attenuated its power.[81] Local party organizations often did not follow orders from the centre, for example, in the 1930s they continued harassment of managers and specialists, despite clear instructions not to do so (Gregory, 2001, pp. 29–31).

What Stalin attacked during purges were horizontal personal networks within the party, which he perceived as hostile.[82] Not omniscient, Stalin 'relied heavily on his deputies and subordinates; within their own fiefdoms, senior party, government, military, and security chiefs exercised considerable authority. To achieve the results desired, the party-state apparatus had to be constantly prodded, directed, and controlled' (ibid., pp. 57–8).[83]

The purges had another significant implication – political turmoil forced an ordinary person to rely primarily on strong ties because one's circle of friends (especially since the 1930s) determined who you were in the eyes of the NKVD. For those who were valuable for the party though, the situation was often different – many directors' mishaps were taken up by the Party Control Commission (KPK is the Russian acronym) and often ended up only with a reprimand, reversed soon after (ibid., pp. 153–6).[84] The value could have been determined by unique or outstanding professional skills, but it appears that most of the time the clique-based explanation carries more weight. 'Members of the elite, especially those with powerful protectors, received mild punishments' (ibid., p. 155). KPK's role directly opened the door for connections because KPK officials, who had discretion in most cases, had at the same time 'imprecise understanding of what was legal and illegal' (ibid., p. 139).

Bureaucratization of the party control became apparent very early on, in the early 1920s. At the start, the authority of the local party control commissions was undermined by their own party secretaries who were centrally appointed and mandated to preserve the unity of the party (Adams, 1977, p. 27).[85] Political networks were at first self-contained and encouraged by the central authority. However, later on, they conveniently blended with other types of networks, for example, industrial.[86] The local party organs preferred people from their own region to be appointed and were successful in making that happen.[87]

Changes leading to this transition weakened the central power. For instance, many appointments were executed locally through networks rather than by a direct order from Moscow. Ministries exhibited autarkic tendencies (Rutland, 1993, p. 21). In a theoretical framework this would mean that networks increased in size and influence and that they no longer remained exclusively top-down, but evolved a complex horizontal structure. Because political networks were not threatened by the purges after Stalin's death, *blat* relationships matured as the turnover rate among party members decreased.[88]

IN CONCLUSION: THE SPECULATOR – KING OF THE MARKET AND WHY NETWORKS FLOURISHED

Ironically but not surprisingly, instead of producing a model commune member who altruistically works for the good of society, the Soviet regime produced an exemplary thief, the versatile liar – a wolf in a sheep's skin. It is worth saying that far from everyone qualified for this description. But the king of the underground market, where everyone, honest and dishonest, went to get the necessities of life, was not the producer – but the speculator.[89] Moreover, so many aspects of people's lives were over-regulated that even the honest ones were forced at times to disrespect the law and, if not their neighbours' possessions, then certainly public property, which included inputs and outputs at the workplace.

The role of networks was very much reinforced by the state's economic policy. The necessity of survival and the legal restrictions on the only possible means to do so – private production and trade – boosted the value of social capital. If the loss of a government job meant loss of everything (even food during famine and nearly everything at other times), then there was a high opportunity cost for questioning ideology and high returns were set on personal connections that kept the job. When rations were introduced, for instance, in the 1930s, distributors of rations depended on personal connections to deliver them to unqualified people for personal profit.[90]

Theft reached astronomical proportions in the Soviet Union. Exact estimates are hard to come by, but losses from theft were large. 'In the Gorky automobile factory cars disappeared right off the assembly line. In the Treugol'nik factory, workers stole over 100,000 pairs of galoshes in 1932. . . . In 1932 nearly 10,000 heads of cattle and thousands of sheep were stolen from state livestock farms.'[91] Arbatov, describing theft in 1922, remarks that it existed in terrifying proportions in all Soviet institutions. Commissars' signatures were forged, and through collaboration with bank clerks and other officials certain individuals obtained millions of rubles, steel, nails, sugar, salt, flour. Commissars themselves stole, often employing the expertise of non-party thieves. Heads of *glavki* (ministry main administration) exchanged state property between themselves by simply writing out orders in the name of the institutions they headed. The head of a provincial department of health, K, prescribed an increased food ration for the Commissar of Transportation, who received meat, butter, chocolate and so on directly from the warehouse and in turn sent to K's home firewood and coal (Arbatov, 1990, p. 122). However, to dispose of goods an informal network was required, as it was illegal to sell even homemade goods at a market price.[92]

Private enterprise often developed under the cover of state institutions. For example, salespeople in state stores, and dining halls sold goods that they either produced themselves or illegally bought for resale from someone else, for instance, a cooperative, a warehouse, or another state store. Bakers in the state bakeries baked bread using state ovens from flour that they had purchased on their own, and sold bread on the side. It would be practically impossible to approach a salesperson in the open and out of blue; some network referral was essential.

Soviet organizations, such as *raikom*,[93] anti-illiteracy groups and the Red Cross, also served as covers for private business.[94] Such business ventures too needed networks to hide. Others, such as underground handicrafts, had to find dealers to dispose of their products because they bought raw materials from the state at lower than market prices, but rarely sold them through cooperatives – the lion's share were sold at market prices illegally (Osokina, 2001, p. 118).

Speculators could not openly advertise themselves, so the network grapevine was crucial here as well. When entire firms operated illegally,[95] their dealers had to know who to bribe in the administration of the flea market and in the police department, because the larger the shipment of goods, the more noticeable it was. The 'organized speculation', which involved groups of people and started developing in the second half of the 1930s, required more sophisticated and wider networks. Speculators employed others to stand in line for them and developed 'connections with employees in state trade'. The store clerks and management sold information about deliveries of goods, or hid them to be sold to speculators later (ibid., pp. 182–3).

Trade fell under the control of the NKVD and those whose lifestyle did not match their salaries were watched closely, so there was even more reason to rely on networks for underground dealings. In August 1940, the NKVD had 490 secret informers working in Moscow's trade system (ibid., 2001, pp. 184–5), therefore a network referral had a high value. For much of the service industry (seamstresses, dentists, tutors), clients were found through acquaintances.

Even legal state enterprises needed networks for illegal barter between institutions, for instance between *kolkhozy, sovkhozy*[96] and factories. 'Steel, wood, cement could be bartered for raw materials and groceries. Agreements took place in person and over the telephone and were not recorded on paper, but the state's threatening antibarter resolutions testify to the scope of this activity' (ibid., p. 181).[97] Evidence shows that arranging a job or barter involved 'a chain rather than a direct connection': a son of a friend who has a friend and so on. Direct bribes were rare and most often it required a connection (Fitzpatrick, 2000, pp. 172–3). 'Senior officials could only be bribed by someone of comparable social status' (ibid., p. 173), therefore, ascending networks formed, except for a few persons[98] who specialized in networking and had access to people of various social ranks.

Surely, without speculators trade would have been less efficient. However, they should not be idealized because the black market was not necessarily an approximation of a freely competitive environment.[99] After all, *snabzhentsy* worked to fulfil the *central* plan, not to help produce *what consumers wanted. Tsekhoviki* – entrepreneurs who operated underground factories and were often directors of state factories at the same time – fulfilled demand of one group of consumers at the price of creating shortage for another.

One example is that of the Dergachevskii factory. The factory was supplied materials to produce children's coats, which would be sold at a nominal price in state stores. The director bribed state inspectors, and instead produced women's coats, which were sold on the black market at a market price. Tin leads were very much in demand in the USSR because virtually everyone made their own preserves, pickled foods and so on. In order to get raw materials for underground production of the tin leads, *tsekhoviki* used their influence to shift the supply of tin from Astrahan' to Ukraine. As a result, production of canned fish at an Astrahan' factory was halted and the director there hanged himself.[100] In a non-market economy this secondary shortage was not readily eliminated because the supply and demand could not be balanced in the absence of a price mechanism, and even the black market production was limited by the extent of its access to resources.

Salespeople at the state commission stores, who engaged in their own private trade under cover, often lied to sellers about the elasticity of demand, forcing them to lower the prices, only then to lie to buyers about the willingness of a seller to sell. The salespeople, naturally, pocketed the difference. Because it was extremely difficult for buyers and sellers to obtain information about each other and because no matter how prolific the black market, demand still far exceeded supply, commissioners could often artificially restrict supply even further. The inverted, seller's market – where fierce competition takes place among customers – is unlikely to produce higher-quality goods. In addition, if such market feeds on shortages and flourishes through redistribution of stolen goods, it places higher value on who you are in the hierarchy, not how good you are at producing something.

Economically and politically the centralized system undermined its own existence by the way it operated. The more centralized it was, the more it tacitly encouraged horizontal networking (Gregory, 2004, p. 264), except for the networks of civic engagement. The plan was expected to be fulfilled no matter what, and horizontal networks sorted out the delivery and production details that the central planner could not. Consequently, '[h]orizontal unofficial networks developed as alternate sources of power and provided a base for vested interest coalitions' (ibid.).

The relaxation of political control and attempts to relax economic control as well performed a greenhouse effect for the development of personal connections. The system stubbornly persisted because production quotas remained in effect, while the supplies were not forthcoming and because it was supported by the existing political and professional elite. These 'existing monopolists . . . [were] unable to cash-in on the capital value of their privileged positions' (Boettke, 2001, p. 145). Gregory notes that among the four models of dictatorship – scientific planner, stationary bandit, power-maximizing dictator and the vested-interest model – only

the first two are postulated to produce good long-term economic performance although questionably so (Gregory, 2004, pp. 186–90, 264–7); in the
end the all-encompassing interest succumbs to opportunism.

NOTES

1. Ideology – one of the crucial, yet puzzling driving forces of changes in Russian life – is
    out of the scope of this work. The importance of ideology underpins the analysis of the
    political economy of socialism between 1918 and 1928 by Boettke (1988). The spirit
    of Pipes's work is also one of a heavy weight of ideological consequences. Somewhat
    surprisingly, in the conclusion, Pipes downgrades the significance of Marxist ideology
    in Soviet Russia (1995, p. 395). Although there are always many conflicting forces at
    work in history, Pipes himself provides convincing evidence that Marxist ideas and
    those that grew out of them are very much at the top of the list.
2. A detailed account of the events surrounding this period is provided by Pipes (1995).
3. Both formed on the same day, the Provisional Government took 'full governmental
    responsibility, while the Ispolkom (the Soviet of Workers' and Soldiers' Deputies)
    acted as a kind of supreme court of the revolutionary conscience' (Pipes, 1995, p.
    83). The coexistence, however, was filled with tension because the political and eco-
    nomic goals of the two governments were very different and because the Provisional
    Government was legitimate – it consisted of elected State Duma members, however
    lame the parliamentary system was, and the Soviet was not – it consisted of nomi-
    nees of socialist parties. Kerenskii was the exception among these nominees since
    he was a member of both governments in the beginning and the only revolutionary
    in the Provisional Government. Even though the Soviet had the real power and the
    Provisional Government did not, the latter still presented an obstacle (ibid., pp. 83–8).
    Z. Gippius, who lived in Petrograd during these events with her husband Dmitri
    Merejkovskii and who was closely acquainted with various prominent political and
    intellectual figures, provides a first-hand account of the events (Gippius, 1990, pp.
    250–332).
4. Pipes (1995) asserts that they remained a minority. Perhaps a misinterpretation on my
    part, but it appears in his account as if the Bolshevik takeover were a surprise. Gippius
    (1990, pp. 305, 309, 317, 321–2) wrote in her diary in August–early September of 1917
    that the Soviet had been completely Bolshevized, and that everyone in Petrograd
    was in panic and waiting for the Bolsheviks to take over. The date of takeover, 25
    November, was apparently announced publicly by the Bolsheviks themselves (ibid., p.
    318).
5. In some remote regions peasant unrest and fighting with local guerrillas (for example,
    Basmachi) in Asian republics lasted as long as 1922, 1923.
6. For more figures, see Shanin (1972, p. 10).
7. For more details, see Shanin (1972, pp. 12–24).
8. Only too late and only in the aftermath of great civil unrest of 1905.
9. This is pointed out in Boettke (1988) many times, for instance, pp. 257–8, Notes 42 and
    43 and p. 231.
10. For instance, if War Communism were a response to war circumstances, then the
    grain requisitioning should have been at the top of the list because bread shortage
    was the most crucial issue. But while it 'was a major policy it *was not* the major
    element in the program of socialist transformation' (Boettke, 1988, pp. 201–2, Note
    79; original emphasis). During NEP, while private trade and private ownership of
    the means of production were allowed, the state had a solid grip on the industrial
    enterprises and the majority of the workforce. 'The result of this [during NEP]
    industrial reorganization was that by 1923 of the 165,781 enterprises that were

accounted for in an industrial census 147,471 or 88.5 per cent were owned by private persons, 13,697 or 8.5 per cent were State owned and 4,613 or 3.1 per cent were co-operative enterprises. While these private enterprises amounted to 88.5 per cent of the total enterprises, they employed only 12.4 per cent of the total number of workers employed in the industry, while the State-owned enterprises, which comprised only 8.5 per cent of the total enterprises, employed 84.1 per cent of employed workers' (ibid., p. 243). Also see ibid., 'Retreat or Advance', especially p. 260, Note 46; pp. 261–3, 270–71. Civil War was not presented as a reason for War Communism by the Bolsheviks at the time of its implementation (ibid., p. 266, Note 55), and War Communism was admitted a mistake only in timing not in the context of its poli-cies (ibid., p. 267, Note 57). Pipes has a similar opinion (1995, pp. 192–3). Lenin expressed his views in print (as were analysed by Boettke and Pipes) and also in private conversations. His intentions seemed pretty clear (Solomon, 1991, p. 273).

11. A very industrious and, in my opinion, correct treatment of causes of shortages in foodstuffs during 1915–17 is given by Struve, Zaitsev, Dolinsky and Demosthenov in Struve et al. (1930). The disarray of the transportation system (ibid., Part II, Chapter IX) inevitably led to significant price differentiation among different regions. In addi-tion to this the banks speculated in grain, sugar and so on (ibid., Part II, Chapter VIII). The industry once again was working primarily for the front, so consumer manufacture goods were in shortage. As a result, there appeared a gap between realized (effective) demand and supply. Otherwise plentiful commodities appeared in limited supply. Peasants were hoarding agricultural goods in the expectation of a higher price and because of inability to spend the money on manufacture goods ('disorganization of commodity exchange', ibid., Part II, Chapter X). As banks were not allowed to participate in food trade the dealers illegally received bank credit. They bought up and hoarded foodstuffs in order to release them on the market in small quantities to make more profit. The disarray of the Russian internal market, uncertainty created by the war and the Provisional Government's policy of price regulation (ibid., Part II, Chapter XIII) prevented prices from stabilizing. In this situation every time the prices went up, it only revved up the speculators' appetite.

12. For more details on price regulation and grain monopoly, see Struve et al. (1930, Part I, Chapter IV). On sugar monopoly, see ibid. (Chapter X); on price regulation of meat and salt, see ibid. (Chapter XI). Under the Provisional Government the grain monopoly effectively failed in its purpose, although it created substantial havoc in the market. The reason it failed was the unwillingness of the Provisional Government to confiscate grain by force and thereby spill blood. The Bolsheviks resorted to this measure immediately.

13. Sometimes referred to also as 'bag-peddling' (Struve et al., 1930, p. 465).

14. Relative to the low value of a peddler's life, as a cynically inclined economist must point out.

15. Rationing produced a similar rise in illegal trading in the end of the 1920s and in the beginning of the 1930s, during World War II and in the 1980s.

16. As a surprise to me, as probably to anyone who was exposed to the Soviet ideology first-hand, comes the 'standard' account, presented by the Western historians who studied the Soviet economy, Dobb (1948), Carr ([1952] 1980) and Nove ([1969] 1984), of the events of War Communism and the NEP. It is argued that nationalization was a response to an emergency war situation. While it is clear that the Bolsheviks viewed this as an adequate response to war circumstances, they nationalized private property out of ideological reasons – the market had to be eliminated war or no war. A very profound and passionate argument against the standard view is provided by Boettke (1988). Particularly interesting is also Boettke's response to Nove's criticisms (Boettke, 2001, pp. 98–102).

17. Because the inflation soared, barter became the dominant method of trade.

18. Flea markets still existed, regularly ransacked by the Soviet police (Solomon, 1991, p. 283).

19. Some claim there were as many as 200,000 *meshochniki* in Ukraine alone in 1921, but precise data do not exist. However, contemporary accounts draw a picture of railways overwhelmed by *meshochniki* as if by a 'legion of ants' (Ball, 1987, pp. 88–9).
20. For more details, see Ball (1987, pp. 20–23).
21. Also, because of lack of cadres to confiscate and, if not run, to at least safeguard the nationalized property, many, in particular smaller factories, eluded government control in the beginning of the 1920s and remained in private operation. The Supreme Council of the National Economy operated between 4000 and 5000 enterprises by November 1920. This was a small part of the industry (Ball, 1987, p. 6).
22. For a good analysis of small-scale industry on the eve of the revolution and through the early 1930s, see Kaufman (1962). Joint stock companies were 'socialist', mixed and private. The number of the latter was never large. And many were *joint*-stock only in name (Ball, 1987, pp. 154–7).
23. Nepmen were entrepreneurs who took advantage of economic opportunities under the laws of New Economic Policy.
24. Even in later years food took up to a half of all traded items (Ball, 1987, pp. 86–7). Even though an impressive (for a communist-to-be state) number of enterprises were leased to private individuals, they were small in size. But more importantly, leases were given on average for three years and probably none for more than six, and were not renewed upon their expiration. Private industry, unlike private trade, was concentrated in the countryside. For figures and more details, see ibid. (pp. 129–32).
25. There was a licence fee, a levelling fee amounting to 3 per cent tax on production and sales; on production and sales of luxury goods the levelling fee was raised to 6 or 12 per cent and additional fees applied; see Ball (1987, pp. 29–30).
26. A decree stated, 'anyone who conspired to raise prices or withhold goods from the market was to be imprisoned or have property confiscated, or both. Interpreted strictly, this decree forbade peasants to store their grain until prices improved and made it a crime for a private middleman to offer peasants or any other producers a higher price for their products than that offered by the state' (Ball, 1987, p. 33). Of course, there were other taxes, such as fees to use business facilities (ibid., p. 30).
27. The state altered its policies and ransacked Nepmen in the end of 1924, only to revert again in 1925; for details see Ball (1987, pp. 38–55).
28. In Transcaucasia and Central Asia, which were further out of the state's grasp, illegal or legal private economic activity enjoyed a lot more freedom than in Central Russia; for figures see Ball (1987, p. 99).
29. Also see Brovkin (1998, p. 204).
30. For multiple examples of such personal connections between state and private sector, see Ball (1987, pp. 114–20).
31. Semen Pliatskii, for instance, who had been a millionaire metal trader before 1917, chose to work for the state after the revolution. During the NEP he set out as 'a buyer and seller of scrap metal and later as a supplier of industrial products. . . . He had a knack for acquiring even scarce commodities by hook or by crook. Here his many connections with state agencies, often established with bribes, undoubtedly helped' (Ball, 1987, pp. 91–2).
32. For more details, see Nutter (1962, Chapter 2). The reason we can be sure of that is because the results of the analysis make economic sense and are consistent with what can be observed directly (ibid., p. 13). Nutter's methodology is very sound. The figures after all were not invented out of this air. The view that Soviet statistics are usable is shared by Gerschenkron and Marx (Gerschenkron and Marx, 1950). Naum Jasny provides very harsh, but to the point cases of where and how Soviet statistics are falsified. In his opinion, the Soviets make more than four out of two, so the official data is hard to use in hope for reasonable accuracy (Jasny, 1950a and 1950b). Regardless of who wins in this debate, the statement that Soviet statistics were manipulated remains a fact; therefore, the use of anecdotal evidence is warranted.

33. For details on Stalin's policies at the end of the 1920s, see Ball (1987, Chapter 3 and pp. 101–7).
34. The shortages were huge, and consequences deadly for many. For details on shortages at the end of the 1920s and in the 1930s, see Osokina (2001, Chapters 2–5). Fitzpatrick (1999) covers the period under Stalin.
35. In the 1930s those who received the best food rations numbered 4500; the second best were received by 41,500, all in all there were about 55,000 families and the majority of them resided in Moscow (Osokina, 2001, p. 98).
36. Osokina (2001) gives a very detailed assessment of the standards of living of the various categories of the Soviet population in the 1930s. The apartments of Stalin and Molotov were quite modest; others created luxury by borrowing pre-revolutionary furniture from the Kremlin storehouses. '[A]bundant food but with little variety, a modest wardrobe, an apartment of average size, a country home for rest, a state car, tickets to the theater, and parties. The Soviet elite did not live lavishly compared to the West, even after the worldwide depression lowered the living standards of the Western upper-middle classes' (ibid., pp. 96–8).
37. For examples, see Ball (1987, pp. 107–8), and Osokina (2001, p. 102).
38. They were certain to be quite modest in size though (Osokina, 2001, p. 111). 'Cooperatives, schools, hospitals, sanatoria, and unions of scientists and artists all acquired their own rabbit hutches, pigsties, and seedbeds. Even Sovnarkom [Council of People's Commissars], and OGPU [Joint State Political Directorate], and the Central Committee all had their own supplementary economies that helped to supply departmental dining halls and buffets' (ibid., p. 110).
39. To clarify the form in which property existed in the USSR, a distinction between personal *(lichnaia)* and private *(chastnaia)* property should be made. Individual plots of land, *dachas* (summer cottages in city suburbs) and peasant houses were permitted to be held in personal ownership. They were not the means of production in the strict sense. This is the difference between socialist and capitalist types of private ownership (www.answers.com/topic/ history-of-the-soviet-union-1953-1985).
40. In fact, centralization of trade continued (Osokina, 2001, pp. 148–9).
41. On how this influenced the quoted figures, see Osokina (2001, pp. 145–6).
42. To describe how desperate the situation was, it is worth quoting at length here an NKVD (People's Commissariat for Internal Affairs) report from the late 1930s about lines at various Moscow stores:

> The line starts to form several hours before the store closes, in the yards of the nearest houses. Someone makes a line list, and, after getting on the list, some people leave to find a place on the street or in a yard to rest. Some citizens bring big winter coats and blankets to keep warm. Some also bring kitchen chairs to sit on.
>
> By sunrise people were standing in line, sitting on sidewalks wrapped in blankets, or sleeping on doorsteps near the store. . . . The clerks started letting people in the store before opening time, and suddenly the lines deteriorate. Everybody starts running to the doors of the store, and people fight and get crushed. . . .
>
> By eight o'clock in the morning there were already over 3,500 customers at the store of the textile industry. . . . When the store opened at 8:30 there were around 4,000–4,500 people. The line, formed at eight o'clock in the morning, extended . . . [for at least a kilometer]. . . .
>
> At eight o'clock in the morning a line of 1,000 people formed at a department store in the Leningrad district of Moscow, but the militia blocked the crowd with ten trucks. Masses of people ran to the square of the 'Spartak' movie theater, to get between the cinema and the police trucks. There was an impossible crush and confusion and shouting. The militia appeared to be powerless to do anything, and in order not to be squashed, they climbed onto the trucks. . . . At opening time the line had more than 5,000 people.
>
> At six o'clock in the morning a line formed at a department store in the

Dzerzhinskii district, taking over the nearest streets, tram, and bus stations. By nine o'clock there were 8,000 people in line. (Osokina, 2001, pp. 187–8)

43. This happened due to lack of expertise, suppression of market forces, which distorted administrative directions, and a fast pace of industrialization, which prevented integration of the shops.
44. For more details, see Shearer (1993).
45. For a discussion of the dictator and managers in the principal-agent framework, see Gregory (2004, pp. 252–7).
46. Supply expediters or *tolkachi* in the Western literature on the USSR.
47. For examples, see Ball (1987, pp. 148–51).
48. The money for this unofficial salary together with expenses for the presents for the local party officials and bureaucrats had to be earned on the side as well, for example, from bribes. Falsifying statistics by factory managers was apparently widespread and often undetected (Gregory, 2001, pp. 145–7). Sometimes a manager would declare products 'defective' and sell them to 'utilization shops' at his factory to be fixed and subsequently sold at the market prices. The factory kept the profit, which was legal in this case (ibid., pp. 147–8).
49. Stalin was, of course, lenient to the victors of industrialization; however, no one could be certain to avoid a show trial. The fact that managers bargained actively for increased rights (more autonomous decision-making) of directors of enterprises even after Stalin's death shows that it was not a piece of cake even then (Hoeffding, 1962, p. 477).
50. Later some managers preferred to seek local party assistance in procuring supplies before addressing *glavki* (ministry main administration) (Gregory, 1990, p. 97).
51. For details, see Berliner (1957, pp. 243–7).
52. Examples in Shelley (1990, p. 15), and Osokina (2001, pp. 183–4).
53. On the desirability of such positions, see Simis (1977–78, p. 42). It is worth quoting NKVD reports on the lifestyle of these millionaires:

> In 1940 the director of Krasnaia Presnia store in Moscow . . . spent 100,000 rubles building a dacha, bought a car and two motorcycles, built a special garage, and even built a one-kilometer asphalt road to his dacha. . . .
> The NKVD considered 'Z,' the director of a store the wealthiest person in Moscow at the beginning of the 1940s. He earned six hundred rubles per month but spent ten to fifteen thousand. . . .
> Underground millionaires enjoyed a lifestyle at least as luxurious as the highest political elite in the country, but their wealth belonged to them exclusively rather than being state property. (Osokina, 2001, p. 185)

For more examples, see ibid.

54. For more on this, see Birman (1988, p. 218). Though official figures are not available, the information in the Soviet press paints a picture of utter dissatisfaction with the supply side in the 1980s. These are just some examples:

> [M]ore than 15 billion rubles of annually planned supplies are not delivered. At the same time, according to the TsSU, in 1980–82 the economy produced about 17 billion rubles worth of products not ordered by consumers – i.e. that were not really needed by them. . . .
> [I]n 1984 about 100,000 state-owned trucks and cars could not be used because there were not enough tyres. Individual owners of cars also 'experience difficulties' with tyres. . . .
> [D]uring the first third of 1987 only 80 per cent of enterprises carried out their 'contract obligations' in full. (Birman, 1988, pp. 216–17)

For more examples, see ibid.

Among others, housing shortages were bad: '[I]n November, 1974, 180,000 families or 590,000 persons made the [waiting] list. This accounted for 7 per cent of the capital's population. Sixty per cent of them averages less than 5 sq. m. of living space. The others lived in dilapidated quarters or lacked basic conveniences such as central heating or hot water. Of the total, 70 per cent were on preferred lists. They will be accommodated earlier; the other 30 per cent may have to wait as long as a decade' (Morton, 1979, p. 805). Amidst this 'local party and government officials, plant managers, state bank directors and others use their connections to build well-equipped, over-sized homes (far in excess of the permitted 60 sq. m. of living space), on illegally assigned plots, using stolen building materials and illegal loaned construction machinery and labor. Sometimes they own several private homes (although only one is legally permitted to each household), while still maintaining a state owned apartment in the city' (ibid., p. 807). More details on the housing market and corruption, ibid. (pp. 790–810).

An excellent study critiquing the CIA estimates of comparing personal consumption in the USSR and the USA was done by Birman (1989). In this study he industriously examines the quality of consumer products in the USSR, arriving at a not so positive picture as presented by the CIA study. Just some of many examples are that only 6 per cent of bread and bread products in 1974 were baked out of flour of highest quality, that in the 1970s colour televisions required on average six to seven repairs a year and after 'improvements' still twice a year and one-fifth soon after purchase (Birman, 1983, pp. 43 and 137). 'In the opinion of American manufactures the quality of almost all American products is higher. The only two exceptions were dried split peas . . . and sugar cubes' (Birman, 1989, p. 36).

There is also a study on the Soviet 'poor', see Matthews (1986). Sedik builds a model of consumer behaviour in a price-controlled economy and tests it on the results of a survey conducted among the Soviet émigrés in the United States. The results support his hypothesis that 'for the purchase of deficit goods in state and cooperative stores, connections are at least as important and probably more important than monetary side payments' (Sedik, 1989, pp. 13–14). Even though data is potentially flawed and methodology controversial, the results are not at odds with what common sense would tell us about the consumer behaviour under shortage conditions and are worth examining.

55. In fact, the population could live for nine months on the hoarded money; more on this in Birman (1983, pp. 70–84). On the disastrous state of agriculture and industry, trade, labour productivity, foreign trade, see ibid. (pp. 178–201). Even in years of good harvest, the USSR had to buy grain abroad. Three-fourths of industry A (light) production did not go for consumption but was absorbed by the industry itself – thus, showing its inefficiency (ibid., p. 185).

56. For an example, see Ofer (1987, p. 1799). For a comparison of food consumption in the USSR and in the United States in the 1970s in both the caloric intake and composition of foods, see Birman (1983, pp. 36–7, Tables 5.3 and 5.4). Soviet caloric intake is slightly behind the American, which is an underestimate if we factor in a lifestyle of more physical labour and more stress.

57. Birman (1989) also discusses military expenditures.

58. Some of the growth has been attributed to the use of the concentration camp labour. These were not planned to be used that way, but soon after their institution, the leadership realized that slave labour was cheap. However, recently uncovered evidence questions the overall positive effect of the camps on the growth – their output did not constitute the majority of any industry's output and quality was poor, such as the White Sea Canal project (Khlevnyuk, 2001, pp. 111–29). On the Gulags, see Jasny (1951), and more recently, Gregory (2004, p. 258, Note 30).

59. Such were the 1957 reforms (Hoeffding, 1962, pp. 475–87). Khruschev's attempts to 'decentralize' governing and reform agriculture only ended in disaster.

60. We now know from the archival sources that there was a strong impetus for reform before, and even right after the purges. This is what resurfaced again in the 1950s and 1960s, unfortunately, with little significance (Gregory, 2001, pp. 79–80).

61. Boettke presents here a discussion of the credibility and reform in the Soviet Union (2001, Chapter 9).

62. Gimpel'son (1997, p. 50) cites a Sovnarkom (Council of People's Commissars) decree from November 1917 stating that people's commissars received 500 rubles in monthly salary plus 100 additional rubles per each non-working family member. Lenin considered rich those with income exceeding 500 rubles a month.

63. The capital was moved to Moscow in 1918 because Petrograd was too close to the border. Interestingly, it was the Moscow, not Petersburg, business elite who used their connections with the Tsarist government most; and it was Moscow bureaucracy that had been most corrupt before the revolution.

64. Besides the Kremlin, the best food rations were given to those who worked in the Food Provision Commissariat, to those who were assigned to live in the nationalized Hotel Natzional' and former Hotel Metropol'. As one might suspect, even though only party members were supposed to live there, mistresses, friends and family of party members enjoyed these privileges unofficially (Solomon, 1991, p. 283). On Voroshilov's and Bydennyi's rich lifestyle, see Arbatov (1990, p. 108). Concerns with the luxurious lifestyle of the party elite prompted an investigation. In 1920 a questionnaire was suggested to find out more details about misuse of status and privileges. Even though the investigation was never carried through, the questions are quite illuminating: What are the salary and the rations? What are the extra rations received in the last month? How many orders were sent for clothing and footwear in the last month? For what personal purposes are personal secretaries used? For what personal purposes are cars used and how many are in possession? How many rooms do the flats have? Feasts, inappropriate behaviour? (Gimpel'son, 1997, pp. 51–2).

65. For examples, see Pipes (1995, p. 367).

66. The rationing (as in limiting of use) never applied to the top leadership. Although electricity use was severely limited in Moscow, the Kremlin and its surroundings were brightly lit (Solomon, 1991, p. 282). Provincial communists, well-fed and happy, drove around in automobiles during famine (Arbatov, 1990, p. 118). Gorki's second wife, who became a commissar after the revolution, expropriated a mansion in Liteinyi Prospect, had two cars and so on (Gippius, 1990, p. 198).

67. Except for foreign workers (Osokina, 2001, pp. 75–7).

68. Lenin, for instance, though his occupation of estate in Gorki might also raise a question. Others, Marxists in the true sense, such as F. Kon, either died of natural causes by the 1930s or had a 'little' help. The new Bolsheviks – those who joined the party after the revolution – were in bulk young, poorly educated opportunists from the streets, whose enthusiasm, dedication and values were questionable (Galeotti, 2000, pp. 277–8).

69. Even earlier, despite of the claims of equality, the Soviet rationing system was one of the most stratified in the world. It emerged during War Communism. Type and amount of a ration depended on the sector of industry. Even children were subject to unequal rationing (Osokina, 2001, p. 201).

70. Besides political elite, *nomenklatura* included scientific and artistic elite. Scientific elite received special rations already during War Communism. There is a claim that (by the 1930s) rations were an exchange for loyalty to the regime; for more details see Osokina (2001, p. 72). My view is that this was an unplanned consequence of the system rather than a deliberate design.

71. A detailed account of privileges in the Soviet society based on interviews with émigrés can be found in Matthews (1978, Chapters 2–4). One of the classic works describing everyday life in the USSR in the late 1970s is *Klass* by Willis. He estimates the privileged Rising Class (middle class) to be 23 million people and 40 million including relatives, or about one-sixth of the total population (Willis, 1987, p. 12).

72. Perel'man provides an example of how privileges of one's status could be rented for a short period of time. Citizen X had a number of friends who were personal drivers of members of Politburo or ministers. A driver would normally meet his boss in the airport to take him home after a trip. But if the driver would unexpectedly call in ill, there was almost certainly a lapse in arranging a substitute. In this case citizen X was ready to rescue a flabbergasted bureaucrat from the public transportation chaos. On the way to the minister's home citizen X would prove a witty and entertaining companion, in fact, so entertaining and obliging that the bureaucrat would offer to hire him as his personal driver. Citizen X would wholeheartedly decline the offer – he does this only out of a genuine desire to help. Bureaucrats like honest people, so X would get a hefty reward for his services and the 'sick' driver – his renting fee (Perel'man, 1977, pp. 64–6).
73. Term used by Los (1990).
74. For details, see Adams (1977, pp. 22–8).
75. For another source on the growth of elite posts, see Matthews (1978, pp. 135–47).
76. Between the two elites of the 1920s – the politicians and the technologists – the latter were educated before the revolution and thus already carried with them the idea of tight relationship between industry and the state (Rowney, 1993, p. 130).
77. In the Soviet period *blat* (or *sviazi*) denotes personal connections which have the ultimate goal of achieving higher welfare and/or status.
78. Quoted in Los (1990, p. 204).
79. Quoted in Los (1990, p. 205).
80. *Komitetchiki* were members of the Communist Party, many of whom were sent to supervise the collective farms or factories and to recruit new members.
81. Education was not the major qualification for selecting chairmen of the collective farms (*predsedatel'*) in the 1930s. There were plenty of educated agricultural specialists at the levels below that of a chairman. 'It is hardly surprising . . . to find evidence that "successful" collective farm chairs owed their success primarily to their good relations with local party and soviet organizations, primarily those on a district level' (Merl, 1993, p. 50). Potential party members were coaxed into joining through personal relationships:

    Every local party cell was required to identify 'politically advanced persons' whose job was working over [*obrabotka*] specific individuals with the aim of recruiting them into the party. A chosen comrade was to name two or three persons who were the targets of his 'agitation activity.' Their names were to be kept secret. The party task of the chosen comrade was to establish regular meetings with them in an informal atmosphere, to invite them for tea, visit them in their homes, and establish friendship. (Brovkin, 1998, p. 49)

    The persons in question had no knowledge of being worked over.
82. Wintrobe (1998, pp. 225–8) provides a nice discussion of purges as a way of dealing away with horizontal networks, which could be detrimental to the vertical ones. Gregory (2001, p. 56) finds from the archives that indeed Stalin's private and public discourses were the same – preoccupied by spies, wreckers and so on.
83. On how purges affected mobility of elite, see Matthews (1978, pp. 147–54).
84. Ninety per cent of managers received reprimands in the 1970s instead of criminal sentences (Shelley, 1990, p. 20).
85. There are some facts in Klugman (1989) on political elite and their career dynamics.
86. Blending networks and politics offered a range of opportunities for average citizens as well, the simplest being an economic value of a *partbilet* (party membership card) – they were traded in the black market (Gregory, 2001, p. 136). There is no evidence though of collusion between the military and industry (ibid., p. 91). Rutland describes collusion between primary party organizations (PPOs) and factory managers. The managers enjoyed a higher status and had better connection, so PPOs' secretaries were

often submissive to managers and stopped serving as a check on them (Rutland, 1993, p. 45).

87.   Careers in the party followed a well-defined path, which as well as the practice of local appointments (Rutland, 1993, pp. 190–94), suggests the use of informal networks in career dynamics.
88.   For figures, see Hough (1977, p. 29).
89.   In fact, the state figured often as a speculator itself. On the operations of Torgsin (state-run hard-currency stores), which sold goods to the population at highly inflated prices in exchange for antiques, gold, silver and so on and enriched the state, see Osokina (2001, pp. 121–9).
90.   On 'freeloaders', see Osokina (2001, p. 104).
91.   For more details, see Osokina (2001, p. 106).
92.   Except for peasants.
93.   The district committee of the Communist Party.
94.   For more examples, see Osokina (2001, pp. 114–17). 'In the village of Lukashevka … thirteen participants organized a complex of services fronted by the Ukrainian Red Cross, in which they had a bakery, confectionery, a mineral water facility, a snack bar, and a barber shop' (ibid., p. 117).
95.   For examples of those, see Osokina (2001, pp. 118–19).
96.   Two forms of Soviet collective farming. *Kolkhoz* (singular), *kolkhozy* (plural) stands for collective farm. *Sovkhoz* (singular), *sovkhozy* (plural) stands for Soviet or state farm. *Sovkhozy* were smaller.
97.   Also see Gregory (2001, pp. 148–9).
98.   In the Soviet literature referred to as *blatmeisters* (Fitzpatrick, 2000, p. 174).
99.   A theoretical exposition of perverse influence of shortages on the behaviour of economic agents is presented by Kornai (1980). On the role of personal connections in a shortage economy, see Kornai (1980, Vol. A, pp. 76–8). For the perverse effect of shortages on a supplier's behaviour and how a seller gains a dominant position in the market, see ibid. (pp. 120 and 122). The soft budget constraint, sellers' market, and institutional peculiarities of a shortage economy will lead to lower quality (ibid., pp. 115, 125, 162).
100. For more information on *tsekhoviki* and their operations, see *Chernyi biznes razvitogo sotsializma* (3 August 2005). For more details on how the underground business operated, see Simis (1982, Chapter 6).

7. Social networks and cultural atavism

WHY NETWORKS PROSPERED OR WHAT CONSTITUTED CULTURAL ATAVISM IN RUSSIA

Particular features of the Russian-Soviet culture, such as retrospective and fatalistic attitudes, collectivism, passivity, negligence, disrespect for law and private property were prompted among others by the economic and political circumstances. Uncertainty produced fatalism, high cost of market transactions combined with the arbitrary power produced disrespect for law and negligence. Absolutism produced political passivity, and strong pressure of the totalitarian regime had a positive effect on the growth of personal networks during the Soviet period.

There was a particular social dualism present in Russian life before the revolution – the cultural pattern of the peasantry was especially backward (Shanin, 1972, p. 26). The other sectors of Russian society were more progressive both in technological and social organization, but the revolution destroyed that progressive element. Although the Soviet Union created its own intelligentsia,[1] it was not an overnight event and values of this group were even more distant from laissez-faire than values of the pre-revolutionary upper classes. The Soviet intelligentsia's values were undoubtedly corrupted by the survival strategies forced upon them by the regime.

The formal regulatory institutions imposed by the Soviet government prescribed honesty, egalitarianism in everyday life and transparency of business relations. These stipulations were inconsistent not only with what economic circumstances demanded but also with centuries of informal practices. Given that the regime apparently could not be toppled, the only plausible outcome was for people to find a way to adapt to the new economic and political circumstances using proven methods. As mentioned earlier, during the beginning stage, the Soviet Republic lacked bureaucratic cadres and had to employ people from the Tsarist bureaucracy to run the state institutions. They had practical knowledge of how hierarchies work.

The Soviet formal institutions meddled in every walk of life[2] and the regulatory pressure from the state became greater in the Soviet period. The transaction cost of market exchanges skyrocketed (if anything because market relations were banned most of the time) but the set-up costs of hierarchies were relatively low. Consequently, networks as a governance method of exchange expanded and became more pronounced in the Soviet period, as people had more incentives and opportunities to use them and acquired more networking skills in the process.[3]

LEGACY OF PRE-REVOLUTIONARY CULTURE

Even though the new regime brought radical economic and political changes, the outcome was not independent of the Russian mentality. By the beginning of the 20th century there were only a few progressive (liberal) minds in Russia. Not only had they had a limited influence before, but both they and their legacy were heavily suppressed after the revolution. Left were largely uneducated peasant and worker populations and social-ist intellectuals whose numbers were small. Commoners practised personal relationships based on reciprocity, reinforced among other factors by *mir* or communes. The commoners also carried into a new era a strong tradition of patrimonialism. The phrase normally used to characterize the Soviet period – 'it is better to have 100 friends than 100 rubles' – has in fact a pre-revolutionary origin (Shul'gin, 1991, p. 163).

The ideas of central planning were popularized and enforced by the Soviets, but they also did not originate with them. Some of the intellectu-als at the beginning of the 19th century, including the Decembrists, also entertained the idea of central planning. So did the workers in a more down-to-earth way. Because industrialization in Russia occurred later and proceeded at a more rapid pace than in Western Europe, workers' unions did not have a strong foothold. When searched upon leaving the factory for concealed tools, when beaten or not provided with minimally adequate living conditions, workers found no mitigating force but the government, as suggested by its presence everywhere in their lives. The worker and peasant alike were fixated upon the state's responsibility for the evils they had experienced, although the peasants did want abolition of state taxa-tion. This unfortunately created the state of mind that produced revolution (Mavor, 1925, Vol. 2, pp. 366–7).

The Great Russian was once truly incapable of defeating the whims of nature, and once passivity becomes a national habit, it is perhaps easier to accept the state as an omnipotent power rather than undertake a long and difficult fight against the state's encroachment on personal liberty. Passivity characterized even the most progressive economic elements. There is no evidence that, for example, the Nepmen (see Chapter 6) resisted their elimination in any aggressive widespread or organized form (Ball

1987, p. 63). OGPU (Joint State Political Directorate) documents reveal that there were strikes, disturbances in queues and so on[4] during short-ages, but there were none that happened on a nationwide scale, and most discontent was not expressed openly.

Instead, people 'adapted survival strategies to fit the conditions. Cunning and versatility filled the gaps in the state system of supply' (Osokina, 2001, p. 94).[5] Likewise, even though at the end of the 1930s there appeared leaf-lets with anti-communist slogans, dissatisfaction for the most part took on a passive form.[6] Individual (not joint!) letter-writing to the state com-plaining about red tape, poor customer service and the like was a popular activity and was also encouraged by the leaders (Fitzpatrick, 1999, pp. 175–8). However, complaints did not materialize into further actions of any significance. In rare cases that they could, a single individual complaint or single individual were easy enough to nullify.

Ironically, personal connections fed political passivity because they helped to 'humanize the system'. If a Soviet believed that he could manipu-late the system through a personal action, he was more likely to have faith in it and less likely to jeopardize it (Galeotti, 2000, p. 275). Strong ties sup-ported the system in one other important way:

> It is among the seeming paradoxes of Soviet life that in a regimented and closely supervised society friendships may flourish in a greater depth and intensity than in a much more free, unorganized, and permissive society like the American one . . . this proposition . . . [could] be an indicator of both the success and the failure of totalitarianism. The failure lies in the inability of the regime to atomize the society completely and to reintegrate the 'atoms' into officially structured and supervised collectivities. The success lies in *partial atomization* which enhances the importance of very small, informal, and intimate units – such as small groups of friends. (Hollander, 1978, p. 287; original emphasis)

Hollander is right, except that because partially atomized networks were unofficially weaved into the system of redistribution they sustained the regime for quite a long time.[7]

Mir

The commune was 'a major factor of peasant life in Russia' before the revolution:

> It proceeded to play that role until the early 1930s to the unending surprise of many peasants-watchers. It was the persistence of the commune and the way it could drop out of sight only to resurface later on, that puzzled most of the non-peasants looking at it. The informal functions and unexpected uses to which the commune was put by its members added to the puzzlement and the debate. (Shanin, 1986)

Since the majority of workers in Russia were yesterday's peasants and many retained their social and economic ties with the village, the urban population inevitably inherited the collective psychology of the *obshchina* (see Chapter 4),[8] in particular that a person cannot be successful without the support of a large group. Although alien to the Bolshevik regime in theory, in practice the communal norms were not at odds with it during the first decades. The Soviet regime benefited from the weak tradition of individualism and of private property that was undoubtedly cultivated by *mir* in Russia:

> Thus the very demise of the mir, which had been sought by Stolypin . . . in the name of individualism, was brought about a quarter of a century later by the Bolsheviks in the name of socialism. And yet it is at least open to doubt whether collectivization . . . could have been effected so speedily, even with the liberal use of force, if the mir system had not hindered the crystallization of the concept of stable individual property rights in land among the Russian peasantry. There is a good reason to believe, therefore, that in spite of the Bolsheviks' hostility and contempt to the mir, their agrarian collective system is indebted to it. (Volin, 1962, p. 498)[9]

The second agrarian revolution was one in which the land was taken by poor peasants from richer ones; redistribution was done through the commune and signified its revival.[10] Apparently during the New Economic Policy (NEP – see Chapter 6) communes enjoyed at times greater power in local matters than the local Soviet government.[11] Going deeper, the relation of the Soviet government to its people was in line with the traditional relation of the Tsarist government towards the serfs. 'To serfs, authority was by its very nature arbitrary; and to defend themselves from it they relied not on appeals to legal or moral rights but on cunning' (Pipes, 1995, p. 386). Soviet life to them was a continuation of a Hobbesian jungle.

SOVIET MORES: THEORETICAL GOALS AND REALITY

The lawlessness of the Soviet society immediately after the revolution, arbitrage power over life or death in the hands of the former have-nots, set masses of the newly born revolutionaries free of responsibilities before their fellow citizens. Dizzy with power they roamed around the Soviet land eager for loot and in search of scapegoats for their own anger, only fuelled in their rage by the orders from the top. As a result, the mores of the new Soviet person were very different from the egalitarian principles of socialism.

Arbatov provides several examples in his memoirs. Due to the impunity that came simply with a proletarian background or a party card, disrespect for private property grew. The so-called 'fives' (*pyaterki*), consisting of five people who were regime sympathizers and yesterday have-nots, were enti-tled to confiscate 'surpluses' from the population. *Pyaterki* conducted con-fiscations at night often leaving no more than a pair of undergarments per person. Petty bourgeois came first but others did not escape the plunder. The official campaign slogan, in fact, claimed that a confiscation must take a form of *robbery*. The confiscated items, such as money, precious metals and stones, simple household attributes, furniture, clothes and the like were supposed to be gathered at a certain location and redistributed to the poor. One might guess that most of the items did not make it to the prescribed location. Having stolen the best of goods for themselves, several days later many communists would ask to leave the party because of sudden 'poor' health. Ironically, one of the core Bolshevik principles – 'to steal the plunder' – previously referring to the bourgeoisie robbing the workers, was fulfilled by the communists themselves (Arbatov, 1990, pp. 111–12).[12]

The behaviour of the Communist Party vanguard, discussed in a study by Brovkin, demonstrates how the Soviet social networks were moulded by culture (Brovkin, 1998, pp. 37–56). The old Bolshevik intelligentsia was not numerous to begin with and had a very limited influence in the provincial towns and rural areas (Fainsod, 1953, p. 222; Brovkin, 1998, p. 55). The enlistment of intelligentsia for the fear of losing control over the bureaucratic-managerial group did not start until the 1930s and was resumed after World War II (Fainsod, 1953, pp. 225–6, 233). In the 1920s and early 1930s the lower ranks of the Communist Party were expanded through enlistment of former peasants[13] and workers, many illiterate, not quite keen on socialist ideology and with a narrow perception of how the mightier should behave. They mostly sought to achieve a higher social status through party membership and imitated their former bosses (pre-revolutionary landowners) in demanding luxury (Brovkin, 1998, pp. 37–46).[14] Socialist asceticism was alien to them. Since the party was the origination of the new class, not the other way around (Djilas, [1957] 1958, pp. 38–41), the new ruling class carried the social norms of the incomers and set the example for the rest of the population.

There were features of the Russian character that the Soviet regime set out to change but reinforced instead as an unintended consequence of public policies. The Soviet leaders tried to do away with Russian fatalism, but could not. The power of the regime over the individual was akin to the mighty power and unpredictability of nature that the Great Russian had accepted long ago. Atheism was propagated so strongly that it took on attributes of faith. Yet, other character traits were encouraged on purpose.

For instance, the Soviets strengthened the self-image of Russians as a 'truth-possessor' people;[15] in this context the regime appeared to be more acceptable.[16] Slavophilism was revived under Stalin (Barghoorn, 1960, p. 578).[17]

Communal spirit, which the Soviets bred so zealously in younger generations, became an integral part of culture:

> The sense of individual desire and personality submerged in the broader group – whether that group is a row of schoolchildren, a department of factory workers . . . or the entire nation – is much more than a fragment of Marx and Engels polished by Lenin. . . . It has been absorbed into the structure of values and mores so that its violation stimulates genuine revulsion in many people. (Shipler, 1983, pp. 71–2)[18]

Boettke points out that ideology was important (and considered important by Lenin) in overcoming the free-rider problem in the collectivist society. Education and brainwashing propaganda were directed at creating a very strong sense of community belonging and of a common purpose (Boettke, 1988, p. 147, Note 23).[19] The work of Klugman (1989) discusses that as a result a person who became successful in Soviet society had by definition accumulated the skill of establishing and benefiting from personal networks.

In some ways the propaganda of communal spirit succeeded, but it failed in many others. Repressive formal rules forced people to break the law and 'help each other out so that all can live'.[20] As Berliner notes, a desire to live peacefully usually motivates one to stay on the right side of law (Berliner, 1962, pp. 418–19), but only when the economic incentives are aligned properly. Soviet enterprises falsely declared part of their goods defective and bartered them for produce from the *kolkhoz*. *Kolkhozy* broke the law by giving the produce away before fulfilling the state plan (Osokina, 2001, pp. 108–9). Workers stole and damaged public property.

One Soviet citizen going through the accomplished weekly list of chores such as food, dry cleaners and so on remarked that in every case he 'had to behave with something less than complete honesty' (Simis, 1982, p. 206). Any transaction involving a connection and/or a bribe was a reflection of a dual reality. Cheating and hypocrisy was already welded into norms during school years. '[H]ypocrisy is taught as a virtue in effect. As children learn what to say regardless of what they think, they grow more responsive to outer form than to inner conviction. There is not always a difference between the two: The incessant saying and hearing of untruth have a numbing impact on thought' (Shipler, 1983, p. 114).

The circumstances forced an honest person either to compromise or to be expelled from the system with dire consequences. Simis provides an example. A former military officer was assigned to the post of manager of a food shop. He accepted and gave no bribes, and did not sell goods at inflated prices on the side. As a result, the bureaucrats above him got angry because they did not receive their bribes and the suppliers stopped supplying food because they did not get theirs. The plan, however, needed to be fulfilled and the store could not just go out of business. The new manager was faced with a choice of either to accept a compromise and resort to corrupt practices or to be fired under scandalous (but naturally fabricated) circumstances. He chose a compromise (Simis, 1982, pp. 218–21). Those who knew how to use the backdoor were deemed as clever; those who did not as failures. The Bolsheviks' attitude to the law stimulated this norm: 'Soviet citizens were to feel that they were legally obliged to behave decently . . . but they were contract-bound to the state, not to each other. Horizontal ties were to be replaced by vertical ones' (Lovell, 2000, p. 143).

But horizontal ties survived in the local administrative circles. Vigilance and unjust laws drove the trust relationship into the underground. Centralization of power and harsh demands enforced administrative micromanagement, where there were political vertical networks of loyal subordinates and horizontal administrative, primarily local, networks. The latter ensured that information on local administration faults stayed within the 'family'.[21]

All in all, these resulting new and old traits were characteristic of a closed society with strong nationalistic and collectivist tendencies. Reshetar (1960, p. 573) says that government policy failings produced a healthy scepticism among Russians. But it was more likely a curse than a blessing because such failings built a higher barrier to overcome in public policy games and promoted general distrust among individuals.

NETWORKS IN EVERYDAY LIFE

How to Get Things

Soviet people exploited networks in order to fulfil everyday needs, such as getting clothes, and to fulfil more ambitious goals, such as achieving professional status.[22] Hierarchical relationships governed ascension to a higher caste. Due to shortages official cash income was not necessarily the sole determinant of one's well-being. A well-connected person had higher standards of living. A higher position brought with it perks and more opportunities to develop high-level connections. Such were the illegal 'millionaires' – the Soviet writers and people with positions in commerce (*Economist*, 1983, p. 69).[23]

Markets in foreign goods through commissary stores (Alexeev and Sayer,

1987), smuggling and resale of foreign clothes and electronics were also embedded in the networks. Those who found employment in the underground economy paid kickbacks to those who provided them with private orders.[24] In the 1960s as much as 9 per cent of total convictions fell on those accused of economic and official crimes (Shelley, 1990, pp. 19–20). However, many cases did not even get to courts – the extent of personal connections determined how successfully one could forestall prosecution (ibid., p. 21).

Functions of Networks

Social networks took on a variety of functions that are served in a free-market society through both formal and informal channels. For example, networks performed an informational function. Sometimes they were just an unofficial channel of information. Among the privileged circle, news could travel remarkably fast. The fate of a hotel director, where a fire had taken place, was decided at a closed meeting and reached a (connected) Westerner on a research trip in Moscow in the 1970s a mere four hours after the meeting had ended (Adams, 2000, p. 16).

Networks were also responsible for scientific progress or regress depending on the circumstances. Mark Adams discusses the role of personal networks in science, in particular the demise of *Lysenkovshchina*[25] and rise of the new approach to genetics in the Khruschev period. The same networks that created Russian eugenics in the 1920s survived its demise only to replace it with 'medical genetics'. The traditional approach to genetics was sustained through continuous networks from the 1900s through the 1980s and 1990s.[26] Lysenko was forced out by the members of scientific networks that had originated before the revolution (ibid., p. 21).[27]

Personal relationships replaced market signalling (advertising), which was present to some extent in commerce but not in industry.[28] Strong ties approximated for market reputation. Other than alcohol (Katsenelinboigen, 1978, pp. 194–6), an instrument for establishing trust was to have a common acquaintance or do someone a favour. Networking saved on search costs – standing in a queue in vain or simply looking for a specific product could be avoided.

Connections were a valuable, positive return capital asset. Wintrobe writes that '*trust* or organizational *networks* are capital assets accumulated by subordinates with each other . . . to . . . allow exchange. . . . [T]his asset may be accumulated by forgoing opportunities to cheat – hence, making an investment in the future relationship' (Wintrobe, 1998, p. 210; original emphasis). So were the Soviet networks, which in addition yielded directly observable benefits in the form of goods. Sedik (1989, p. 3) treats connections as one of the multiple currencies. Connections could be exchanged, and they served as a store of value, although depreciating over time without a fresh investment flow.

Structural Issues, For Example, Size versus Sustainability

During the Soviet period networks grew in size and complexity. First of all, networks were a response to economic shortages and much has been said in this regard. Second, Russia was culturally predisposed to network expansion and informal institutions proved to be quite strong and adaptive. Third, one can distinguish between horizontal networks (family, friends) and vertical (bosses and *snabzhentsy* [suppliers], political networks); between ideologically based (science, dissident, early communist) and economically based (industrial) and friendship-based networks.

For the lower and intermediate groups, the exchange of favours was usually localized, that is, both strong and weak ties lost significance with large geographical distances because of deficiencies in communication and low mobility of population. The situation was different for people of certain social and professional groups, such as politicians and directors of factories – for example, the network of suppliers and intermediaries spanned all geographical regions (Berliner, 1976). Such networks were qualitatively different from localized horizontal networks (friends, *blat*) because they were primarily based on economic motivation.

With persistent shortages the value of connections grew. Along with huge industrial capital investment went social capital investment. Hence, networks expanded. From those at the top of perk distribution to the lower level there extended a line of loyalty to the system. But there were simply not enough goods to go around for everyone as shortages remained, growth slowed down and the demands of the population along with its size increased.

The connections currency suffered inflation – more and stronger connections were required towards the 1980s to obtain and sustain the lifestyle that fewer connections could support earlier. The networks started collapsing from outward in. It is plausible that the culmination point in the evolution of networks occurred prior to the collapse of the Soviet Union and that the structural integrity of personal connections networks weakened by their size contributed to the fall of the central planning system.[29]

IN CONCLUSION: THE DETRIMENTAL ROLE OF CONNECTIONS

Black markets emerged towards the end of the Soviet system to a greater extent than they had existed anytime before in Russian history. Social

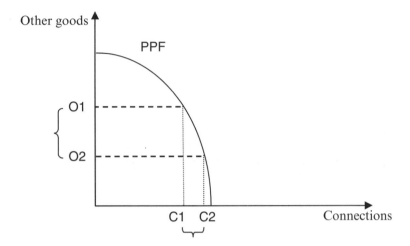

Figure 7.1   The production possibilities frontier (PPF) of the Soviet economy

networks served many positive functions in a life of a Soviet citizen. They were an efficient economic mechanism from a normative standpoint and when viewed in a static environment with set constraints. After all, what was a Soviet person to do when he needed necessities or desired luxuries if networking was the law of the land? However, when viewed in a dynamic environment, strong ties appear to have played a detrimental role. There was a great social waste due to investment in personal connections. Connection maintenance required significant economic resources to be drawn away from other productive uses. Time spent on 'friendly' visits, phone calls and so on, money spent on gifts, all had an opportunity cost.[30]

The graph in Figure 7.1 outlines the nature of the relationship between connections and other goods in the national economy of the Soviet Union. Connections are an output of an individual and of the national economy. The production possibilities frontier is steep: a lot of other goods (O1O2) need to be sacrificed in order to produce a relatively smaller amount of connections (C1C2). The law of diminishing marginal returns applies – as more connections are being produced the cost of producing one more unit of connections rises.

Yet it is unclear how much and of what quality goods would a move from C1 to C2 yield. One characteristic of the Soviet life that would strike a Westerner as odd and inconvenient is the 'round-aboutness' of methods used to get things done. A connection transaction lacks the straightfor-wardness of financial transactions in a free-market environment. By that I mean: if I choose to buy a good, I can do so without making sure first that it will be delivered to me, that I will not get a horse buggy for the price of a foreign car, that the steering wheel will not fall off the next day and so forth. While a connection certainly may provide access to a good or a service not available under the existing circumstances, it does not guarantee such access; there is no written enforceable contract.

Many of the unwritten rules are, of course, observed diligently in an underground trust network if everyone's survival depends on it.[31] But what if it does not? What if a bureaucrat is offered a bigger bribe by B when he had agreed to help A? Will he cheat on the agreement? This depends on the strength of the tie with A. If it is equal or weaker to a connection with B, he will most likely cheat because he is in a privileged position of power over a resource and A cannot ostracize him next time. A, in turn, might want to increase his investment in this personal connection trying to outbid others' future bids.

There is a big difference between an agreement that stems from the long-standing practice of written contracts and contract enforcement and between unwritten rules that were such from origin. Most of the time, it is impossible to foresee all contract loopholes because multiple contracts are being informally held over one good. Rational economic calculation under the system dominated by hierarchies is impossible: no expected value can be assigned to the benefit from a connection transaction. Since benefits and losses are unpredictable, economic planning is extremely difficult.

As an institution, social networks cultivated beliefs that influenced economic outcomes[32] as well as the distribution of property rights. There are three forms of distribution: formal rationing, queues and connections: 'The goods shortage first and foremost creates chaos in the distribution of *real* income. The distribution of real incomes no longer corresponds to the distribution of money incomes. . . . Under conditions of goods shortage the winner is he who stands closer to the sources of the flow of *goods*'.[33] Once in place, strong ties promoted such distribution. Connections successfully complemented the rationing system by giving the privileged class an extra source of income and others access to shortage goods, and substituted the queues in some cases. This substitution effect supported the system because queues with no way to resolve a shortage for at least a part of it would have undoubtedly produced more anger and social unrest. Social networking dampened the potential political crisis.

Property was indirectly concentrated in the hands of the political bureaucracy, who, just as a regular private owner, has self-interests. However, not all self-interests are equal, and Soviet bureaucrats' self-interest lay in a quiet life. They were risk-averse and stalled economic initiative (Rutland, 1993, p. 21). Thus, bureaucratic self-interest in the

USSR was different from the one confined by free-market rules. The latter increases the wealth of the society; the former (confined by the rules of game within personal networks) increased the distribution of wealth, but not necessarily the amount of it.

A society can take a number of paths where gains from trade are exploited but standards of living remain low compared with other societies with similar endowments. Even though social networks in the Soviet Union permitted all gains from trade to be exploited, they yielded an inferior economic outcome.

NOTES

1. By the end of the 1930s 'the functionaries and their descendants were clearly overrepresented at the universities in relation to their relative proportion of the total population' (Edeen, 1960, p. 291).
2. Government meddling in personal and business affairs was, of course, present under the Tsars, and was also continued by the Provisional Government. The Provisional Government was not shy in declaring state control over production, distribution, mobilization of labour and so on; Boettke (1988) provides citations from reports on pp. 171–2. The Provisional Government though lacked the nerve and resources to implement it fully.
3. Many start the countdown of the *blat* (see Chapter 6) system from Stalin's time, for example Fitzpatrick (2000, Chapter 9). This research shows that it happened earlier.
4. The largest strikes took place in Ivanovo (near Moscow) in 1932 and 1933. The largest strike in the Urals involved 580 people; for more examples see Osokina (2001, pp. 93–4).
5. On the heritage of 'self-help', which increased bribery in the earlier Soviet years, see Kelly (2000, p. 77).
6. For examples of leaflets, see Osokina (2001, p. 157).
7. For more on American and Soviet friendships, see Hollander (1978, pp. 282–8).
8. Some scholars find that peasant migration brings the culture of kin or networking into the city, others believe this interpretation to be a mistake; for a list see Los (1990, pp. 212–13).
9. In the mind of a peasant the land belonged to him but only through the allocation mechanism of the commune; thus, he or she did not recognize private property (Pipes, 1995, p. 387). Of course, differences between *mir* and *kolkhoz* must be pointed out here (Volin, 1962, pp. 499–505). In *kolkhozy* the land was not redistributed to households any longer; instead every collective farm member was supposed to work the fields and the product was to be redistributed by the central authorities throughout the country.
10. For more details on the agrarian revolutions and land redistribution, see Shanin (1972, pp. 145–61).
11. For a discussion of commune-gathering during the NEP, see Shanin (1972, pp. 162–9).
12. High figures for crime, theft, murder, which might have been exaggerated but are still worth considering, can be found in Sorokin (1990, pp. 407–8). An excellent sociological analysis of the Soviet society is provided by Hollander (1978).
13. The figures describing the social composition of the party members in the late 1910s and 1920s are subject to interpretation. For instance, while 65.2 per cent of members were classified as workers in 1932, only 43.5 were workers by occupation (Fainsod, 1953, pp. 214–15). The data collected by the Soviets split categories based on social origin, but many had moved to different occupations at the time of joining the party. At the

beginning of 1918 the peasant element in the party rose to 28.2 per cent, with workers constituting 41 per cent (Fainsod, 1953, p. 212). This percentage went up and down in the course of the next 15 years. Some peasants joined the Communist Party simply to get out of *kolkhoz*, although it became harder after 1936 (Merl, 1993, pp. 45–7). 'Later evidence suggests that political convictions or even a rudimentary knowledge of the political aims of the party itself played only a minor role' (ibid., p. 45). Either way, the most important factor is the low level of education among the peasant, worker and party members alike. In 1922 80.5 per cent of workers, 70.3 per cent of peasants and 72.8 of employees had lower-level education. By 1927 the respective percentages decreased to 63.9, 60.9 and 62.8 (Fainsod, 1953, p. 221, Table 7).

14. Higher-ranking officials surrounded themselves in luxury as well; for many of them it was a return to the pre-revolutionary lifestyle they enjoyed in Europe (Brovkin, 1998, p. 38).

15. A people who follow the historical path, which is superior to other nations; who have the best possible form of government, the most superior set of values.

16. For interesting points on Russian ethnic values and their transformation in the Soviet period, see Reshetar (1960, pp. 559–73).

17. The stronger the dictator, the more nationalistic are the tendencies. Putin is another example.

18. For examples of 'unfortunate achievers', that is, those who were very successful in terms of personal achievements and were then deemed by the regime too individualistic because of that uniqueness, and punished – for instance, brilliant scientists who dared to contradict what the Party wanted of science at that moment – see Shipler (1983, pp. 71–2). 'In a field of wheat, only the stalk whose head is empty of grain stands above the rest' is a Russian proverb (ibid., p. 73). For more on the collective and individual in the USSR, see ibid. (pp. 71–93).

19. There is a large literature on the Soviet propaganda, the usage of films, schools, theatres, literary journals, newspapers and so on to engineer the new Soviet citizen. For example, see Clark (1993, Chapter XI) and Fisher, Jr. (1960, pp. 625–35).

20. Quoted in Berliner (1962, p. 418). Some people did not use personal connections because they either did not have them, or were apprehensive of them for various reasons. The new generation of the 1930s more readily 'jumped into the *blat* deals' (Fitzpatrick, 2000, pp. 176–7).

21. For a discussion on this, see Fitzpatrick (1999, pp. 32–3).

22. For a comprehensive sociological study of *blat*, see Ledeneva (1998).

23. For disseminating state propaganda Soviet writers were rewarded with access to closed establishments, such as restaurants and stores; see Osokina (2001, pp. 79–80).

24. Treml determines that 41 per cent of survey respondents paid between 50 and 10,000 (with 500 median) rubles in kickbacks in the 1970s (Treml, 1992, p. 26 and Table A on p. 45).

25. Lysenko was Director of Soviet Biology under Stalin. Lysenko rejected Mendelian genetics and replaced it with theories of environmentally acquired inheritance. *Lysenkovshchina* was the term for the scientific movement promoting Lysenko's theories.

26. For more examples, see Adams (2000, pp. 18–20).

27. Network relationships are described in Adams (2000, pp. 21–6). On how the leading physicists, who supported genetics, used their influence (after they had made it in to the Presidium of the Academy of Sciences by 1956), to push Lysenko out, see ibid. (pp. 26–9). Under Brezhnev, Soviet science became bigger, fatter, freer, but not better (ibid., pp. 30–31).

28. Such as queues or word of mouth; see also Hanson (1974).

29. Another way of looking at the collapse is that 'by the mid-1980s the cohort which had collectively controlled the bureaucracy since Stalin's rule began to die or retire. With them went the structure of informal quasi-contracts within and between the bureaus which formed the basis of the stability of the Soviet power structure' (Boettke, 1993, p. 83).

30. As the Soviet citizens debased themselves before bureaucrats and other miserable individuals of power their moral principles became inevitably compromised and the whole value system of the population got distorted further away from the one that accompanies free-market transactions.
31. Here the circle of full mutual responsibility is the mechanism for internalizing externalities from potential cheating.
32. For a discussion of and literature references to a connection between beliefs and economic outcomes, see Di Tella, Galiani and Schargrodsky (2005).
33. Quoted from Novozhilov, who wrote this in 1926 (Sedik, 1989, p. 2; original emphasis).

PART IV

Perestroika and the Post-Soviet Era

8. The political economy of the Russian state: elite networks

Our country offers great potential not only for the criminals
but also for the State.

(Vladimir Putin, 2003, *Interes*, **46**, 6)

US reporter: 'Do you trust Vladimir Putin?'
George W. Bush: 'Yes'.
US reporter: 'How do you know?'
George W. Bush: 'I looked in his eyes and saw his soul'.

(Interview with RTR TV of Russia, 29 May 2003)

THE COLLAPSE OF THE EMPIRE, RETREAT OF SOCIALISM AND THE RETURN OF THE TSAR

By the 1980s, following a period of economic stagnation, the Soviet Union started to collapse from within. Charles Rowley (1993, pp. 1–2) stressed that since the USSR fell apart from an internal failure and not from an external defeat or shock, not many rents were left for grabs.

The leadership attempted to salvage the system. Andropov targeted corruption and excessive privileges of the higher party officials in a series of reforms, which he largely failed to implement, partly due to his death. The food production and distribution systems were failing. Life expectancy continued to decrease and reached the low of 57 years for men and 75 for women in the 1990s (Brady, 1999, p. 24).[1] In 1986 the oil prices collapsed, severing the flow of hard currency at a crucial time.

Gorbachev too tried to recover the deteriorating system.[2] The structure of ownership under the Soviet regime yielded inefficiency.[3] Perestroika intended to restore the socialist economy by officially allowing some market relations and redesigning the structure of ownership.[4] Yeltsin intended to increase private ownership even further, but, just as in 1917, an abrupt change of a political regime left no time for the new government to build its own administrative apparatus.[5] The post-Soviet Russia inherited the Soviet bureaucracy and political elite. The opposition of the old political cadre to the government reformist activity created a momentum during which new, although also politically connected, elements managed to creep up to the top and secure control of the new phase of rent redistribution.

The impact of the collapse of the USSR on the lives of the Russian population was tremendous, as it was a collapse of a huge empire with satellite states suddenly pulled away and the whole order shaken up severely and unexpectedly. The emergent order was rather an unordered anarchy, a Hobbesian jungle, in which fraudulent ventures, such as pyramid schemes, flourished.

During the transition the vertical networks were shaken, and lack of trust presented a major problem. Shortening time horizons due to political and economic uncertainty set up the stage for the return of the Tsar. Whether or not there is social contracting among the political elite to bring the Leviathan back is not clear. However, it is clear that many in the broader population hanker for a return to Soviet order and are afraid of the upheaval of anarchy.

GORBACHEV, PERESTROIKA AND THE ROLE OF PARTY IN THE REFORMS

Regardless of whether Gorbachev was sincere in trying to implement the market reforms, 'the impact of perestroika was to disrupt the operation of the central planning system, without replacing it with a functioning market mechanism' (Rutland, 1993, p. 211). The new leader found very few genuine supporters among the regional party apparatus.[6]

Gorbachev faced the same problem a dictator faces trying to manage an overgrown bureaucracy toward his goals. A powerful brake from below stalled the initiative. Party interventions into the economy continued as before, despite cutting down the numbers and merging ministries because the economy was not effectively privatized and initially needed a great deal of direction. Innovators running for management positions were left out by the careful orchestration of the elections by the local party and the old management cadre. Even if a reformist were elected, he faced a hostile circle of political and economic colleagues and had a difficult time putting changes into practice. By 1990 it was clear though that the party's function as a regional coordinator of supply was damaged.[7]

Once the resources were no longer centrally coordinated, the black market slowly started coming above ground. The rules of the black market undoubtedly created a vision of an alternative to the central planning system, which later on was labelled 'free market' because it was the only familiar approximation at hand and was in line with the rhetoric of the day.

In 1987 Grossman took a very positive view on the role of the black market in the transition period. Contracts in the black market had to rest on the spoken word only and violent enforcement seemed to be rare. Trust and threat of ostracism seemed enough to avoid cheating. He concluded that 'learning to operate on trust – and building up one's own probity – is also a step in the direction of a market economy' (Grossman, 1987, pp. 2.7–2.9).

It does appear afterwards that just as all self-interests are not equal, so all trust relationships are not equal. The outcome depends on the rules confining these trust relationships. When de facto property rights entered a new phase of distribution, when boundaries between legal and illegal became even less clear, violence indeed became widespread because ostracism was no longer a legitimate threat.[8] Black market procedures originated a very strong pattern that proved harder to break than many thought at the time. Boettke (1993, p. 67) points out that: 'The discipline of repeated dealings provided an incentive for most individuals to act in a cooperative fashion. But the opportunity for strategic cheating was always there. . . . The underground economy of the former Soviet Union cannot be relied on completely to transform the economy into a functioning free market system'.

The state in the late 1980s and 1990s failed to do so as well. Most policies in Russia before the revolution and today can be called half-measures because the goals of the leaders have not always reflected the interests of the majority and because interest groups have always existed and have been accommodated. Often, the goals were incoherent or incentives were misaligned.[9] 'Perestroika failed in large part because it was not tried. Gorbachev between 1985 and 1991 announced at least ten radical plans for economic restructuring, *not a single one was ever implemented*' (Boettke, 1993, p. 2, emphasis in the original).

Gorbachev's decrees in practice were quite different from what they claimed to be. The law on non-labour incomes (May 1986) was in fact very prohibitive and punitive, but not liberalizing. The law on permitted individual labour activity (November 1986) was still very restrictive in many respects. The resolution permitting the existence of cooperatives (January 1987) was not new in nature – they had been encouraged under Stalin although closed down later on. Besides, a Russian cooperative is more socialist than free market in its form.[10]

Cooperatives were regularly harassed by the local party, so to avoid problems and secure supply many operated 'under the roof' (protection or sponsorship) of state factories and public organizations like the Komsomol youth organization, thus continuing the tradition from the early Soviet years. 'In fact, more than 75 per cent of coop turnover in 1989 was generated by selling materials to state firms' (Rutland, 1993, p. 216).

'Some cooperatives found ways to get cheap and subsidized supplies, from the state or shadow markets, and sold them for fast profits' (Hoffman, 2002, p. 40). All in all, because of a clash between economic and political logic,[11] the reforms were stalled. Gorbachev backed out on various policies and that ruined the credibility of his reforms.[12]

YELTSIN, TRANSITION AND THE OLIGARCHS

The economic chaos of 1991,[13] and the nascent social unrest, prompted an immediate government response, which did not, however, lead to an optimal outcome. One of the problems was the factions within the government. For example, the head of the central bank was opposed to the reforms and adhered to cheap-credit policies, which fuelled inflation (Yergin and Stanislaw, 1998, p. 282).[14] Introducing hard budget constraints for all enterprises could have been the best scenario in theory, but in practice Yeltsin was faced with a difficulty – the economy would crash if the insolvents weren't bailed out, and they would take the good enterprises down with them. Therefore, in 1992 he decided to bail out net debtors and give in to inflation (Cochrane and Ickes, 1995, pp. 92–3). Allowing bankruptcies would have been a better solution in the long run, however, the Russian government had a reasonable fear of losing control and bankruptcies were not considered an option.

Yeltsin intended to reform the economy, but by 1993 the president, his team of economists and the parliament were deadlocked over the reforms.[15] Chubais allegedly had to compromise with parliament deputies in order to get approval for the privatization programme.[16] In fact, it was altered significantly – various concessions had to be made, and that undermined not only the credibility and the fairness of the process but also its effectiveness. By the designers' own account of the reform '[o]f the politicians who grabbed control rights from the center, none got more under Gorbachev, and subsequently Yeltsin, than local officials' (Boycko et al. [1995] 1996, pp. 41–2). For instance, local governments exercised direct control over the privatization of small shops and at times even collected spoils from it.

All in all, '[t]o secure political support, Russia's privatizers had to make compromises and give in to the demands of major interest groups. Local governments, managers, and workers all got much more out of privatization than most observers would consider reasonable'.[17] Large state-owned companies were to be 'corporatized' with the state holding all the shares initially and managers appointed not by the ministries but by the GKI (the State Committee on the Management of State Property headed by Chubais).

The apparent success in the number of privatizations, such as that by 1996 roughly 18,000 industrial enterprises had been privatized, over four-fifths of small shops and retail stores transferred into private hands, 70 per cent of GDP generated in the private sector (Yergin and Stanislaw, 1998, p. 288), were indeed meaningless if bureaucracy still had a strong grip on business and economic success was linked to networking. In the mid-1990s the state sector accounted for half of total employment. Many 'privatized' firms behaved economically just as before – they had not changed managers, workers, products, and suppliers, and received bailouts from the state (Cochrane and Ickes, 1995, p. 76 and Boycko et al. [1995] 1996, p. 131).[18]

Privatization did not succeed everywhere – in fact, relative success of the small shop privatization may be attributed to the local governments' initiative by bureaucrats who were eager to raise more rent for themselves because they exercised great power over newly privatized stores.[19] Most managers were indeed interested in voucher privatization, but not in 'public' support through voucher ownership, which was ineffective because the general public was poor and easily influenced by mass hysteria. Since the old supply network was in disarray, a manager was looking to find a niche in the new one. If he had connections to arrange the supply of inputs he wanted the shares for himself; if he could not, he preferred that someone else should fix the supply problems for him in exchange for a large block of shares.[20]

The so-called 'romantic wave' in the history of business development, when many restrictions on business activity were lifted and just about anyone tried a private venture of some sort, passed by the mid-1990s and 'only the structures close to political circles survived' (Kukolev, 1999, p. 295). In the beginning of the transition, it paid for everyone to use previously established network relationships and to invest in the new ones, especially for the political elite and for those who were well connected with the influential party members.[21] This path – the political career was on average most profitable – had been defined already by the 1980s. The predominance of those who followed a political career among the *Obkom*[22] elite in the early 1980s supports this (Rutland, 1993, pp. 199–201). Hyperinflation wiped out the savings of the majority but created fortunes for the few. 'The lure was especially strong for those who already had connections, such as the cooperative businessmen, nascent bankers, Komsomol activists and ex-KGB agents' (Hoffman, 2002, p. 212).

Kukolev (1999) explains further that most Communist Party (CPSU) district committee members quit their jobs and were appointed in 1991 to work in the regional administration. The 'old boys' networks' – personal connections to or membership in the regional authorities' inner circle – had been a prerequisite for a career already prior to the transition (Stykow, 1999, pp. 204–5).

The new administration exploited this path and connections from previous jobs as well. They began to include in their sphere of influence the most prospective sectors of regional economy, cultivating perks from their contacts even further. Other, abandoned sectors had to compete for favours on the basis of strength of their personal connections. It was usually followed by a formation of a few large financial-political groups (Kukolev, 1999, p. 294).

When it came to large business ventures at the end of the 1980s and the beginning of the 1990s, rent seeking through political connections was becoming ever more successful. This process segregated top economic elite to a relatively small interest group at the federal level. Vertical connections provided tremendous opportunities for enrichment at the expense of the rest of the country.

The oligarchs manipulated government funds, loans, bonds,[23] and actively participated in redistributing the natural, industrial and techno-logical resources of the country. They negotiated agreements with the government for exclusive provision of goods and services. They arranged a bail-out for the reformist government in 1996,[24] which the government paid back with a favour in 1998.[25] The tie between the government and the oligarchs seemed very strong. In several cases, as Hoffman mentions in *The Oligarchs*, even in most economically devastating situations the tycoons managed to stay afloat. How? Even an experienced journalist has no answer; although one might guess that the answer is through connec-tions (Hoffman, 2002, p. 52).[26]

The state policy in the late Soviet period contributed to high pay-offs from hustling, which in turn led to economic instability and put production in complete disarray:

> In the late Soviet period, trading companies run by young hustlers and well-connected bureaucrats made quick fortunes. . . . They bought oil cheap inside the country, paid bribes to get it across the border, sold it at world prices for hard currency, bought up personal computers from abroad, paid bribes to get the computers back inside the country, and sold them for fantastic profits, to be reinvested in the next lot of oil. The state created the conditions for this hustle by keeping oil prices low, by making the computers scarce, and by collecting bribes. (Hoffman, 2002, p. 47)

Russian businessman, Khodorkovsky, acknowledged in 1991 that all the ventures started at that time 'succeeded only if they were sponsored by or had strong connections with high-ranking people' (ibid., p. 101). Political organizations plunged into business sponsorship to save themselves. The first experiment was with the Komsomol youth organization.[27] Some made fortunes manipulating the imbalance between cash and non-cash accounts in enterprises.[28] In December 1987 the central committee of the Komsomol approved a new set of financial rules allowing local organizations to raise and spend money as they pleased and to set up their own bank accounts. Importantly, they were allowed to mix cash and non-cash. 'It is possible that the new rule came out after the practice had already begun that year' (ibid., p. 110) and had been found advantageous. It might be that friends 'in high places' were prompted to formalize this practice.

During Yeltsin's reign a new set of laws was written to bring about and regulate markets in Russia. These laws, however, were written by individuals with a strong personal interest in the outcome. The negative effect from localized spoils was felt by the whole country. The absence of clarity and uncertain speed of the reform raised the pay-offs from networking. In the early to mid-1990s Yeltsin supported liberalization, in 1997 he reversed the state's policy: 'From the policy of non-intervention, we are going . . . over to a policy of preemptive regulation of economic processes' (Yergin and Stanislaw, 1998, p. 292).

The Russian state was no different in the post-Soviet era – in Roy Medvedev's (2000, p. 4) words, in implementing the reforms the government 'had no base of support in the form of a political party; they did not even have a publicly stated program. They used exclusively administrative methods, sometimes employing force and violence'.[29]

Continuous reshuffling of the administration to find scapegoats or to spite political opponents, empty promises of economic stability, reformist programmes that were not thought through and driven by impatience and political ambition – all discredited the government in the eyes of the general public. Needless to say such dubious actions on behalf of the state as 'Harvest-90' in which the peasants were swindled (Shevchenko, 2004, pp. 44–5) undermined credibility even further. And, by 1998, a crisis was imminent. Cash 'had almost disappeared from the economy. Large enterprises did 73 per cent of their business in barter and paid only 8 per cent of their taxes in cash' (Hoffman, 2002, p. 411).

Structural continuity between the political networks of *nomenklatura* and the post-Soviet political networks should not mislead us into the assumption that the new political elite has not changed its face. In fact, its sociological portrait is different from the Soviet one, although it still harbours the old cadre. The relevant question here is just how much politics and business are juxtaposed. Evidence suggests they work in consort. Many of the hierarchical networks that started under the Soviet rule persevered and brought prosperity to their members during the transition.

The depolitization of the economy succeeded only to a very limited extent – Boycko et al. ([1995] 1996) claim that the ministries were now left out of the picture. But arguably this was not so – '[m]any of the new banks were carved directly out of government ministries'; for instance, the Ministry for Automobile Production created Avtobank and the Ministry of Oil and Chemical Engineering created Neftekhimbank (Hoffman, 2002, p. 46). Networking with politicians and bureaucrats still remained a key to business success; only new players had an opportunity to enter the game. The means by which the oligarchs[30] build their fortunes serves as a proof. The order in which their stories are briefly retold here are of no importance.

There is a strong indication that Berezovsky already had many important vertical connections in the Soviet era. After two decades at the Institute of Control Sciences he was remembered as a man with 'a flair for making things happen in a world of lassitude and false pretenses' (ibid., p. 131 and also pp. 130, 133–4). He 'was one of the first people at the institute who established very profitable contacts between his lab and Avtovaz [automobile factory]' (ibid., p. 137). Later he used his connections in Moscow and his connections with the managers of an automobile factory to create his own company – Logovaz.[31] His new business though was nothing more than resale of finished products – the new system of redistribution where Berezovsky was a clever intermediary who exploited the state production and the artificially low prices for his own profit (ibid., p. 146).[32]

Alexander Smolensky was disadvantaged under the Soviet system, uneducated and initially unconnected politically. While serving in the army in Tbilisi, his street-smart caught the eye of one Mr Krasnyansky. Krasnyansky, a journalist, was apparently well-connected, since he was able to get away with stealing Smolensky's release papers from the army, fixing him an airplane ticket to Moscow, and arranging for Smolensky's admission to the Polygraphic Institute in Moscow. Later Smolensky became the head of a state-owned apartment building and repair enterprise and often used his skills as a *tolkach* (supplier) (ibid., pp. 32–8).

In the late 1980s he was ordered to form a cooperative by the local party bosses because they saw his potential as a hustler. 'The first private entrepreneurs had to rely on their wits – on *blat* and *sviazi*, on theft, bribes, and bargaining – to get supplies' (ibid., p. 42). Smolensky was successful and party elite became his clients. This was a welcome outcome for him because they 'may well have had some leverage over his lumber supply' (ibid., p. 43).

Gusinsky started disadvantaged as well, but over time acquired a large network of useful contacts due to his communicativeness.[33] 'He enjoyed good connections with the Komsomol and the KGB' (ibid., p. 157). Gusinsky showed his temper inappropriately in dealing with some KGB officials, but he was protected on at least two occasions in the 1980s. One protector was Voronov – a deputy head of the Culture Department of the Central Committee. Gusinsky also established a connection with

Bobkov, a deputy KGB director who headed the Fifth Main Directorate, which persecuted dissidents, by allegedly becoming an informer (ibid., pp. 158–59).[34]

At the beginning of perestroika he was able to arrange printing of metal-stamping moulds for his cooperative at a closed military facility (ibid., p. 151). A personal letter from the Soviet Prime Minister Nikolai Ryzhkov permitted him to export his products for hard currency, even though his cooperative was registered as a part of a government foundation, which was prohibited by law from engaging in commercial activity (ibid., pp. 159–60).

Befriending the mayor of Moscow, Luzhkov, gave him the opportunity to strike a profitable business deal with the city in real estate. The city gave Gusinsky permission to reconstruct one of the prime real estate buildings at his own expense but keep about half of the proceeds from sale. The rest went back to the city. Although not a direct bribe to Mayor Luzhkov, the cash undoubtedly moved the bureaucrat's career forward (ibid., p. 163). In turn, the Moscow mayor advanced the prospects of Gusinsky's MOST bank. 'The bank snared the city's main accounts in the early 1990s, a privileged status that allowed Gusinsky to play with municipal deposits, earning handsome profits for himself while he paid a small percentage back to the city' (ibid., p. 165).[35]

In order to privatize the telecommunications industry in Russia, Gusinsky 'had to work hard'. Literally that meant he 'drank vodka with the generals and persuaded them that the Spanish telephone company would not threaten their prerogatives. It was certainly not a disadvantage that Filipp Bobkov, the former KGB general, was now on Gusinsky's corporate team'.[36]

Alekperov and Vyakhirev were chief executives in the petroleum and gas industry. Vinogradov was the chief of a Soviet bank (Rigby, 1999). Yury Luzhkov was a senior-level administrator in the city government of Moscow when Yeltsin summoned him to straighten out the food supply in the capital (Hoffman, 2002, p. 56). Educated as an industrialist, Luzhkov went through several posts in the city administration.[37] Vladimir Potanin came from a *nomenklatura* family (Hoffman, 2002, pp. 302–5 and Brzezinski, 2002, pp. 176–83) and occupied a senior financial post in the Soviet Union. Khodorkovsky was deputy chief of the Komsomol at the Mendeleev Institute of Chemical Technology, and accumulated a few friends 'in high places' (Hoffman, 2002, pp. 107–8, 119).

Transactions transforming useless non-cash reserves into cash and sometimes even hard currency would have been impossible if not for Khodorkovsky's good connections (ibid., p. 112).[38] The Komsomol-based centres for youth initiative were simply centres for making easy money (ibid., p. 113). To milk the state was by far the most profitable venture; and the value of investment in high-level bureaucrats was obvious to people like Khodorkovsky. Expensive receptions at the bank's expense would give thousand-fold returns (ibid., p. 124).[39] Connections allowed them to buy state companies for a trifle. Apparently Chubais did not care (or it was in his own interest not to care) at the time – as long as something was sold into private hands, no matter to who and no matter for how much (ibid., pp. 199–200).[40]

The oligarchy was much more deeply embedded than the few names mentioned above and the infamous seven banks. In Yegor Gaidar's[41] words, the oligarchy 'included representatives of former Communist structures and socialist-era enterprise directors in leading positions of power all across the country' (Brady, 1999, p. 230). Politics kept large foreign investors out for quite some time, and whenever they dared in, the law was not on their side.[42] Many of the successful post-Soviet entrepreneurs enjoyed their fathers' heritage. The All-Russian Central Institute on Public Opinion (VTsIOM) surveyed '1812 individuals, identified as the political, economic and cultural elite in 1988 and in 1993' (Rigby, 1999). The new business elite was defined as 'owners and managers of large enterprises which were private from scratch' (ibid.):

> To start with, their fathers' standing and education were a good deal higher on average than those of all other new elite categories except the scientific and cultural elite, fully 49 per cent of them (the fathers) having been tertiary-educated and 40 per cent members of the old party nomenklatura. They themselves, however, were somewhat less likely than other elite categories to have acquired a tertiary education (91.9 per cent compared with the 95.5 per cent of state enterprise executives), far less likely to have been Communist Party members (50.7 per cent – other elite categories ranging from 77.7 to 84.9 per cent), and on average far younger. (Ibid.)

The sociologist Olga Kryshtanovskaya, of the Institute of Sociology of the Russian Academy of Sciences launched another survey: '61 per cent of the new business elite were identified as coming from some branch or other of "the Soviet nomenklatura"';[43] '37 per cent had been Komsomol officials at the end of the 1980s';[44] 'another 37 per cent had been in high managerial positions (*khoziaistvennaia elita*)' (Rigby, 1999). Slightly over half of them were born in Moscow and republic capitals and two-thirds of them received their tertiary education in Moscow (ibid.). Most were well-launched before the 1990s' privatization. Slightly less than half started through cooperatives and only half by using their chief executive positions in Soviet banking, industry and manufacture to accumulate personal wealth (see Table 8.1).

Table 8.1   Launching pads of the new business elite

	Finance	Non-finance	Total
Soviet bank chiefs	15		15
Chief executives, extractive industries	2	5	7
Chief executives, manufacturing		3	3
Department minister, Soviet government	2		2
Cooperatives and so on	14	4	18
Other entrepreneurial moves	4	6	10
Post-Soviet politics	2	2	4
Total	39	20	59

Source: Rigby (1999).

But these results must be interpreted with caution. As Rigby puts it:

> Nearly all the businessmen examined here have been involved in some formal capacity (or capacities) in the political life of post-Soviet Russia, by serving on advisory bodies or *ad hoc* committees attached to the Government or Legislature, on bodies representing business interests generally or those pursuing specific sectional interests, or as open or behind-the-scenes supporters (if not patrons) of candidates for parliamentary, gubernatorial or presidential office. Business success in contemporary Russia, moreover, is unthinkable without building informal or formal relationships of mutual advantage with the appropriate politicians and administrators. (Rigby, 1999)[45]

Steen's investigation found that Soviet political capital was highly convertible into post-Soviet political capital, but not directly into economic capital (Steen, 2000, pp. 16–17). Undoubtedly though, the *social capital* accumulated by the politicians and well-connected managers alike due to their position in hierarchical networks was very much convertible into economic assets.

POST-SOCIALISM: PUTIN'S MALLET AND THE RETURN OF THE TSAR

For better, or worse, the oligarchs cooperated too closely with the government.[46] During the period of easy money their power was corrupted by wealth. Financial scandals surrounding Yeltsin's circle, increasing concerns about the president's health in mid-1999, the approaching end of the last presidential term and the rise of Prime Minister Primakov's popularity – all prompted Yeltsin to look for a loyal successor.

On the eve of a new millennium Yeltsin unexpectedly announced

Vladimir Putin as his political heir.[47] Putin started his term by granting immunity to Yeltsin and his family and next set out to establish his own personal power and to put in place safeguards to preserve it.

The first point on his agenda was the business of the tycoons, which had become unruly. He declared a new era – dictatorship of the law. Big, politically connected business now had to either keep the money and keep quiet on political matters or be prosecuted. On the surface it looked like the end of government favours for the oligarchs, and was intended to send a triple message – a positive one to the foreign investors who were now too important to ignore, a threatening one to the still refractory businesspeople[48] and a reassuring one to the supporters who now knew to expect a piece of the pie.

A deeper investigation reveals that the basis for relations between business and the state has not changed fundamentally since 2000. However, the structure may have been altered. An invisible hand (shortly after revealed to be Putin's) directed the tycoons to join something like a labour union – the Russian Union of Industrialists and Entrepreneurs – which is loyal to the Kremlin. This union was a hallmark of a new agreement between the tycoons and the government. Theft entered an organized stage. The cooperative tycoons got to keep their share and were not to interfere with Putin's readjustment of property holdings.

The new redistribution took place among the group of *siloviki* (men of power, of either former military or secret service background), now gathered in Putin's circle in numbers greater than under Gorbachev. These new supporters demanded a stake in the country's wealth. Many former KGB took administrative positions. The head of the Defence Ministry, Sergei Ivanov, for instance, got hold of most of the renationalized Yukos petroleum company. There are quite convincing indications that the Yukos affair was partially a scheme to enrich the new generation of oligarchs (Baker and Glasser, 2005, p. 352).

Members of the Yeltsin circle, Finance Minister Kudrin and Economic Development and Trade Minister Gref were kept in their positions, by some accounts, to keep up the pretence of reform and to serve as scapegoats (ibid., p. 374).[49] After reshuffling the inner circle, Putin moved on to number two on his agenda. The next important task was to secure ubiquitous loyalty across professions and social groups – in the administration, in the media, in the judicial and legislative system, among the youth, among the small businesspeople, farmers, or homemakers.

Forming the Vertical of Power or Ends versus Means

Putin went a long way to consolidate power back to the Kremlin, prosecuting big businesses that persisted in their own political ambitions, and pressuring fiefdom-seeking regional governors (Baker and Glasser, 2005, p. 6).[50] Shortly after the Beslan terrorist attack, Putin announced that as a means to fight future terrorist attacks the regional governors would be appointed by the president and no longer elected, only after time and again denying this arrangement. But, in fact, the project of severing the regional elections had been in the works for some time before Beslan (ibid., pp. 371–2). Out of seven envoys appointed by the president, five were *siloviki*.

The Kremlin took over the last semi-independent[51] television station, NTV, in April 2001, again, after months of denying any intentions to do so (ibid., p. 78). When some of the journalists from NTV formed another channel, TV6, it was shut down too. Their next escape, TVS, was closed as well. Berezovsky was forced to transfer his management rights of ORT (a major channel) to a Kremlin-friendly oligarch, Abramovich, who then gave it to the Kremlin.[52]

Shortly after this successful takeover, the journalists conveniently became self-censored (ibid., pp. 91–8).[53] On Fridays Putin and the directors of top television networks had met for years to share information about the government's new legislation and the like. In 2003 the structure of these meetings changed – 'a written agenda was handed out, with the week's expected topics and recommended approaches' (ibid., p. 294). Very soon it included: 'recommendation – don't cover' (ibid.).[54]

Many switched loyalties to the Kremlin, ranging from politicians, journalists and political rights activists.[55] The Glasnost Defence Foundation reported that in 2005 alone:

> six Russian journalists were murdered, sixty-three were assaulted, forty-seven were arrested, and forty-two were prosecuted. The editorial offices of twelve publications or broadcasters were attacked. Twenty-three editorial offices were closed. Ten were evicted from their premises. Twenty-eight newspapers or magazines were confiscated outright. Thirty-eight times, the government simply refused to let material be printed or distributed. (Politkovskaya, 2007, p. xiii)[56]

The talk show, *Freedom of Speech* was taken off air with Putin's comment, 'Who needs a talk show for political losers?' referring to the democrats who lost in the 2003 Duma elections (ibid., p. 12). *Freedom of Speech* was completely closed in July 2004, as well as *Personal Affairs*, also a relative outlet of freethinking on NTV (ibid., p. 149).[57]

The country's judicial system has undergone reform attempts. A jury system was introduced and the prosecutors were forbidden to go back and fix the cases that did not convince the courts the first time around. However, the improvements are questionable if the Kremlin still uses the system to its advantage. NTV takeover is just one example.[58] 'The system Putin had built was based not on the rule of law but the rule of the state'

(Baker and Glasser, 2005, p. 242). Khodorkovsky's trial is another demonstration of due process violations. On one occasion, for instance, the lawyers were not allowed to see the original court records, while the copies were falsified (Politkovskaya, 2007, p. 316).

Overall, the number of institutional agencies overseen directly by the president increased under Putin (Shevchenko, 2004, p. 164). The upper house, the Federal Council, lacks democratic legitimacy of its own. The State Council, created by Putin to offset this limitation, serves only as an advisory body to the president, thus increasing the federal powers (ibid., p. 161).[59] In the Duma, business is done as usual; the votes are bought (Baker and Glasser, 2005, pp. 85, 281).[60]

The administration was populated with agents loyal to Putin, which inevitably increased the efficiency of policy execution, but not necessarily the efficiency and relevance of policies themselves.[61] Krishtanovskaia called this a snowball effect – Putin brought, for instance, ten FSB agents into the government, they in turn brought ten each and so on. The process worked quickly:

> When Putin created seven presidential envoys to oversee the Russian regions, five came from military or secret service backgrounds, as did 70 per cent of the fifteen hundred staff members each of them eventually hired. . . . Deputies at the press, transportation, foreign affairs, and economic development ministries were also from the special services; overall, 35 per cent of the deputy ministers named during Putin's tenure were siloviki. . . . Hundreds more were named to less public postings in the government. FSB generals came to power with Kremlin support as elected governors in the regions of Ingushetia, Smolensk, and Voronezh. In the two houses of parliament, as many as thirty deputies and senators from the special services formed a powerful caucus. (Krishtanovskaia, cited in Baker and Glasser, 2005, p. 253)

The tradition of rigged voting continued in the 2003 Duma elections. All possible means, including instructed agitation from the media, buying people, ordering governors to deliver a certain number of votes were used to secure the majority for the political party United Russia,[62] the president's tool. United Russia challenged its opponents' legitimacy in court and used political pressure to resolve the issue in favour of United Russia. Other minor scheming occurred as well. For example, one day during the campaign some opponents found their contracts for advertising billboards in Moscow mysteriously cancelled.[63] In Saratov free vodka was dispensed outside the polling station, urging people to vote for a United Russia candidate (Politkovskaya, 2007, pp. 4–5).[64]

Presidential elections in Chechnya were similarly rigged; candidates were taken off ballots on a questionable technicality or lured out of the race (Baker and Glasser, 2005, pp. 300–301); and 10 per cent more votes than the registered population were miraculously cast (Politkovskaya, 2007, pp. 4–5). The president's own elections in 2004 were heavy-handedly directed – the orders stated employing talent shows, disco dances and so on, to ensure the victory of the incumbent with at least 80 per cent turnout. In a Khabarovsk hospital, patients were ordered to vote or be thrown out of hospital; yet others were offered discounts upon coming to vote, like a discount on utility bills.[65]

Renationalization

Putin knew full well that the Soviet Union collapsed, among other reasons, because of economic inefficiency, and was aware of a risk associated with renationalizing private companies. However, to maintain power, bureaucratic appetites had to be fed and private capital had to be controlled. To that extent, state-connected financial holdings such as Vneshekonombank, Vneshtorgbank and Mezhprombank bought up collateral in successful enterprises through intermediary companies. For instance, the Baltic Factory – the largest shipbuilding yard in the northwest of Russia, was purchased[66] in 2005 by Mezhprombank, run by Sergei Pugachev – the so-called Orthodox oligarch – now its de facto head after he had become a senator.

As the saying in Russian goes, 'killing two rabbits with one shot', Putin went after the oligarchs,[67] but only after those who dared to present an opposition to him as the personification of the Russian State.[68] Putin's former fellow officers, now in government positions, Igor Sechin and Viktor Ivanov, 'were reported to have close ties to massive state-controlled natural resource companies such as the oil firm Rosneft and the natural gas monopoly Gazprom, giving them financial heft in the backstairs political machinations' (Baker and Glasser, 2005, p. 271; Politkovskaya, 2007, p. 153).

With the exception of three major figures (Khodorkovsky, Gusinsky and Berezovsky) the oligarchy has prospered – Roman Abramovich, Petr Aven, Mikhail Fridman command large oil resources, Oleg Deripaska is Russia's aluminium king (Baker and Glasser, 2005, pp. 277–78), Chubais heads the country's electricity monopoly (ibid., p. 290):

> Midway through Putin's first term, eight oligarchic clans had accumulated control of 85 per cent of Russia's top sixty-four privately held companies, and the combined sales of the top twelve private companies alone matched the entire annual revenue of the Russian government. Putin permitted the oligarchs to get richer while sometimes swindling minority shareholders and manipulating the pliant court system in battles for control of the country's most precious economic resources. (ibid., p. 277)

Consolidation of business and government brings stability, but not of the rule of law. When the state went after Khodorkovsky and the chairperson of Group Menatep, Platon Lebedev, one of them was denied a lawyer on one occasion and another's attorney was simply locked out of the courtroom, as the judge denied bail to his client (ibid., pp. 274, 284). The state acquired Yukos by employing the same scheme that Khodorkovsky had exploited years earlier and that put him in jail (ibid., p. 352).[69] This does not make the oligarchs right, but under the rule of law the state does not have an authority to deny the elemental right of due process to anyone.

'Even companies that remained private learned that in Putin's Russia they were obligated to demonstrate fealty to the state first and their shareholders second' (ibid., p. 351). Lukoil one day just transferred $200 million to the state without any apparent coercion. Lukoil's vice president said that the state's domineering is good in his opinion. 'Oil is a strategic thing and of course the state should participate' (ibid.).[70] However despicable the financing of media by the rich may have been, now oligarchs do not finance such or any other non-governmental organizations – they finance autocracy instead.

DMITRY PUTINOVICH MEDVEDEV[71]

Mimicking his predecessor's appearance in the Kremlin, little-known before[72] Medvedev is now the president. Just like eight years ago, we know little about the selection process of the successor and about the motives and plans of Putin and the people behind him. We know that Medvedev has promised to continue the general line of public policy started under Putin. This promise, and mostly the belief that Putin will continue to have a very strong influence over the course of public policy, reduced some of the Russians' uneasiness about the future.

There was hardly any political campaign, no effective opposition, no debates and no political programme presented. A lot of people believed that a sweeping victory, with over 70 per cent votes cast for Medvedev was at least partially staged, but few, perhaps only three people have bothered to formally analyse the results so far. One of them is Sergei Shpilkin,[73] who has said that the votes followed the expected bell-shaped distribution, but only until the support of 63 per cent. The series of spikes above that percentage showed that the local administrations were trying 'to improve' the results (Halpin, 2008 and Podmoskovnik, 2008b), but did not act as a unified group. Therefore 'number fraud' became apparent. (The author of this analysis cleverly called this the Churov distribution, after the head of the Central Election Commission.) While this is not surprising, and was probably not necessary for Medvedev to win, it shows that Putin controls not only the political and administrative processes in the country but also the informal vertical networks. The farce concluded with the Central Election Commission presenting awards to those polling stations that accurately predicted the results (Halpin, 2008).

There is a reason to believe that stuffing ballot boxes was only part of the stratagem. Multiple cases of coercion to turn up and to vote for Medvedev were reported. Some people were instructed at work to vote 'the right way', lest they would receive no bonuses; students at universities, patients at hospitals were told both implicitly and explicitly to vote for Medvedev (The *Other* Russia, 2008a).

In one Moscow district voters using absentee ballots (30 per cent of the total votes cast) allegedly each received 200 rubles in cash; in the north and north-east districts several buses transported people from one polling station to the next, where they successfully voted at each one (The *Other* Russia, 2008b). In Novosibirsk, the school managing the polling station that produced the largest turnout was promised 100,000 rubles (ibid., 2008b). Monitors, both Russian and foreign, noticed that the number of people entering a polling station was at times as little as one half of the official turnout reported at the end of the day (Coalson, 2008).

Predictably, the pattern of voting discovered in the 2008 presidential election followed a routine already tested in the 2007 Duma elections. In both the Duma and the presidential elections, all other parties and candidates exhibited expected Gaussian distribution of votes. The winners' votes, United Russia and Medvedev, had pronounced spikes at exactly 70, 75, 80, 85, 90, 95 and 100 per cent of ballots cast (Figures 8.1–8.4).

If such peaks for the December 2007 election were to be explained by anomalous voter behaviour, it would mean that supporters of United Russia (and analogously the Medvedev supporters four months later) are extremely predisposed to collectively voting for their party and their candidate, but only when the turnout is at its peak (Zigfeld, 2008). In other words, the more people that show up, the less is the diversity of their opinions.

How the dual power will work is hard to predict at this point. Russian history has some examples of double rule (Whitmore, 2008a). It is unlikely that Medvedev will use his constitutional powers to change the existing order. Putin's presence is powerful – he not only accepted the post of the prime minister under Medvedev but also the leadership of United Russia, the most influential political party, on 15 April 2008. The nature of the dual power is likely to be shaped by conflicts and compromises between current

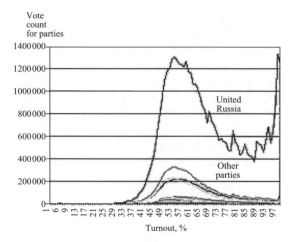

Source: Zigfeld (2008) and Podmoskovnik (2008b).[74]

Figure 8.1   Duma elections, December 2007, Podmoskovnik's analysis

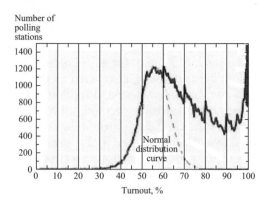

Source: Pshenichnikov (2008),[75] and Zigfeld (2008).

Figure 8.2   Duma elections, December 2007, Pshenichnikov's analysis

interest groups, particularly by war of the *siloviki*, one episode of which occurred in 2007 (ibid.).

Already many analysts notice that Russia's political system resembles the Soviet one. Krishtanovskaia explains in RFE/RL (Radio Free Europe/ Radio Liberty) that leadership of United Russia, which has the majority in Duma, Federal Council and regional parliaments, gives Putin unprecedented sovereignty over those political bodies. Since regional parliaments

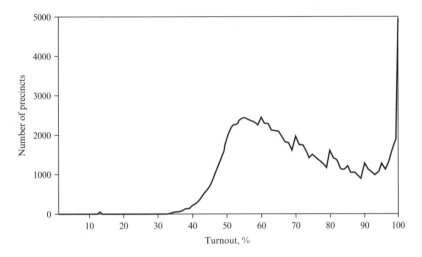

Source: Petviashvili (2007).

Figure 8.3   Votes for United Russia

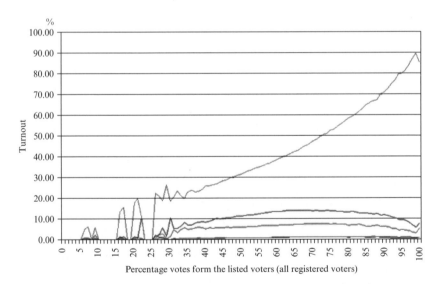

Note: Percentage of votes given the turnout. Highest curve represents Medvedev, lower ones, Zuganov, Zhirinovski and Bogdanov respectively.

Source: Podmoskovnik (2008b).

Figure 8.4   Presidential elections, March 2008, Podmoskovnik's analysis

confirm governors, he will control this process as well (Whitmore, 2008b).

IN CONCLUSION: RUSSIAN GILDED CAGE ENTREPRENEURS

Neither historical institutionalism nor the rational choice approach can be discounted in analysing the profound changes that Russia's governance has experienced over the last 20 years. Russian formal and informal institutional legacies, as the historical approach predicts, plays a large part in the post-Soviet events. And as rational choice asserts, the conflict between politically and economically powerful actors competing for benefits shapes the direction of the governmental redesign.[76]

In this struggle the cartel of oligarchs occupies a special place – oligarchs serve as transmitters of informal networking principles into the effective governing structure. While the relations between the executive and legislative branch are undefined, while the limits of bureaucratic authority are in constant flux,[77] while lawlessness, subjectively granted by the state, has become the law of the land, old and new elite networks fill in the legal gap. The persistence of informal rules, as Steen (2000, p. 20) correctly points out, can be explained by serving some useful organizational and problem-solving functions in the legal void of the 1990s.

Vertical connections prove to be the most important. Among the horizontal networks the most prevalent are clan- and family-based, as well as industrial exchange networks. Connections between ministries, state and private enterprises are very strong (ibid., p. 18). Networks of civic engagement have yet to appear and are not encouraged by the state.

The Russian 'capitalism with Putin's face' promotes the formula 'the state is always right', conveniently dropping the reference to its 'customer' – the citizen. Some oligarchs try to object. Must Russians embrace such attempts as Khodorkovsky's to promote liberal values with embezzled money? Are ordinary Russians, many of whom are now entrepreneurs too, ready to accept the word of a tycoon? At this moment, it seems that no category of the Russian population can harbour a belief in an honest Russian entrepreneur. They prefer the mallet. The very possibility of a Putin lackey like Dmitry Putinovich Medvedev becoming the president is yet another proof.

NOTES

1. 'From 1991 to 1995 deaths in the 20–29 age group increased by 61 per cent, 30–39 years – by 75 per cent and 40–49 years – by 73 per cent' (Tikhomirov, 2000, p. 169).
2. A brief description is in Yergin and Stanislaw (1998, pp. 273–4).
3. An excellent exposition of why socialism did not work is found in Boettke (1993). Some details on Soviet inefficiency are in Boycko, Shleifer and Vishny ([1995] 1996, pp. 33–8).
4. Gorbachev tried to reallocate control rights to the managers from bureaucrats and politicians. But because the managers still did not control cash flow, they managed inefficiently. For more details, see Boycko et al. ([1995] 1996, pp. 38–44).
5. Yeltsin was quite unsure of what to do, as he had been in the opposition when power suddenly fell into his hands. He had no plan (Medvedev, 2000, pp. 10–11).
6. Reference to a 1990 study by Brovkin in Rutland (1993, p. 207).
7. For more details, see Rutland (1993, pp. 212–16).
8. For a vivid description of violence surrounding the redistribution of property rights in the automobile industry, see Hoffman (2002, p. 147). On criminalization of business in the 1990s, see Ryvkina (2001, pp. 39–45) and a very informative study by Satter (2003).
9. '[A] half-liberalized system is often worse than either a fully controlled or a fully liberalized system: The liberalization allows people to scheme the remaining controls, and the reform breaks down' (Cochrane and Ickes, 1995, pp. 67–9).
10. For more details on the perestroika measures and limitations of laws in the 1980s, see Grossman (1987, pp. 2.11–2.18). For a critical analysis of reforms, see Boettke (1993, pp. 38–42). Cooperatives were dependent on the official system for supplies, which they obtained illegally (ibid., p. 168, Note 29).
11. For more details on this, see Boettke (1993, pp. 84–6).
12. For a discussion on the duality and the lack of credibility of reforms, see Boettke (1993, pp. 99–104). For more details on the policies and governmental structure under Gorbachev, see Shevchenko (2004, Chapter 2).
13. No one controlled the army; there was a serious fear that major cities would be left without heat in the winter, state deficit was 20 or more per cent of the GDP; grain reserves had been depleted; see Yergin and Stanislaw (1998, pp. 280–81 and Chapter 10) for more details. As Cochrane and Ickes (1995, p. 66) rightly point out, 'the microeconomic, institutional changes are unlikely to be implemented if the economy is in a state of macroeconomic chaos'. Although later years brought some political stability, the economic stability must not be overestimated – in 1993 and 1994 Russia was running trade surpluses, which indicated large capital flight. In 1992 it was evident that many of the inter-regional suppliers' networks had been broken and new ones had to be built (ibid., pp. 78–9).
14. Chernomyrdin, who was not necessarily a pro-reformist, was appointed the prime minister in December 1992 in an attempt to stabilize the political situation (Yergin and Stanislaw, 1998, p. 282). After Gaidar resigned in 1994 and Chernomyrdin took direct responsibility over the economy, cheap credits were opened again to appease the opposition. Inflation ensued, and Chernomyrdin had to pursue reforms once more (ibid., p. 283). The same scenario was repeated later as well. In 1993 the inflation rate (800 per cent a year) was more than four times that of the discount rate of the Central Bank. Naturally, connections allocated cheap credit among the enterprises (Cochrane and Ickes, 1995, p. 73).
15. In addition to the old parliament Yeltsin inherited the old directors from the previous government (Boycko et al., [1995] 1996, p. 4 and Hoffman, 2002, p. 183).
16. For this skilful politicking and for ability to enrich himself in the process, he earned the name of 'cunning fox' among the general public. And not for nothing – Chubais and other senior officials in the Ministry of Privatization each got $100,000 for fixing the sale of Svyazinvest in favour of Potanin's Oneximbank and Jordan in 1997. Given that

properties worth billions of dollars changed hands under Chubais's supervision, this seems quite a petty fee (Brzezinski, 2002, p. 225).

17. Although the ministries got nothing (Boycko et al. [1995] 1996, pp. 93–4).
18. After the ministries had been dismantled and before attention was drawn to the clan of oligarchs, the dominant structure on the industrial Russian landscape was the financial-industrial group (FIG). These firms developed ties with each other through cross-ownership, lending of resources, serving on each others' boards of directors and so on. By diversifying among various sectors, these firms kept risk down. Needless to say, they were organized around the informal relationships held by their leaders. For more details, see Rutland (2001, pp. 17–18). State policy was in no small part responsible for FIGs, which, although stabilizing the economic environment, are structures less responsive to market signals in the long run. More on FIGs in Chapter 9.
19. For instance, through real estate, which remained in government ownership (Boycko et al. [1995] 1996, p. 127).
20. *Privatizing Russia* (Boycko et al. [1995] 1996) is a very good source on the voucher privatization written by the insiders, but some assertions must be taken with caution. For example, the claim that 'the program turned into a rare success story' proved to be historically unwarranted. Moreover, it is unscholarly to claim that 'a group of scholars commonly known as Sovietologists, who built their careers studying the Soviet economic and political system' disagreed that Russians respond to incentives 'because it contradicted their [Sovietologists'] image of the Russian people' (pp. 10 and 97). The first thing that the designers of the reform did was to assume that Russians like other people respond to economic incentives. Russians, of course, respond to incentives, but rules of the privatization game were tainted by the peculiar institutional make-up. To simply acknowledge the fact that there is no history of private property and contracts is not enough. Russians are interested in becoming rich, but not necessarily by honest means; and some become wealthy often at the expense of others. They are also accustomed to windfall fortune and bankruptcy. To say that history and social norms do not matter and Russia is no different from another capitalist culture would be to copy the Bolsheviks in 1917 who believed they could create a new Soviet citizen on the ruins of history. Still, I would not argue that the privatization could have been done better, given that the Russian regime had quickly become subject to powerful influence of interest groups and that the government would not want to create any more economic havoc than it did. There was a good chance that lesser concessions would have led to a civil war.
21. On the importance of *nomenklatura* background and how political capital affected wealth in post-Soviet Russia, see Krishtanovskaia and White (1999).
22. The *Obkom* was the regional committee of the Communist Party.
23. One way to successful banking was accommodating dirty money or obtaining budget accounts and profitable contracts from the authorities; yet another was speculating on exchange rates. Loans were risky; for more details see Hoffman (2002, p. 48).
24. Details in Hoffman (2002, Chapter 13). Although the oligarchs pushed and organized the campaign, it was allegedly financed by laundered cash from resale of government bonds, and much of that cash was pocketed in the process (ibid., p. 349).
25. There were also immediate rewards, such as loans for shares; for more details see Hoffman (2002, pp. 361–3). After the August 1998 crash Russian banks and companies were allowed not to pay foreign debts for three months. 'It was an invitation for the tycoons to run away from their obligations forever, more than $16 billion in loans' (ibid., p. 430). The very fact that the default and devaluation were discussed the night before the public announcement between Chubais (acting on behalf of the government) and the oligarchs would be unheard of in a Western economy, yet quite acceptable in Russia (ibid., pp. 433–4). Later in the year the Central Bank 'made a series of mysterious "stabilization loans". . . . The Central Bank dished out a $345 million loan to SBS-Agro' – an oligarch-owned company (ibid., pp. 438–9).
26. Before the crash of the ruble in 1998 some investors were able to get liquidity and run for

the exit, while others were not. The success of the former depended on 'a combination of factors – connections, luck, rumors, bribery, and sheer timing' (Hoffman, 2002, p. 427).

27. For more details, see Hoffman (2002, pp. 104–5).
28. For instance, Khodorkovsky. For more details, see Hoffman (2002, pp. 109–10).
29. Medvedev (2000) provides an excellent account of the state's policies in the 1990s.
30. Lists of oligarchs between 1995 and 1998 'vary in number from six to sixteen, and twenty-eight names appear at least once' (Rigby, 1999).
31. For more details, see Hoffman (2002, pp. 142–5, 148).
32. More on Berezovsky in Klebnikov (2001).
33. To bring 12 people to see a highly sought performance required good connections. He was the only one among his class to have a car, and he consistently supplied his friends with shortage goods (Hoffman, 2002, p. 154). He worked as a stage director for Ted Turner's Goodwill Games in 1986 (ibid., p. 157).
34. Bobkov later came to work for Gusinsky as Chief of Security, drawing elite military and KGB personnel under his command (Hoffman, 2002, p. 165).
35. The banks were engaged in making easy money. In 1996, for instance, 90 per cent of credits were 'disbursed for short-term transactions on government debt' (Hoffman, 2002, p. 231). Bank Menatep 'had direct lobbying links to key ministers. . . . The bank thrived on a web of government lending programs, ranging from defense spending to food purchases; the Russian Finance Ministry was one of its first major clients and loans for the state made up more than half of Menatep's lending activity in 1995' (Hoffman, 2002, p. 232).
36. The military and security services were convinced they had a rightful claim to the telephone lines (Hoffman, 2002, pp. 374–6). The Spanish telephone company was a co-investor.
37. More details on Luzhkov's political career in Hoffman (2002, Chapter 2).
38. By his own acknowledgement, it was the old friends and not the money that did the trick (Hoffman, 2002, p. 113). Because non-cash was 'a virtual money that existed on ledgers only, Khodorkovsky must have had permission to keep it in an account or perhaps got control of someone else's account. It was not the kind of money that could be kept in a shoebox. . . . The fact Khodorkovsky was dealing in hard currency was a clue that . . . he had patrons in high places' (ibid., p. 114). The State Committee on Science and Technology, which was a conduit between the Communist Party and the state scientific institutions, gave Khodorkovsky a hand as well (ibid., p. 115).
39. Other oligarchs included brothers Chernoys – their company Trans-CIS the biggest metal trader in the world in the 1990s (Brzezinski, 2002, pp. 172–5), and Roman Abramovich – the Far East oil magnate.
40. For a list of rigged values of Russian state companies, see Hoffman (2002, pp. 205–6 and Boycko et al. [1995] 1996, pp. 109, 117–19). An implied aggregate value of the Russian industry was short of $12 billion, ibid. (p. 117). For a good collection of essays on the 1990s' political economy, see Rutland (2001).
41. Yegor Gaidar was Prime Minister under Yeltsin and an architect of Yeltsin's shock therapy.
42. Tatum built a Radisson Slavyanskaya hotel in Moscow. Then the city government wanted a stake in the hotel's profits. As a result, Tatum acquired an unwanted and sudden partner. The lawsuit against the Moscow City Council was unsuccessful (Brzezinski, 2002, pp. 242–3). Even though foreign investors owned 51 per cent of shares, they were not even allowed through the doors by the Russian directors and had no access to the books (ibid., pp. 169–70). Khodorkovsky successfully defaulted on $236 million in loans to Japanese, German and British banks, and executed a plan to force out an American investor, Kenneth Dart, who held 12 per cent in Khodorkovsky's company (Baker and Glasser, 2005, p. 276).
43. Although 'this was far less than all other elite categories except the leaders of political parties' (Rigby, 1999).

44. Interestingly, only 5 per cent of new party leaders had Komsomol careers, only 2 per cent of the regional elite did, and not a single member either of the government or the president's entourage was launched from Komsomol (Rigby, 1999).
45. Kukolev (1999) covers the sociological portrait and background of the elite in the 1990s. Lane (2001, pp. 111–13) examines the elite's origins.
46. For instance, Gusinsky regretted this closeness later, as his television channel NTV had come to be viewed as the state's puppet after the 1996 campaign (Hoffman, 2002, pp. 347, 363).
47. In 1999 the general prosecutor Skuratov (ironically bearing the same last name as Ivan IV's [Ivan the Terrible in English] right-hand Maluta Skuratov), started digging into the affairs of Matebex construction company, which pointed to large bribes of government officials in Yeltsin's circle and his immediate family. The investigation was made possible, although not directly ordered by acting Prime Minister Primakov who enjoyed growing political popularity and hinted at prosecuting Yeltsin's circle upon becoming the president. Putin demonstrated military-like loyalty to his bosses in the Kremlin in forcing Skuratov's resignation, although he might have had personal reasons as well. This quality appealed to Yeltsin (while lip service to liberal reforms appealed to the oligarchs), who named him the prime minister several months after the Matebex affair, thus dismissing Primakov. For more details, see Jack (2004, pp. 80–87).
48. This speculation was prompted by a statement of the head of Uralmashzavod stock company, Bendukidze: 'We all are convinced that Gusinsky has not failed as a businessman per se, but has got into trouble as a businessman who was not loyal to the regime. Now everything will depend on how we react, how we interpret this situation: as one person's foolishness or a calculated provocation on the part of the regime' (*Itogi*, December 2000).
49. Voloshin, a holdout from the Yeltsin 'family', resigned when Khodorkovsky was arrested. Kas'yanov, also a holdout from the Yeltsin era, was relieved of his post as the prime minister during the presidential elections in 2004. When Putin's opponents withdrew from the elections, refusing to follow through with the farce, Putin was faced with a remote possibility that Kas'yanov might have temporary presidential authority.
50. Yeltsin's regime defined a new system of budget relations between the federal centre and the local bureaucracy. The Soviet system of relations between the centre and the republics gave the latter a predetermined share from fixed taxes and allowed them freedom to set some tax rates in order to cover the rest of the expenditures. If this was not enough, the republics received subventions, as the system 'involved substantial discretion, and it encouraged negotiation over budgets, sharing rates' (McLure, 1995, p. 205). The new code was supposed to be more objective than the Soviet system; however, case by case negotiation persisted with oblasts' (administrative divisions') governments now replacing the republics'. At least to the mid-1990s the government was not able to make oblasts contribute an appropriate share of taxes to the centre (ibid., pp. 205–7 and Berglof et al., 2003, pp. 54–5).
51. Although not directly financed by the state, the station was used to promote Putin's image in the previous year's elections.
52. On the confrontation with NTV during the theatre production of *Nord-Ost*, see Baker and Glasser (2005, pp. 174–6).
53. For more details on the NTV takeover and pressure on print media, see Jack (2004, pp. 131–73).
54. Andrei Babitsky, a reporter for Radio Liberty, dared to contradict the official version of events. He was first arrested by pro-Moscow Chechens and then handed over to the rebels in a manufactured exchange. Putin appeared to be well aware of this (Jack, 2004, p. 117). Examples of self-censorship also in Politkovskaya (2007, p. 78), especially in the case of Beslan (ibid., pp. 178–9).
55. Whether to avoid the wrath of the Kremlin or to earn the Kremlin's protection against criminal elements is not so much relevant as the result of reporters' loyalty to the regime and not to the truth.

56. Censorship is practised especially in cases of national emergency. For instance, when the nuclear submarine *Kursk* sank in 2000, only select journalists were allowed to attend the press conference and only one channel – loyal to the Kremlin RTR – was allowed to record. The video that was shown on television had been carefully edited (Satter, 2003, Note 7 on p. 258). On at least two occasions the newspapers were forced to retrieve articles regarding *Kursk* (ibid., p. 23).

57. To keep up the pretence of democratic process, a Kremlin-sponsored human rights movement was created, headed by a former People's Deputy of the USSR, a former member of Supreme Soviet of the USSR, and a former Duma deputy, Ella Pamfilova. The organization is called the Civil Society Institutions and Human Rights Council *under the President of the Russian Federation*.

58. For more details on the failure of the rule of the law, see Baker and Glasser (2005, Chapter 12). 'Just 8 per cent of cases went to juries, and those that went to judges held no more suspense than in Soviet days' (Baker and Glasser, 2005, p. 247). Jury trials, with only 15 per cent acquittal, face a 32 per cent successful overturn of a verdict by the Supreme Court (ibid., pp. 247–8). For an overview of the judicial reform, see Berglof et al. (2003, pp. 69–97). Jury trials are expensive; the process is not well-polished yet, and Putin has recently questioned the efficacy of trial by peers, as there were too many acquittals in his opinion of people accused of high-profile killings; see Faulconbridge (2007). That is, of course, assuming that the accused were the guilty ones. It is entirely possible that the accused had a history of assaults but were not involved in the case they were tried for.

59. On centralization of power, see Shevchenko (2004, Chapter 7).

60. The Duma is successfully manipulated by Putin (Jack, 2004, pp. 219–29).

61. Absolute and relative numbers of bureaucracy at the local levels were on the rise between 1994 and 2001. The federal bureaucracy declined slightly in 2001 (Gimpel'son, 2002, pp. 30–31).

62. Sometimes also called Unified Russia.

63. For more details, see Baker and Glasser (2005, pp. 294–311).

64. Candidates not approved of by United Russia were sometimes roughed up or had various body parts, such as a human ear or heart in a plastic bag thrown through their window. Most pulled out of the race (Politkovskaya, 2007, pp. 4–5).

65. For more examples, see Baker and Glasser (2005, pp. 322–3). Putin's campaign is covered in Chapter 16, ibid.

66. The Baltic Factory followed suit after defence company Almaz-Antei and Milya Helicopters (Politkovskaya, 2007, p. 354).

67. For more details, see Baker and Glasser (2005, pp. 83–7).

68. Khodorkovsky, for instance, openly opposed new politics and planned five tours around the country to deliver criticism of the regime at educational establishments and on television. He had been financing the Yabloko Party, which opposed Putin, as well. Moreover, he had an open plan to control the Duma (by *buying* the majority, of course), to rewrite the constitution and to become the acting prime minister (Baker and Glasser, 2005, pp. 280–84 and Jack, 2004, pp. 206–15). Khodorkovsky was arrested during his second tour (Baker and Glasser, 2005, pp. 273–4).

69. There have been other cases of renationalization, for instance, in the vodka industry (Vladykin, 2002 and Zarakhovich, 2002).

70. The new deal between the state and the tycoons looks more transparent on paper than it is in reality. The latter still exercise influence – oligarchs continue to meet one on one with the country's leader but not in the open. The emphasis has shifted to buying votes in the parliament and to appointing loyal-to-business people into the government. In fact, this direction started taking shape already in late 1998 (Jack, 2004, pp. 191–206). John N. Paden (Clarence Robinson Professor of International Studies and Professor of Public and International Affairs at George Mason University, Fairfax, VA, USA) suggested that in the Russian case we may be looking not necessarily at an authoritarian form of government, but at the form that is associated with oil-rich states where there is a great deal of centralization of power as well.

71. *-ovich* is a suffix in Russian added to the father's name to form a patronymic, for instance, Vladimir Vladimirovich Putin is the son of Vladimir.
72. That is, little known to the population, not to Putin. Medvedev and Putin have known each other since the time Putin served in St Petersburg administration.
73. Cited as a computer programmer who made a formal presentation of his findings at a think-tank in Moscow (Halpin, 2008).
74. More analysis, graphs and discussion on Podmoskovnik's blog; see Podmoskovnik (2008a).
75. Original and more graphs.
76. For a brief description of both approaches, see Shevchenko (2004, pp. 3–5).
77. For more details, see Shevchenko (2004).

9. Social networks and economic efficiency: everyday networks

Let us suppose for a moment that after the fall of the Soviet Union property rights to land, enterprises, real estate and other things of economic value were distributed through a fair auction system. Let us suppose further that a sincere attempt at representative governing and allowing free markets was made, and let us ignore the difficulties in setting up such a framework. Even though the price mechanism will regulate some exchanges relatively quickly, problems of long-term investment that are risk-sensitive cannot be ignored. Time lags and the complex structure of modern economy pre-suppose the existence of formal or informal exchange governance (but not necessarily government-engineered or government-instituted).

Therefore, even in a near ideal situation it is difficult to set up free markets where there has been no history of the rule of law and private property. In addition, people are very likely to rely on the informal accepted ways of doing business, especially when the formal rules are being changed as abruptly as they were in post-Soviet Russia. During the Soviet period personal success was often determined by how well an individual could con the system; in the beginning of the transition many people were defrauded by pyramid schemes and many more felt involved through sympathizing with the victims. Naturally, in the post-Soviet Russia an expectation of opportunism persisted.

SOCIAL NETWORKS AND THE ROLE OTHER INSTITUTIONS PLAY IN FACILITATING PRODUCTION AND EXCHANGE

What Ledeneva (1998) calls 'non-monetary forms of exchange' are claimed to have lost their importance by comparison with monetary forms in the post-Soviet period. This is certainly true of most everyday purchases, such as food. However, in some cases, the value of network capital remains intact, and perhaps even increases.

In the aftermath of the breakdown of the system of centralized eco-nomic regulation and standards, the informal network provided a set of institutions that had already proved functional in the underground market. These institutions helped the newly born *above*-ground economy to function (de Soto, 2000). Consider first, the shortage of professional competency and highly reputable long-standing firms in the market, second, bureaucratic arbitrage in business licensing and regulation, and it becomes clear that this institutionalization of informal networks within the Russian 'market' economy and even the legalization of some informal practices were prompted by shortcomings of the environment.

One instance of legalizing networks is customs operations. Already, in Soviet times, work in customs was rightfully considered a golden mine.[1] Customs employees had first-hand pick of high-quality imports, which they either stole or bought at a minimal price and then resold on the black market. In the 1990s, as my respondents indicated, 'it went without saying' that out of ten items of clothing packaged together, one would be taken out by a customs employee either for personal use, for a family member or as a gift for someone else.[2] On top of that, the imported goods could be damaged, stolen, indefinitely delayed or overly taxed with no good explanation or legal recourse.[3]

Russian start-ups, most of which at the time made all their business through imports, explored existing connections to customs employees and developed new ones as well, to prevent such looting and to secure leniency. Given that the number of importing start-ups grew, while the number of customs officials remained roughly the same, there was a market niche for intermediary firms, which organized the bribing process and made customs inspection less chaotic and nerve-racking for entrepreneurs.

These firms now not only provide 'customs services' but also transportation services. They compete against one another; the customers are treated quite decently, and in fact, many businesspeople say it is no shame to pay for such a civilized (!) service (Klyamkin and Timofeev, 2000).[4] Although the firms are legal in form, this market is still network-based. A firm-importer employs a specialist with *sviazi* (see Chapter 3) to deal with intermediary firms. While in the end of the 1990s this was somewhat of a novelty that entrepreneurs talked about, now towards the end of the 2000s, it is quite a routine procedure that no one thinks of mentioning unless prompted.

In cases such as getting food and clothes, deep-involvement horizontal social networks have become redundant. Still, in my observation, buyers seek personal contacts with shop assistants because, with a growing variety of products and cost-cutting practices, the market is full of 'lemons', while shop assistants often possess better knowledge about quality.

When gathering data in the early 2000s, it appeared to me that networks in medical services might soon become redundant. The uncertainty about the quality of the end product made it very hard to achieve a consensus on price, and could have led to 'black market failure'. Did the patient die because the bribe was too small and the connection too insignificant or because the doctor was truly helpless to change anything? The bribe would be pure extortion if the doctor knew he could do nothing. On the other hand, if the patient recovered, it was still unclear how much the doctor had to do with it.

At the time I believed that the nature of the product in this market was vague enough to question the resiliency of the illegal market for medical services as compared with other types. But the reality turned out differently. Among the newly sprung private clinics, there are only a few of relatively high quality, and, to discover those, people rely on word of mouth. To get into a high-quality medical establishment, state or private, requires either a connection alone or a connection and a bribe. At a state clinic it is best to have a connection to at least one of the doctors, even better to the head of the department, in order to have testing administered. Richer Russians keep a personal doctor on a payroll. These doctors find their jobs through personal networks. Those who lack the financial opportunity turn to the state medical providers. There, medical personnel compensate their low pay by taking bribes, theft or neglect of duties.[5]

Networks in bureaucracy have taken an especially strong foothold.[6] Even though the Soviet state has been destroyed, its backbone – the bureaucracy – is very much alive and well and arguably has privatized important functions of the state (Ryavec, 2003, p. 104). Much as the Bolsheviks inherited the Tsarist bureaucratic apparatus, post-Soviet Russia inherited the Soviet one. About three-fourths of civil servants have continued in their positions since the Soviet times (ibid., p. 157).[7] And now allegedly up to three-quarters of high administrative posts spanning both private and state-supervised industry are occupied by formerly KGB-connected officials.

Even though many resources have been transferred into private hands, 'many' does not mean that rank-and-file citizens possess a majority of *quality* resources. Urban real estate is one source of enrichment for local bureaucracy. Bureaucrats trade assets without actually owning them, much like the party elite never owned dachas, airplanes, and servants during the Soviet era. Whereas a problem between a bureaucrat and an ordinary citizen can often be solved by a one-time transaction, long-term investment pays in for bureaucrat–business relationships.

Indeed, there are numerous opportunities for 'productive' relations between business and local government. Bureaucrats officially control legal markets. Favourable administrative decisions, for instance granting a business licence or a contract, are very valuable and officials want to sell them at a high price.[8] Naturally, information about the size of a bribe for various economic activities and the ritual of gift-giving is communicated through the informal network only. Unless a person has sufficient investment in hierarchical networks, he will not succeed.[9] Once allowed, the bureaucrat never gets off the back of an entrepreneur – payments are expected as long as the business plans to function.

Thus, effectively business becomes a joint venture with local government, and the bureaucrat becomes a stationary bandit. The official then tries to legalize concessions from the business. For example, a business may turn into a permanent donor, making an entrepreneur responsible for financing banquets, car repairs, microwaves for offices and so on.

At the same time, the official is very interested in the stability and well-being of his branch establishment. He needs to protect 'his' business from parasites in other branches of government, such as the technical inspection committee, the committee for artistic appearance standards, and so on. For a coveted fee he arranges that others do not interfere with his protégé business. This is called having *krysha* ('roof' in Russian) or protection – an arrangement remarkably similar to feudal relations. Protection of business by criminal elements is also called *krysha*. Small businesses often used the protection of a criminal gang in the early 1990s. Larger businesses, however, need protection by both local administration and criminal elements, which in this case often work in consort (Ryvkina, 2001, p. 41). Many of the mafia clans of the early 1990s have dissipated but their members now work for perfectly legitimate 'security' firms.

The relationships between public servants and private parties have spontaneously grown out of the everyday necessity to survive and are already being habituated. Firms have incorporated structural innovations, such as creating a special category of employees – government liaisons – whose sole responsibility is to regulate business–bureaucrat relations. It is crucial that liaisons develop strong ties with the officials so that a business deal can be discussed over a cup of tea, intermittent with friendly inquiries about each other's families. The intermediary then becomes a guarantor not only of business profitability but also of the official's safety because it is harder to give up a long-standing friend for prosecution.[10] Quite significant too is the cost of ostracism for being a traitor since hierarchical networks are extensive and information is disseminated well.

Bureaucratic corporatism of the 1970s and 1980s had undergone a transformation with the appearance of a private business sector in the late 1980s. There is regional variation in the models of relations between bureaucracy and business depending on the relative powers and position in hierarchy at the time of change. Lapina (1998) distinguishes between the patronage model, the partnership model, the privatization of power model and the fight of everybody against everybody model.

The patronage model exhibits 'regimentation in the economy and/or strict control of the economic players' and is found in 'national republics (e.g. in Tatarstan and Bashkortostan), in Russian territories with a pro-communist orientation (e.g. in Ulyanovsk and Krasnodar), and in Moscow' (Lapina, 1998). The partnership model is 'found in regions in which market economy reforms are being carried out . . . and the political and economic players have succeeded in entering into a dialogue (e.g. in the territories of Novgorod, Nizhny Novgorod and Leningrad, and in St. Petersburg)' (ibid.).

The privatization of power model has evolved where 'an economic elite has emerged which at the same time forms the power elite (e.g. in the republics of Kalmykiya and Khakassiya and in the territory of Tyumen)' (ibid.). The fight of everybody against everybody model 'prevails in subjects of federation with a weak political leadership and tight economic resources and which, consequently, are largely dependent on meagre financial support from Moscow (e.g. the territory of Kirov)' (ibid.).

So far I have concentrated on the advantages of connections, but there are some limitations as well.[11] In the labour market in the 1990s employment through connections was the logical path for business, but was not problem-free. In the Soviet Union most people worked as private entrepreneurs on the black market and only occasionally for hire (Treml, 1992, p. 24),[12] so they had little opportunity to experience the organizational culture of a market firm. Before Gorbachev's reforms, many Russians had acquired some experience of entrepreneurship of one kind or another. Such entrepreneurship, however, even where it was not illegal, was for the most part dependent upon the operation of bureaucratic-administrative structures (Rigby, 1999).

During the transition the law on labour contracts lacked clarity and enforcing power.[13] This increased the already existing probability of getting 'lemon' employees. Just some of the difficult questions of newborn businesses were: how to pick an employee from a pool where an overwhelming number are cheaters and shirkers, or how to find a supplier when the government offers no formally institutionalized fraud protection. In a thin market for knowledge of 'who is who', the logical solution was to rely on the practice of strong personalized relationships. So friends became employees, friends arranged supplies for each other and gave each other recommendations.[14] Many businesses were organized with only family members as employees (19.5 per cent), friends and family members as employees (26.4 per cent), close acquaintances as employees (47.7 per cent), strangers or distant acquaintances (13 per cent) (Radaev, 1993, p. 73).

The first advantage of this practice resulted in fulfilling positions that could not be openly advertised because initially a significant part of the economy was still underground. In this situation employees had to be trustworthy, and trust was supported by a 'personal recommendation' – a new euphemism for *blat*.

The second was that, with non-trivial unemployment, any announced job opening produced such a storm of phone calls (translators from Hindu, miners, typists and so on) that only a firm with an abundant staff could handle it. However, many businesses did not have a human resource manager or even a secretary to take the phone calls. It was easier then to call friends.

The third was that in Russia, where people were still only learning how private businesses operate, not every job had a clear description and/or requirements. Many positions combined tasks from different spheres of competency. Turning to a recruiting agency or placing a newspaper advertisement was futile simply because specific knowledge of the situation was required in order to fill in the job opening with an appropriate candidate. The fourth was that friends could confirm skills and education, certification of which could be easily falsified.

The fifth was that recruiting agencies did not find it cost-effective to place individual unemployed workers who possessed no outstanding skills. Recruiting agencies were very few anyway, but those that existed preferred either to look for expensive specialists with unique skills and experience (commission was calculated from five-to-six figure salary) or to take 'wholesale' orders (for example, find 35,000 messengers with 1000 salary each). This, of course, did not mean that one could not find a job in the 'open' market; a position of distributor of Herbalife's cure-all products was readily available (Karpova, 2001).[15]

Certain US economists conclude that networking practices in Russia differ little from those in the West:

> In a survey taken of a random sample of entrepreneurs and nonentrepreneurs in Russia over the 2003–2004 period, a team of scholars found that Russian entrepreneurs were more than twice as likely to have had family members running a business . . . than other Russians. . . . We find this a clear demonstration of how in a society where formal entrepreneurship was not allowed until 1986, entrepreneurial activities have taken root in less than two decades through the same channel – family background – as one sees in highly entrepreneurial societies like the United States. (Baumol, Litan and Schramm, 2007, p. 124)

Such a panglossian judgement of the new Russian experience with capitalism is simply unfounded.

There were several disadvantages too associated with connected hiring. Some connected employees turned out to be less skilful, but it was impossible to get rid of them. Many employers felt that information about new technologies, products, partnerships and so on was not completely secure when there were employees connected with other, perhaps competing organizations. Of course, the situation has been changing gradually. For example, at first not many understood what a marketing director was supposed to do. Thus, marketing directors as well as public relations and financial directors were chosen from the pool of connected individuals. Today a marketing director is one of the key people in a firm, on whom its success or failure depends, and he is, therefore, chosen primarily on the basis of expertise.

The new generation, educated in the late 1990s and early 2000s, has an easier job search and is more adaptive to the new environment than were their parents. Russia's labour market tends toward a prevalence of weak ties among the new job seekers. It must be noted, however, that these positions, though decently salaried, on average do not allow a young person to buy an apartment or a reliable car, attend restaurants regularly, travel regularly and the like. Young people in high-paying positions today got their jobs through their parents' connections or through strong ties of their own in the 1990s.[16]

Money, not necessarily connections, will buy a cucumber or a coat in today's Russia. But if any good or service has a risk associated with its delivery, be it delay in shipping, adherence to the terms of contract, physical damage, or securing payment, reaching an agreement between the two parties may become problematic. In order to hold, implicit contracts need to fall back on something like market reputation.[17] During the first decade of transition this was often established by a recommendation or word of mouth. Other times trust on both sides was established through transactions in *black cash* – cash turnover that is not recorded in the books, in US jargon 'green is unseen'.

There are three types of firms operating in the Russian market, although the proportional relationship between them has changed over the years – officially registered firms, firms registered officially but partially accepting payments under the table, and businesses that are not registered and work for black cash.[18] The black cash or simply a cash transaction without receipt is a preferred form of payment for both seller and buyer. First, it is more convenient, second, less costly,[19] third, ensures better service, fourth, more attractive from networking standpoint,[20] and fifth, facilitates tax evasion. Black cash establishes an informal relationship between the provider and the recipient of the service and suggests mutual benefits from future repetitive dealings. Repetitive dealings in car repair service, for example, guarantee that the technician knows the problems of a particular car very well – this saves time for both sides, increases gratitude on the part of the car owner and cash flow to the technician.

In price and service, underground businesses operating for black cash often beat their officially registered competitors. They also have wider bargaining margins. Black cash businesses will exist as long as consumers find them beneficial and as long as consumers must rely on connections rather than on the reputation of a firm in order to obtain good service (Klyamkin and Timofeev, 2000).

SOCIAL NETWORKS, RUSSIAN INDUSTRIAL ORGANIZATION AND TYPES OF OWNERSHIP

Along with the breakdown of supply and retail networks, the transformation within hierarchies left its impact on the industrial organization and ownership structure in Russia today. Management connections to the ministries remain important even after privatization. On the one hand, private industry enjoys a great deal of government concessions, both officially and unofficially and, on the other hand, it bears government intervention.[21] The larger the venture, the more likely it is to rely on state subsidies and contracts.

Business leaders called integration a desired form in surveys taken in the beginning of transition (Avdasheva, 2000, pp. 45–6). Large companies were looking to internalize externalities, such as inadequate supply system, undeveloped shareholders' market and unreliability of employees, by integrating vertically. The soft-budget constraint, still operating in the post-Soviet environment and the lack of an efficient legal system, prevented official vertical integration. In other words, bounded rationality, asset specificity, and opportunism gave way to 'quasi-integration' where relational contracts were the dominant form of enforcement.

Profit was redistributed through financial-industrial conglomerates or through holding companies[22] and financial-industrial groups (FIGs) (ibid., p. 84).[23] This form of industrial organization only reinforced the importance of social networks because the legal structure of Russian FIGs was not functional in coordinating action between members if one or more of them disagreed.

Therefore, hierarchies grew stronger and often became the only guarantee of stability within a group. Ties remain pertinent with regard to the organization's mobility as well – it determines how quickly and successfully ownership can be redistributed within a FIG or outside of it, to a more effective outside owner. Because a formal institutional framework is lacking and because formal redistribution of property rights can be tremendously costly, relational-based agreements or handshake agreements are the most efficient ones given the prior accumulation of social networking.

Informal networks, which sustain *unofficial* vertical *integration*, allow enterprises to rip off benefits of the *official disintegration*. Disintegration provides several advantages – when factual ownership rights are distributed[24] it is more difficult to take control of an enterprise, managers act opportunistically by privatizing part of an enterprise, soft budget constraints allow accumulation of debt to the government, which is more likely to be forgiven when property rights are not concentrated (ibid., pp. 86–7), tax evasion and financial machinations are easier to implement.

Difficulties of the transition, such as no independent legal system, low level of competition and the uncertainty of contract enforcement, which shortens the business planning horizon and raises opportunism among managers, often prompt the de facto boundaries of a firm to exceed its de jure limits, and to create a disjoint ownership and management, thus placing extra weight on relational contracts. As Avdasheva (ibid., p. 117) points out, many owners view shares not as a profit-making device, but as a rent-seeking device. The fact that ownership distribution and the books are not transparent often deters a potentially more efficient outside investor (ibid., p. 118).

STANDARDS OF LIVING: HOW WELL DO RUSSIANS LIVE IN THE NEW MILLENNIUM?

During the 1990s real incomes fell, and many savings as well as confidence in the economy were wiped out by the 1998 default. Economic indicators, such as household income related to expenditure and average income related to the official poverty line, point to a steady decrease in the standards of living over the 1990s (Zherebin and Romanov, 2002, pp. 33–4, 53). Some 22.4 per cent lived below poverty line[25] in 1996, while 20 per cent of well-off Russians claimed 46.5 per cent of aggregate household money income (ibid., p. 49).[26] In 1999 the top 10 per cent income category claimed over 50 per cent of aggregate household income (ibid., p. 110).

Differentiation between the lowest and the highest income categories was 1 to 13 in 1994 and remained so until 1997, increasing to 14.7 times in 1999 (ibid., pp. 109–11, especially Table 5.1).[27] The difference in income between the bottom and the top 10 per cent category in the mid-2000s is 1 to 14. Interactive Research Group classified just 3 per cent Russians as rich, 30 as middle income, and 67 as disadvantaged (Jack, 2004, pp. 32–3). Average *annual* income was $2160 in 2003 (ibid., p. 253). In addition, many low-income categories were not paid on time.[28] And they are still not. On average, 375,000 people in 2007 were not paid on time; in the first quarter of 2008 it is already at 200,000. Wage arrears have been carried over from the previous years (*Informatsiia o sotsial'no-ekonomicheskom polozhenii Rossii* (*Russian Socio-Economic Data*), 2008, Chapter VI).[29]

By November 2007 the average Russian *monthly* wage had risen to approximately \$580, a 15 per cent increase in real terms from a year earlier,[30] although much of the gain is eaten up by the double-digit yearly inflation. About 50 per cent of the population have an income of around \$380, and nearly 13 per cent of the population lives on less than \$150 a month (*Country Report, Russia*, 2007).[31]

Inevitably there is a large regional variation, with even the second largest city, St Petersburg, falling much behind Moscow, which was calculated to be the most expensive city on earth in 2007. Life in Moscow in the 2000s is a life of contrast between social strata, much like it contrasts with the regions. Average income is 40 per cent higher than in the rest of the country; it receives 42 per cent of foreign investment, and almost 30 per cent of the country's retail takes place there (Baker and Glasser, 2005, p. 143). The capital has 33 billionaire residents, with the middle class earning under \$500 a month; one-fifth of Muscovites live below the poverty level.[32] Muscovites actively participate in the mass consumer culture (ibid., Chapter 7). Since 70 per cent still refuse to put money in a bank, they spend as much as 80 per cent of their income on housing and consumer goods (ibid., p. 146).

The income discrepancies in the country as a whole appear to have been improving over the last few years. But the fact is that the lowest income categories, which also happen to be the oldest age categories, are simply dying out. Recent life expectancy figures are not significantly better than the ones cited for the 1990s. Life expectancy at birth for females in 2005 is estimated at 72.1 years, for males, at 58.6 years (*Human Development Report, Russian Federation*, 2007/2008). The population has been steadily declining, despite recent increase in births and economic stimulus package for couples having a second child (see Figure 9.1).

It is expected that living standards will improve when markets operate in at least some sectors of the economy. But will this share of markets be enough, will their institutional structure be strong and flexible enough, will they be positioned in the right sectors of the economy to be able to bounce the country back in case of world economic shocks? Similar to the beginning of the last century the positive trend of Russian macroeconomic indicators, such as private consumption, stock market, GDP, has been sponsored by favourable terms of trade. Russia has been especially dependent on the oil prices, and many negative effects of Putin's restructuring have been offset by the high energy prices. In real terms the rate of economic growth has been positive, but not impressive.[33]

In recent years Russia's economic boom is still mostly concentrated in the retail and construction sectors (*World Bank Russian Economic Report*,

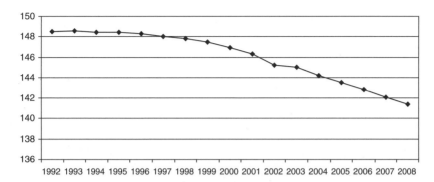

Source: Chart compiled from IMF data in *World Economic Outlook* (2008).

Figure 9.1 Population, in millions

2007, p. 3). Construction is not surprisingly one of the leaders. Even though Russians started investing some of their disposable income in shares, they prefer to buy up real estate property for subsequent resale or rent. In addition, many are looking to buy property overseas.[34]

Levelling growth in manufacturing reflects the inflationary pressure on wages pushing them ahead of the productivity growth, and foreign direct investment remains[35] concentrated in resource extraction industries (ibid., pp. 5–7), which are heavily dominated by government and this is precisely where the presence of foreign capital cannot produce institutional changes.

Rosstat reports that real disposable money income, as a percentage of the previous year, went down in 2006, and real fixed monthly pension was down 4.5 per cent in 2006 (*Russia'2007*, p. 11). In 2007–08 real disposable income growth was positive, but seems to be levelling off with a possible downward trend in 2008 (*Informatsiia o sotsial'no-ekonomicheskom polozhenii Rossii* (*Russian Socio-Economic Data*), 2008, Chapter VI).

The inflation rate for 2007 amounted to nearly 12 per cent. Already in the first quarter of 2008 it is reported to be 5.3 per cent. The largest price increase is on flour; by my estimates prices on bread products in St Petersburg have gone up nearly 7 per cent in the first four months of 2008. Given the historical prognosis, the inflation rate is not likely to flatten (see Figure 9.2).

Apart from wages, consumption basket or inflation, there are a number of indicators of quality of life that are not directly measured, but are conventionally observable. Daily routines are complicated by the roundabout ways of paying utilities, finding a contractor, returning damaged goods, or by projecting the next month's inflation rate.

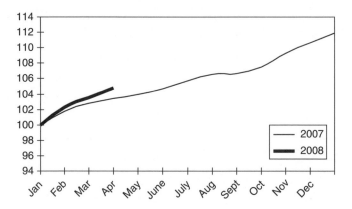

Source: Chart compiled using Rosstat figures (*Informatsiia o sotsial'no-ekonomicheskom polozhenii Rossii* (*Russian Socio-Economic Data*) 2008).

Figure 9.2   CPI increase in 2007, and 2008, in percentage toward December rate of the previous year

IN CONCLUSION: RUSSIAN MIDDLE-CLASS ENTREPRENEURS AND 'ROACH' CAPITALISM

One St Petersburg wealthy businessman remarked on the occasion of the government tax reform, which intended to break up the informal links between businesses and their tax inspectors: 'We [Russian entrepreneurs] are like cockroaches[36] – they sweep us up with the broomstick and out through the door, but we crawl back in through the windows'. By that he stressed the uselessness of attempts to sever informal networks and exemplified the unprecedented resilience of the Russian businesspeople, as well as their forced and habitual reliance on connections.

More often in the 2000s than before, small businesses claim that they fear competition more than red tape (*BBC News World Edition*, 6, 2003).[37] However optimistic it may sound, in reality it does not mean that there is less red tape and that businesses have switched the freed resources to cost-cutting production methods or to boosting product and customer service quality. Following an unsettling standoff in the beginning of the transition, business and bureaucracy have now found a way to be partners. These partnerships are precisely the competition that businesses are most afraid of. And if businesses do try to cut costs, they usually look for a better connection to forgo a larger portion of tax, to pay less for a licence, to privatize yet another piece of state property for a pittance, or to lobby local government for government contracts, subsidies and special regulations against competitors.

Russia is still not a consumer-oriented market, and the question of lack of any substantial middle class remains nascent. In the 1990s many professionals abandoned their low-paid positions in health care, science and so on, for more lucrative market opportunities, such as taxi driving. In the early 2000s government expenditure on administration as a share of GDP started growing, which increased the number of bureaucrats, arriving at almost 30 per cent of non-market employment in 2004 (Illarionov, 2006, especially slides 21–25). In the 2000s the state broke up the petroleum company Yukos – a smart move politically, but not economically. Long-term investor confidence is still very low in Russia. There is little incentive to invest in R&D. Both of these are significant variables effecting long-term economic growth.

NOTES

1. My grandfather was scorned by his friends and considered quite foolish for refusing a job at Petersburg customs; this was usually a one-time life opportunity because connections to customs 'Human Resource Department' were too valuable.
2. Private interviews in August 2005.
3. Looting behaviour and pay-offs were, of course, different for clothes and electronics.
4. Direct link to chapters from the book at http://liberal.ru/Library_DisplayBook. asp?Rel=9.
5. These conclusions are based on my respondents' practices and personal observations and experiences during my visit to Russia in 2005 and follow-up telephone interviews.
6. Overall figures, some demographics, and turnover of bureaucrats at different government levels are mentioned in the previous chapter.
7. For more businesses and bureaucracy, see ibid. (pp. 181–91).
8. With the new Land Code (2002) and new law on licensing, the business climate has presumably become friendlier (Berglof et al., 2003, pp. 103–4).
9. For vivid examples, see interviews in Klyamkin and Timofeev (2000) at http://liberal.ru/ Library_DisplayBook.asp?Rel=9.
10. Interviews in Klyamkin and Timofeev (2000) at http://liberal.ru/Library_DisplayBook. asp?Rel=9. INDEM (Russian NGO – Information Science for Democracy) estimates that corruption has increased four-fold in the first half of the 2000s (Kostikov, 2005, p. 4).
11. A number of studies show that connections affect the performance of firms and agents in the market, for example, Steen (2000). A careful study, although with a small sample size, found that strong ties do not facilitate firms' better performance, while the weak ties do increase sales (Batjargal, 2000).
12. Support from Berkeley–Duke émigré survey. For an acute sociological portrait of a Soviet worker and his economic attitudes, see Ryvkina (2001, pp. 107–18).
13. It is perhaps worth noting that this enforcing power was concentrated in the hands of the few and was redirected to benefit a narrow circle of politicians and rising oligarchs.
14. This also refers to the period of mafia capitalism of the 1990s. Space prohibits me from discussing it here in detail.
15. The catch was that the distributor's licence was given for a fee.
16. Many respondents during my visit in 2005 said they still had to work hard after they had got the job.
17. This does not mean that these contracts are mostly moneyless – INDEM carried out a survey across Russian regions and estimated corruption in industry to be at about $30 billion, with most significant side payments in health and education (Jack, 2004, p. 39).

18. In an interview to the magazine *Chelovek i trud*, Varshavskaia (2001) cited the results of an opinion poll, which indicated that in the early 2000s at least 15–17 per cent of the urban population was employed in the underground market. Forty per cent of self-employed were not officially registered. Together with secondary employment, which was very common, the unregistered self-employment rose to 54 per cent. More than half of the illegally employed were in trade and food industries, 20 per cent in service industries. Goskomstat reported that informal economic activity was especially present in agriculture, trade, industry, transportation and investment. For instance, industrial output had to be corrected upwards by 12–13 per cent (7–9 per cent for illegal production, 5–4 per cent for other unregistered economic activity). For 2000 the correction was estimated to be 12.7 per cent, for 2001, 12.4 per cent (www.gks.ru/news/Tezis/1705.doc). In spite of optimistic reports, for example, by Moscow-based think tank CEFIR that 'for the first time since the collapse of communism, Russian companies are more afraid of their competitors than of the government' (BBC News, 2003), the size of informal economic activity is expected to remain large and the use of networks important. RIA Novosti news agency reported that in 2005 more than 80 per cent officially registered businesses turned out to be fictitious (*Metro*, 2005, p. 2). My respondents indicated that much of the business is either black or grey market operation (author's interviews, August 2005).

19. Black cash practices are easier to use for small to medium-size firms (Yakovlev, 2001).

20. The insurance market is still underdeveloped and manufacturers' or store warranties are not popular.

21. A 2000 survey showed that state ownership retains 42 per cent of industrial enterprises, AO (a joint-stock company, *aktsionernoe obshchestvo* in Russian) with state participation is 33 per cent and AO without state participation – 25 per cent (Ryvkina, 2001, p. 341). As Kaufmann and Kaliberda (1996, p. 4) correctly note, state and non-state economic activities coexist and many unofficial activities extract resources from the state.

22. Forward and backward integration occurred more often than horizontal. For an analysis of Russian holdings, see Avdasheva (2000, Chapter 4).

23. For more details on FIGs, see ibid. (2000, Chapter 5).

24. Usually in a very complicated fashion, for examples see Avdasheva (2000, pp. 104, 109, 112).

25. The consumption basket indicates only slightly larger caloric intake for Russians than Americans (Zherebin and Romanov, 2002, p. 65). Russians on average have a much more physically active and stressful life, which was noted by Igor Birman already in the 1980s. Food expenditures took over 50 per cent of household income in 1998 (ibid., p. 238). For an analysis of food prices, composition of the consumption basket, and regional variations in consumption patterns, see also Tikhomirov (2000, pp. 179–86). In 1996 an average Muscovite could purchase four to five times more than a person living in the poor region of Russia (ibid., p. 184). For percentages of population below the poverty line in the 1990s, see Zherebin and Romanov (2002, p. 125, Table 5.3). The numbers in 1998 are lower than the numbers in 1992; however, this may be explained by the older, and mostly disadvantaged, people gradually dying off.

26. The figure of 46.5 per cent is likely downward biased as unofficial incomes are not featured in the official statistics. Although many poor households supplemented with unofficial income as well, the magnitude would be much smaller than in the category of the rich.

27. Detailed analysis in Zherebin and Romanov (2002, pp. 277–99). On poverty, see ibid. (pp. 302–9); only 5.8 per cent belong to the category earning around $80,000 per household member (ibid., p. 312); the middle class of entrepreneurs comprises approximately 7–15 per cent of total population (ibid., p. 328). Russian researchers put around 20 per cent into a loosely defined category of middle class, and only about 7 per cent as its stable core (Maleva, 2003, p. 432).

28. On wage arrears, see Tikhomirov (2000, pp. 202–20).

29. Shifts in occupational wages were significant as well; for more details, see Tikhomirov (2000, pp. 194–202). Several papers use the Russia Longitudinal Monitoring Survey (RLMS) to estimate economic conditions in Russia. For a study from 1992 to 2004, see Mroz, Henderson and Popkin (2005).
30. Registered wage income does not account for all income in Russia, some additional income may come from bribes, side business, investments and social payments, in the latter case most are received by the already disadvantaged categories, such as the pensioners and invalids.
31. For more figures, see also World Bank Russian Economic Report (2007, p. 13).
32. On the city of contrast, see Baker and Glasser (2005, p. 140 and Chapter 7).
33. For figures, see Illarionov (2006). Andrei Illarionov is the former economic advisor to the president of Russia.
34. Capital flight has been steadily increasing in the five years since 2000 (Illarionov, 2006). My recent telephone follow-ups indicate that despite the seeming economic stability, Russian mid-level businesspeople are still more interested in investing in resort properties in Europe rather than in domestic manufacturing.
35. In 2005–06 the lion share of FDI was in 'other' investments with 74.8 and 69.4 per cent respectively, that is, commercial and other credits, which presumably includes credits to the government sector as well (*Russia'2007*, pp. 41–2). Curiously, the solid leader among countries investing in Russia in 2006 was Cyprus, followed by the United Kingdom (*Russia'2007*, p. 42). A lot of Russia's profit from illegally acquired assets was channelled to Cyprus in the 1990s and 2000s.
36. Ironically, this resonates with Walter Williams's statement where he equates roaches and humans in their economic rationality. Walter Williams is John M. Olin Distinguished Professor of Economics at George Mason University, VA and Townhall.com columnist.
37. The survey, conducted by the Centre for Economic and Financial Research (CEFIR) in partnership with the World Bank, reports that businesses complain less about red tape, not that there is less of it. There is large regional variation; St Petersburg and Moscow saw an increase in bureaucracy.

10. Networks and post-Soviet culture

In the transition period most people found themselves in an economic and social vacuum. Both new economic strategies and new social values emerged in the midst of the destruction of the Soviet legacy, the resurrection of the pre-revolutionary legacy and the introduction of Western norms. Different generations and different social strata adapted each in its own way to these changes, which determined the nature of their interaction in economic and social spheres, shaped the system of post-Soviet social networks and ultimately, defined the relationship between markets and hierarchies.

MORES IN THE 1990S AND THE 2000S: A DISJOINT SOCIETY

Russian society, held together by the informal networks and corruption, faced a shock in the 1990s. The presence of the state and, particularly bureaucracy, in everyday affairs remained overwhelming. The leadership legalized markets but provided no governance, which allowed opportunists and bureaucrats to make easy money. The formula 'everything is possible' transformed into 'everything is permissible'.[1] 'Those with connections now not only have money, but also spend it without shame. And those that have money usually have influence – or the ability to bribe their way out of trouble' (Jack, 2004, p. 28).[2]

Many in Russia still view free-for-all freedom, with no rules, as the only alternative to totalitarianism. It would appear that the presumption among Russians about the nature of humankind and about social contract is Hobbesian, not Lockeian. The belief is that the human being by nature is not a social animal, and that society cannot exist except by the power of a state. Charles Rowley (1996, pp. 6–7) points out that for a society that has focused its concerns on the Hobbesian spectrum between anarchy and totalitarianism it is all but impossible to relocate its concerns onto the Lockeian spectrum ranging from freedom to dictatorship.

Ironically, Lenin's interpretation of the capitalist state – exploitation of the many for the benefits of the few – was correct, in fact is correct to this day, in describing the order of things in Russia. 'Capitalism' of the 1990s meant corruption, theft, impoverishment and mafia:

> For managers, workers, and pensioners in the older generation, the 'market' was a source of great stress, indeed some alien creature that invaded their lives, attacking the body of society, disrupting all they knew, and devaluing their experience, throwing into question the very rationales that had governed their lives and justified their sufferings. (Yergin and Stanislaw, 1998, p. 282)

The distorted concept gained a strong foothold in the minds of Russians. 'New capitalist' ventures, such as cooperatives in the 1980s and early 1990s gained public antipathy. 'The coops were widely perceived as mere shelters for black marketers seeking to launder their ill-gotten gains. Surveys showed that while 14 per cent of the population used coops regularly (and another 37 per cent occasionally), only 38 per cent thought that they were a good idea' (Rutland, 1993, p. 216).[3] Problems of the 1990s led to over-romanticization of the past, even the terror, and to a costly misunderstanding of the nature of democracy and free market.

Since the mid-1980s practically everyone has experienced a change in status. In a short amount of time the value of network property went up for some and plummeted for others. Structural holes in the networks widened and this opened an opportunity for many to improve their income – new social strata of opportunists emerged in the society. Again, these changes were not independent of the mentality of the agents. Given the Soviet social heritage, most people viewed themselves only as pieces on a chessboard in the game of government policy. This taught Russians to rely on alternatives to the state's distribution network for food and clothing and to fight their way through red tape. As they understood the value of strong ties and realized by trial and error that any bureaucratic favour can be bought, they learnt to disregard the formal law.

At the same time the state's heavy presence in social and economic affairs left the government an easy scapegoat to blame for the inefficiency of the social net. It also made public property a convenient (and a first-at-hand) economic resource to steal. Luneev (1999, p. 75) calls the Soviet predecessor of this phenomenon the 'psychology of "justified" embezzlement'.

The success of the free-market experiment in the 1990s demanded optimistic individuals, with an independent outlook and a healthy attitude towards government. There emerged many optimistic and *opportunistic* individuals who, however, did not believe that all must be equal in the eyes of the law. For those few who might have believed in equality, there was *no law* to fall back on while pursuing economic goals. Such incompatibility of economic opportunity and formal governance forced the majority to rely on either previously established connections or in general to apply familiar methods of networking to business transactions. Social networking between business and bureaucracy was so persistent that one of its informal practices – bribery – became ingrained as a norm for new businesspeople.[4]

With the changes taking place in the 1990s, the clash between the generations and the clash between the rich and the poor became inevitable. The new generation has pushed the older one out of modern economic life. Age discrimination in hiring is widespread. There are tensions within firms where 20-year-olds manage people twice as old. Whether the young generation, raised and educated in the time of easy money of the 1980s and 1990s,[5] and moral vacuum of the early 2000s, possesses the right human values for building a free-market society is questionable.

As Avinash Dixit correctly points out, many social norms do not evolve completely spontaneously, but instead are a conscious choice of individuals to instil these norms into the minds of citizens with the help of educators, public figures, media and parents (Dixit, 2004, p. 7). One would expect, or at least hope, that the initial distribution of property in a transition economy would single out a group of people with a free-market 'bias', perhaps even classical liberal views. Presumably the fruits of their labour would give them understanding, incentives and financial resources to promote free-market values among the general public.

But the choice set of social norms that Dixit talks about was limited by the already socially accepted alternatives. The initial group of propertied elite in Russia did not have classical liberal roots and, therefore, had different goals and incentives.[6] When selling off the state's assets in the 1990s, Chubais (see Chapter 9) perhaps was hoping that eventually the haves, regardless of how they became the haves, would help fight for property rights and justice for all. History has yet to make him right. Honesty in business, respect for law and for customers, and openness to new ideas were not among the values on the propaganda list; nationalism, however, was.

IDEAS AND THE ERA OF NASHE

Ideas spread differently in Russia than in the United States. Ideas do not originate with the academics in Russia. They originate partially with the political trends[7] and partially with more creative professions, such as theatre directors, writers, TV commentators,[8] and are consequently spread to the public through media, books and films.

Post-2000 it became respectable to be Russian again. Propaganda of '*nashe*' – 'ours' – appeared, such as the radio station *Nashe*, created by Kozyrev (Baker and Glasser, 2005, p. 64).[9] Russians were unhappy with their national identity of the 1990s – that of an impoverished and unsuccessful country. The era of *nashe*, when it became adequate to recognize the achievements of the Soviet science and culture and be proud again, appealed to the people much more (ibid., p. 65).[10]

In the 1990s Russians were lost and they turned retrospective. Future viewed through the past – such has been the trend since the late 1980s (Elfimov, 2003). I would argue that retrospective attitude and glorification of the past was reinforced by the government. As Elfimov notes, it is much less costly to reconstruct a historical landmark than to undertake a public project, such as repair of roads. Rebuilding an old church, like the Church of Christ the Saviour in Moscow, 'paradoxically attracts more social attention and approval, for people normally tend to take for granted the duty of the government to perform public works or carry out social reforms' (ibid., p. 74). Deteriorating historical landmarks should not be ignored, but I agree with Elfimov's point that in many ways cultural restoration came to determine the progress of national life (ibid., p. 82), and often serves as a convenient distraction from social and economic problems. Elfimov cites Karl Popper here quite appropriately – the 'encompassing positivist cultural-historical morality . . . makes "a moral criticism of the existing state of affairs impossible, since this state itself determines the moral standard of things"' (ibid., p. 102).

The campaign of *nashe* has indeed been successful. 'Before 1998, according to the firm Comcon, only 48 per cent of Russians said they preferred to buy domestic goods when considering quality and not just price. By 1999 that figure was 90 per cent' (Baker and Glasser, 2005, p. 70).[11] The ratings of the president inevitably went up, as well as the acceptance of government policies.

There is, of course, nothing wrong with healthy patriotism. The Russian trend though is alarming in two respects. First, the Russian sense of uniqueness and fear of foreign have been reinforced (the concept of 'otherness' has resurfaced once again). In a way the disagreement between Westerners and Slavophiles has been revived. Russians have a bipolar attitude to Western values – they desire the Western style of life and at the same time hate many of its attributes.[12] Opposition of 'theirs', Russian, as opposed to 'alien', Western, has been growing, and can potentially restrict the positive effects of globalization. In fact, cultivating chauvinism would be the best strategy against the influence of ideas from abroad now that borders cannot be shut. Second, a swelling national pride prevents a Russian from criticizing the authorities and legitimizes the game where individuals are reduced to pieces on the chessboard.[13]

Popular literature is much more telling about the ideas driving the society in Russia than in the West. Perhaps as the downside of globalization, most books cater to an average reader's poor language and primitive themes, but the main idea in both high- and low-quality fiction is the nullity of a human being.[14] An observation and a motto from this literature, which prompts a pessimistic outlook, is that the pawns and the higher-valued pieces on the chessboard are all conscious of accepting their role. Hierarchical networks propagate this acceptance because they provide an alternative way to improve or maintain an individual's standard of living.

Just recently, after the results of the presidential election of 2008 were announced, the head of the country's election commission, Vladimir Churov, had warm words of praise for the vote, saying: 'There is no more open, more transparent, and more organized election system than the election system of the Russian Federation' (Coalson, 2008). Ironically, it is all true.

Kim Zigfeld reflected on the opinions of Russians about truth and justice in their own country after the 2007 Duma elections on *PubliusPundit*: 'On the one hand, one can see that there are still brilliant and creative people in Russia who are willing to stand up to power on behalf of truth and democracy. On the other, there's no indication whatsoever that the mass population has any intention of listening to them' (Zigfeld, 2008). Never has, I would add.

Passivity even among the very rich is quite common nowadays in Russia. The oligarchs' union (the Union of Industrialists and Entrepreneurs) decided to abandon Khodorkovsky and not to protest his arrest. By the account of one of the oligarchs it was 'worse than capitulation' (Baker and Glasser, 2005, p. 292). Nevertheless it was done, because the 18 richest Russians were afraid for themselves. When NTV was taken over by the state, most journalists barricaded themselves inside Ostankino TV centre. There were several supporters in the street who held out for 11 days. But the country on the whole seemed indifferent (ibid., pp. 79, 97), possibly because they thought any undertaking useless.

SOCIAL COHESION

Some of the most commonly shared values in Russia today are national pride, a future seen through the past and a belief that strong ties and money solve most problems. Vertical networks are one of the obstacles to creating social cohesion in Russia. As Dixit writes, in the absence of an external governance mechanism, trust within a group is needed to enforce contracts. Intergroup cohesiveness is reached at the expense of intragroup cohesiveness (Dixit, 2004, p. 40). The weaker the external governance, the stronger intergroup cohesiveness is required, and the stronger will be the hostility between groups in the society, the less weak ties will be formed and smaller amount of them will be bridges. Partially because of the latter and partially because many lives are still dominated by mere survival there can be found little of networks of civic engagement, and in this sense collectivism has not been replaced by the social cohesion.[15] Transaction costs of transition from intergroup to intragroup cohesiveness are simply too high.

There are many examples showing the unwillingness and the inability of Russians of varying income and social status to work together towards a common goal, especially when opportunism is present. One example is the failure to form effective condo associations (TCJ is the Russian acronym). Everyone is encouraged to join TCJs because the local city governments want to redirect responsibility for renovations to the residents. Those who reside in older buildings, are resentful of joining TCJs. Older structures require large (private!) finances and skilful organization to restore adequate living conditions (Ganiushkina, 2005). Apartment residents often lack finances, let alone organization.

The 'uneven' privatization, when the government, for a small fee, allowed citizens to privatize apartments where they had been officially assigned to reside, ignored the market value of these apartments. Such a non-market move was probably the most 'fair' and politically prudent at the moment. But it created large income inequalities between residents in the same building, and any private efforts by the rich to improve the conditions of the building meet with envy and resentment. Often, the improvements are vandalized.[16]

Besides private governance and private social organizations, another way to promote social cohesion is through consumer culture. But cohesion does not simply increase after an exchange between a consumer and a store clerk at the register. Consumers need larger participation in the production and selling process by knowing that their opinion is taken into account. There has to be a procedure to vote out bad businesses, such as through participation in the market of shares. Public participation in the shares market is low in Russia, and the distrust toward companies on the part of the general public is not unfounded. By Khodorkovsky's own words, for example, his bank Menatep needed shareholders only to prevent the state from cracking down on the venture, as it would produce a public outcry then (Hoffman, 2002, p. 123).

THE RULE OF LAW

The Soviet personal networks provided an alternative to the central distribution of goods and services. They also acted as an alternative method of governance and a trust bank. Post-Soviet government offered no effective legal framework for economic activity and contract enforcement. Both hierarchical and horizontal networks were shaken up, and for a time in the 1990s their effectiveness somewhat dropped following the rise in externalities, imperfect information and quickly changing market conditions. With trust banks running half empty, people found themselves as hostile agents in economic and social settings and were not able to form a socially cohesive society. This tottering society persists to the present, despite the unifying, yet superficial sense of national pride. Historically, a society without social cohesion and rule of law has not been able to effectively support free-market institutions.

Moreover, there cannot be social cohesion in the society where the state does not respect individual rights and when public officials can arbitrarily select winners and losers.[17] A rich person, standing in the way of politics, can become a beggar overnight.[18] In the Russians' mentality nowadays, it is *normal* to expect an arrest[19] for a public expression of an idea disapproved of by the authorities or to expect an oppositional newspaper to be closed down.[20]

Often, the authorities do not act illegally because *they* write the law.[21] Some businesses lobby to write regulations. Yet others lobby politicians not to act, so as to preserve the status quo and protect the existing property rights. As McChesney points out, 'Status as a legislator confers a property right not only to create political rents but also to impose costs that would destroy private rents. In order to protect these returns, private owners have an incentive to strike bargains with legislators' (McChesney 1997, p. 41).

The courts are also unable to resolve consumer complaints efficiently. When the terms of the contract are not fulfilled by the provider, not many resort to courts because they presume a long, costly and ultimately lost battle. Those who go to court get just that.[22]

Both a mutually consistent set of laws and a belief by the population in the enforcement of these laws is important (Litwack, 1991, p. 78). There are cases where local courts ignore the Supreme Court rulings.[23] And common law (judge-made law) is not practised in Russia – a previous ruling is not referred to in a new case with similar circumstances unless the parties are the same. Such instances are a rule rather than exception in contemporary Russia, and discourage the belief in the fairness of 'economic legality'.[24]

Logic points to private arbitration, which uses information and enforcement mechanisms often not feasible to gather or implement by a formal court at a low cost. But in Russia, private arbitration that could lay the foundations of the rule of law is absent. Such private arbitration as between businesses with mafia as an enforcer is outright criminal. Semi-private arbitration as between law firms, businesses and the government resembles collusion. It lacks formality, equal and fair treatment of the parties, and favours the strongest, the most cunning and the most connected.

IN CONCLUSION: NETWORKS' VERDICT

Ultimately, it is the economic agents who will sentence the strong ties to death. In some areas, personal networks have already become redundant, in others, such as the labour market, they can often be a hindrance. In the seller's market though, which Russia still is,[25] repeated dealings do not guarantee honest behaviour on the part of the seller. Strong ties are an alternate form of guarantee. They are also an alternative governance mechanism. In need of an efficient formal law, public law in Russia could in theory adopt private arbitration mechanisms. But currently there is nothing adaptable. The fact that formal law is so underdeveloped and informal agreements, which are country-specific are so prevalent, may be detrimental to long-term investment and integration into the international economy.[26]

Shocks to the system cannot kill the propensity to trade or nullify the benefits of exchange. They can, however, corrupt it. If the economy does not experience negative shocks consistently it is possible that strong ties will eventually lose their importance. Every time the system encounters a shock though, it falls back on personal networks instead of a formal rule of law, thus giving personal networks a new cycle of life.

Undoubtedly, personal networks have proved invaluable to the Russians. They remove many obstacles on the way to private economic activity and permit the realization of some gains of exchange. However, as an institution they are not supportive of the rule of law and of free markets where *impersonal* exchange is prevalent – in that lies the weakness of strong ties.

NOTES

1. Jack (2004, p. 38) quotes a French analyst, Jacques Sapir.
2. A minister was fired from the government, shortly after he built an Olympic-size swimming pool costing $1 000 000 (Jack, 2004, p. 29).
3. A number of cooperatives in the beginning were indeed set up by mafia and many became monopolies because the shortages permitted them to charge exorbitant prices. Thus, they earned a bad name from low-income buyers (Matusevich, 1992, pp. 49, 53). A study by Shiller, Boycko and Koronov (1991), investigating popular attitudes toward free markets in Moscow and New York City by the means of telephone interviews in 1990, found that Americans and Russians are not too different in their attitudes, although Russians have less of a positive attitude, for instance to individual entrepreneurship and have less belief in entrepreneurs' honesty. As much as this can suggest

    capitalization of the Soviet Union, it can suggest *socialization* of America. Moscow also stands out in its development. The survey had been taken before the wild privatization of the 1990s when a lot of people developed a negative attitude towards large business and banking.

4.   Russian businesspeople themselves approve of the practice. They define the scope of 'legal, justified' bribes as those that are predictable, negotiated or contracted for ahead of time, and 'illegal, unjustified' as those that are not agreed upon prior to the deal.

5.   For a good study of the values of a younger generation in the end of the 1990s, see Kliger (1999, Chapter 22).

6.   See Chapter 7 of this volume on the new elite's background.

7.   Such as nationalism.

8.   For a discussion, see Elfimov (2003, pp. 10–11).

9.   Kozyrev claims his notion of *nashe* was meant to be patriotic not nationalistic. To his regret the more chauvinistic *nashe* has been winning so far; for more details see Baker and Glasser (2005, Chapter 3). For more on *nashe*, see Ivanova (2002). The title is roughly translated as *Nowstalgia*, which is a clever neologism invented by the author.

10.   The American scholars, conducting an opinion poll, concluded that there is no reason to assume that younger generation Russians embraced democracy. Not only a large number would vote for Stalin as the president (26 per cent), 15 per cent were not sure. Many young people approve of authoritarianism (Baker and Glasser, 2005, p. 357). *Poryadok*, order, was one of the most powerful attractions of Putin's presidential campaign (ibid., pp. 5–6). Pipes claims that Putin's popularity is linked to the unpopularity of a Western-style democracy. The citizens in Putin's state are relieved of political responsibility and forged into artificial unity by imaginary foreign enemies, cited in ibid. (2005, p. 376). Some enemies are made quite real though. Creating the threat of terrorism was exploited to quite a tragic extent. Chilling facts point to the Kremlin's involvement in bombings of the apartment buildings in 1999 and 2000 (Satter, 2003, pp. 24–33, 64–70).

11.   On the trends of Russian nationalism, from regionalist to heritage nationalism, see Tikhomirov (2000, pp. 311–17). The Russian Orthodox Church and the state found each other as natural allies in the process of encouraging the nationalistic tendencies among Russians.

12.   One instance of this is Kara-Murza's book *Manipuliatsiia soznaniem* (*Manipulation of Minds*) (2002).

13.   In the 2004 presidential elections many voted for Putin even if they did not like him, because they felt they had no other choice, there were no other real, capable contestants. At the time no one seemed to pose a question of why there are no other real contestants, or why they are not known. A simple suggestion would be that they are not allowed to be heard.

14.   Unlikely to be ordered by the state, this trend is nevertheless a reflection of today's perception of an individual as a piece on the chessboard both by the state and by the individual himself. Ironically, this perception is the quintessence of harmony between the state, the people and the Church. Examples of these works are Vladimir Sorokin's 'Russkaya babushka' in *Ochered'*, Moscow: Ad Marginem (2002), *Pir, Goluboe salo* in *Sobranie sochinenii*, Vol. 3, Moscow: Ad Marginem (2002); Viktor Pelevin's *Generation P*, Moscow: Vagrius (1999), and *Svyaschennaya kniga oborotnya*, Moscow: Eksmo (2004).

15.   It is questionable how much social cohesion collectivism provided. Envy played a large role in the Soviet society. Envy of higher incomes was carefully concealed (for an example and a discussion see Katsenelinboigen, 1978, pp. 148–51), but nevertheless it was there. It is obvious though that collectivist propaganda did provide a lot of sense of unity and common belonging and cooperation, for instance, on big industrial projects. Their usefulness is not evaluated here.

16.   Several of my respondents indicated this in August 2005. Those in newly constructed or relatively new buildings willingly, even enthusiastically, do join TCJs as they rightly expect nothing but negligence from the municipal organizations. They are, of course,

in a similar income category and are willing to work together. But they encounter discouragement from the local bureaucracy that does not wish to recognize the new TCJs' status. In August 2005 a boiler pipe broke in the attic of one of St Petersburg's newly constructed buildings. The emergency crew did not arrive for several hours, while the water in some apartments accumulated up to several inches, only because the local emergency department refused to recognize the new building as its responsibility and its board of residents as a legitimate organization who placed an emergency call (interview with Vladimir Frolov and Nadejda Frolova, August 2005). I was present at the meeting of the residents where they were deciding whether to sue the emergency department or the builder. After some discussion, they leaned toward not going to court because the prospects of success would be thin but decided to find the *right* lawyer or the *right* person in the administration to make appropriate arrangements for future emergencies.

17. A husband and wife, wealthy, by Russian standards, running a hotel business in Ivanovo, acknowledge in 2004 that 'everything is possible' as long as the right bribes are paid and the right officials are paid. They said: 'When we got property . . . we started to feel very insecure'. 'Because when you have property, there is always someone who wants to take it away from you', the husband added (Baker and Glasser, 2005, p. 321).

18. Khodorkovsky's case vividly proves it. In fact, Ryvkina noticed that entrepreneurs stopped being as open in interviews following 2000 (Ryvkina, 2001, p. 309).

19. Although without significant consequences so far.

20. For example, in Smolensk, see Baker and Glasser (2005, Chapter 12). For details on a temporary close-down of *Novye Izvestia* newspaper for 'Putinization of the Whole Country' article, see Aris (2003).

21. For an example of how the Moscow authorities colluded with one firm to monopolize the market of ritual services and drafted laws for Moscow parliament with the help of this firm's lawyers, see Coulloudon (2001, pp. 90–91).

22. For instance, one of the interviewees in 2005, Anatolii Astrelin, tried to sue the builder of his condo. After moving into their newly constructed condo in 2000, Mr Astrelin's family discovered that many of the construction contract specifications had not been fulfilled and many of the sanitary norms in the building do not conform even to Russian standards. The drinking water was polluted, the ventilation was inadequate and the construction parameters were violated which could make the building structurally unstable; for more details see Nikolaeva (2002, p. 3). Requests to the builder to correct the defects solicited no adequate response. In the consequent civil litigation judges followed neither the law nor the ruling of a higher instance, the Supreme Court; the minutes were falsified. Anatolii Astrelin formally complained about undue process, but the complaints were forwarded for resolution to those who he complained against (interview with Mr Astrelin, 11 August 2005).

23. This is what happened in Mr Astrelin's case. Even after Mr Astrelin had demonstrated to the Supreme Court the inconsistency between two pieces of legislature (the Civil Rights Code and the Law on Consumer Rights) and the Supreme Court had ruled to use the latter, local courts ignored it (interview with Mr Astrelin, 11 August 2005). More details on the deficiencies of the Russian formal legal system in Rubin (1997, Chapter 6).

24. For more on 'economic legality' in the post-Soviet economy, see Litwack (1991).

25. It is not the lack of goods that determines this now. Elimination of shortages does not eliminate the seller's market if the hard budget constraint is not there, as Kornai pointed out in *Economics of Shortage* (1980). The mentality of the Russian consumer is also such that he or she is a passive recipient of low quality, poor service and uncompetitive pricing.

26. One example of Maghribi versus Genoese traders comes to mind here. It is often cited in the institutional literature and law and economics literature, for example, in Dixit (2004, p. 65). Incidentally, relation-based governance works best in small groups bound by family relations, *ethnic* or linguistic ties, as pointed out by Dixit (2004, p. 66). The campaign of *nashe* emphasizes the ethnic and linguistic ties.

11. Conclusion: the reality of Russian political economy

This book presents a description of the events in Russian political economic history since the 10th century to the present with particular attention to how hierarchies prevailed over markets in resource allocation. My goal was to provide a sensible and balanced account of how Russia has arrived at its current state. Since Russian statistics are inherently unreliable and qualitative evidence is not all-inclusive, I have used a middle-ground approach where each complements the other. It is my hope that at the very minimum this book has provided an intellectually stimulating reading and brought a greater appreciation of the importance of freedom of choice in market interactions – a freedom that many Russians even now do not possess.

The wave of enthusiasm for political and economic reconstruction immediately following the collapse of the Soviet Union has subsided; it is now understood that Western values cannot produce the same result, when simply transplanted into a non-Western society. Several attempts to rebuild Russian institutions since then have failed as well. Intellectual aid, as in the case of US economists delegated to help the reconstruction of Russia failed. Support for Yeltsin in 1996 to help the country avoid the return of communism made the oligarchs even stronger.

When Putin raised a mallet over the oligarchs, he was praised by the West as a righteous fighter for democratic values, but failed to be recognized as a rising autocrat. Diplomacy through media relations failed. Human rights protests failed. Dissemination of free-market values through foreign direct investment failed as even global giants have to play by Russian rules. The dissemination of Western values through greater access to information and technology, such as through the Internet, has also failed as the Russian population remains still very susceptible to domestic propaganda and is self-censoring. Historically, public policies intended to alter the Russian economic or political system have proved to be insignificant compared with other institutional variables in the system.

Seventeen years since the collapse of the Soviet Union the institutional framework is being addressed more, but now the real danger of failure comes from political correctness in interpreting economic systems. In line with this current trend it is said that *different* forms of capitalism can coexist and produce some level of economic prosperity. Capitalism, however, amounts to much more than some form of private enterprise under state guidance. The economic institutions of capitalism presume private ownership of the means of production, free labour markets and prices, ease of starting a business and customer preferences as the decisive force behind who stays in the market and who goes. The smooth workings of capitalism must also rely on the rule of law. The social institutions of capitalism imply a set of norms that secure a certain level of trust to ease market transactions. None of these factors are present in contemporary Russia sufficiently to define it as capitalistic in any form.

Throughout its history, Russia has been a connection-based society, not a contract society, because strong ties have always played a large role. Rent seeking was part of the game as early as the formation of the Russian state, probably much like in other parts of the world. However, the especially strong grasp of the state in domestic economic affairs and foreign trade, the peculiar position of merchants as a class, as well as peculiar social norms prevalent in the Russian society made this practice a fruitful venture thereafter. The activity of monopolizing, though very often done with direct impudence, was never formally legal. Therefore, it derived support through hierarchies.

After centuries of monarchic feudalism, the economic hardship and failure of political leadership during World War I opened a path for Lenin's political extremism. As a result, the Soviet Union emerged as a heavily totalitarian power. Centralization, growing regulation of economic activity, and the system of privileges, which assigned an economic value to one's position of control over the allocation of goods and services, were added to economic shortages and government monopoly in the Soviet period. Under the Soviets, opportunism skyrocketed and hierarchical relationships evolved into a unified system interweaving practically all spheres of personal and economic life.

The collapse of the totalitarian state in 1991 presented a possibility of a market economy based on a Lockeian notion of the rule of law. But the people were still sufficiently feudal in their attitudes and sufficiently dulled by tyranny, so, instead, a Hobbesian Leviathan order followed.

Post-2000 Russia falls into a framework not exactly of a tyranny, but where the population still allows itself to be subjugated to autocracy. From here on, it is not clear in which direction the Russian society is headed, but history is far from promising. It is not my intention here to make policy recommendations on how to ensure that institutions of capitalism emerge, but I must point out that, historically, an autocrat in Russia who supports market institutions in practice is quite a rarity. In addition, authoritarianism shapes social networks in such a way that they are not supportive of a free-market environment.

In such circumstances, the future of Russia's political economy at this time is as uncertain now as it was in 1939 when Joseph Stalin hitched his skirts to those of Adolf Hitler in an unsuccessful attempt to destroy Western democracy. Updating Winston Churchill's famous quote about 1939 Russia: *Russia at this point in history is a Hobbesian society, wrapped in opportunism, inside an autocracy.*

Appendix A: war statistics

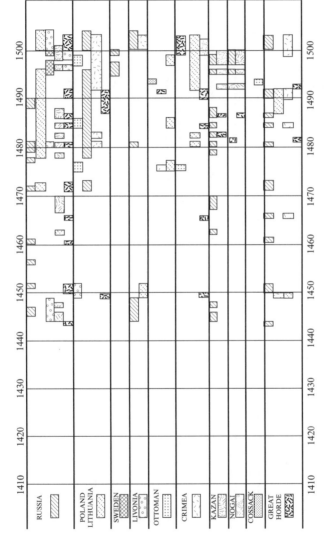

Source: War figures for the 15th through 18th century are compiled by John Sloan; see Xenophon Group International, http://www.xenophon-mil.org/rushistory/battles/ruswar.htm.

Figure A.1   Russia's wars of the 15th century

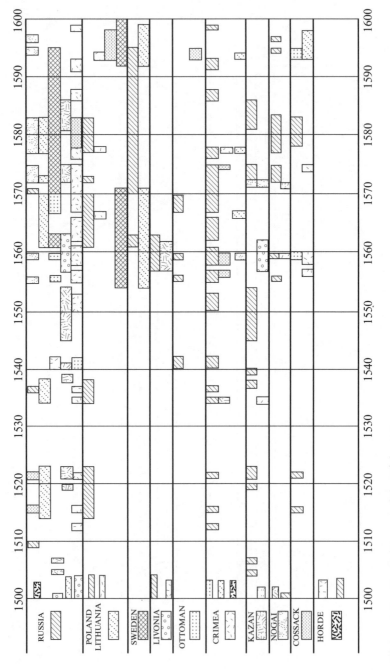

Figure A.2   Russia's wars of the 16th century

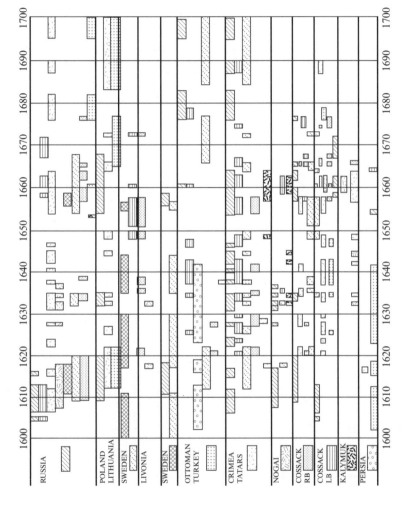

Figure A.3   Russia's wars of the 17th century

209

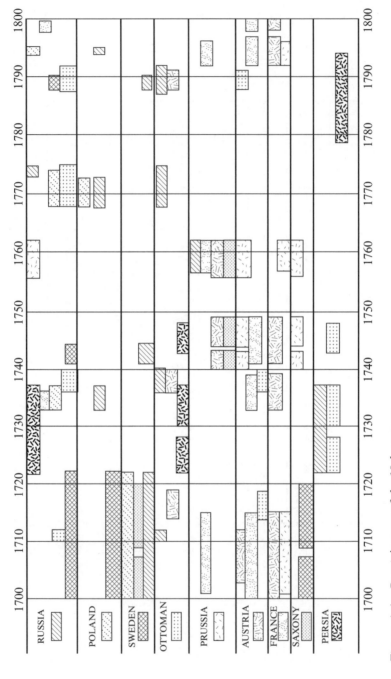

Figure A.4   Russia's wars of the 18th century

Blum, J. (1961), *Lord and Peasant in Russia from the Ninth to the Nineteenth Century*, Princeton, NJ: Princeton University Press.

Boettke, P.J. (1988), 'The Political Economy of Soviet Socialism, 1918–1928', an unpublished PhD thesis, George Mason University.

Boettke, P.J. (1993), *Why Perestroika Failed*, New York: Routledge.

Boettke, P.J. (2001), *Calculation and Coordination*, New York: Routledge.

Bokhanov, A.N. (1994), *Delovaia elita Rossii, 1914 g.*, Moscow: Institut rossiiskoi istorii RAN.

Boycko, M., A. Shleifer and R. Vishny ([1995] 1996), *Privatizing Russia*, Cambridge, MA: The MIT Press.

Brady, R. (1999), *Kapitalism: Russia's Struggle to Free its Economy*, New Haven, CT and London: Yale University Press.

Brovkin, V. (1998), *Russia after Lenin: Politics, Culture and Society, 1921–1929*, New York: Routledge.

Brower, D.R. (1990), *The Russian City between Tradition and Modernity, 1850–1900*, Berkeley and Los Angeles, CA: University of California Press.

Brumfield, William Craft, Boris V. Anan'ich and Yuri A. Petrov (eds) (2001), *Commerce in Russian Urban Culture, 1861–1914*, Washington, DC: Woodrow Wilson Center Press.

Brzezinski, M. (2002), *Casino Moscow: A Tale of Greed and Adventure on Capitalism's Wildest Frontier*, New York: Touchstone.

Burt, Ronald S. (1992), *Structural Holes: The Social Structure of Competition*, Cambridge, MA: Harvard University Press.

Bushkovitch, P. (1980), *The Merchants of Moscow, 1580–1650*, New York: Cambridge University Press.

Carr, E.H. ([1952] 1980), *The Bolshevik Revolution*, 3 vols, New York: Norton.

Chernyh, P.Y. (2002), *Istoriko-etimologicheskii slovar' sovremennogo russkogo iazyka*, 2 vols, Moscow: Russkii Iazyk.

Chernyi biznes razvitogo sotsializma: Tsekhoviki (2005), documentary on channel Rossiia, 3 August.

Clark, K. (1993), 'Engineers of Human Souls in an Age of Industrialization: Changing Cultural Models, 1929–41', in William G. Rosenberg and Lewis H. Siegelbaum (eds), *Social Dimensions of Soviet Industrialization*, Bloomington, IN: Indiana University Press, pp. 248–64.

Coalson, R. (2008), 'Russia: How the Kremlin Manages to Get the Right Results', in *RFE/RL*, http://www.rferl.org/featuresarticle/2008/03/6d7990a4-5217-4b82-b685-3ec7435ed2bf.html, 7 March.

Coase, R.H. (1937), 'The Nature of the Firm', *Economica*, New Series, **4** (16), 386–405.

Appendix B: distribution of serfs around Moscow

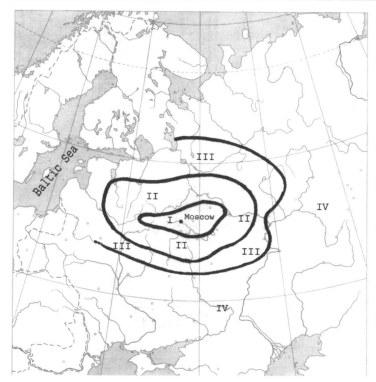

Note: Based on population census of 1782. Borders are approximate. The proportional relations between the populations in these regions were, of course, in place much earlier.

Region I: Moskovskaia guberniia – 66%; Vladimirskaia guberniia – 67%.
Region II: Smolenskaia, Kalujskaia, Tul'skaia, Ryazanskaia, Nijegorodskaia, Kostromskaia, Yaroslavskaia, Pskovskaia gubernii – 83–69%; Tverskaia – 64%.
Region III: Orlovskaia, Saratovskaia, Tambovskaia, Pensenskaia, Simbirskaia, Novgorodskaia gubernii – 68–45%; Vologodskaia – 34%.

Source: Kliuchevskii (1959, Vol. 6, pp. 407–8).

Figure B.1   Distribution of serfs around Moscow

Bibliography

Adams, J.S. (1977), *Citizen Inspectors in the Soviet Union: The People's Control Committee*, New York: Praeger Publishers.

Adams, Mark B. (2000), *Networks in Action: The Kruschev Era, the Cold War, and the Transformation of Soviet Science*, Trondheim Studies on East European Cultures and Societies, Vol. 3, Trondheim, Norway: Norwegian University of Science and Technology.

Alexeev, Michael V. and A. Sayer (1987), 'The Second Economy Market for Foreign Made Goods in the USSR', in Gregory Grossman and Vladimir G. Treml (eds), 'Studies on the Soviet Second Economy', *Berkeley–Duke Occasional Papers on the Second Economy in the USSR*, No. 11, December.

Allilueva, S. ([1967] 1968), *Dvadtsat' pisem k drugu*, New York: Harper & Row Publishers.

Anan'ich, B. and S. Beliaev (2001), 'St. Petersburg: Banking Center', in William Craft Brumfield, Boris V. Anan'ich and Yuri A. Petrov (eds), *Commerce in Russian Urban Culture, 1861–1914*, Washington, DC: Woodrow Wilson Center Press, Chapter 1.

Anderson, G.M. and P.J. Boettke (1997), 'Soviet Venality: A Rent-seeking Model of the Communist State', *Public Choice*, **93** (1–2), 37–53.

Arbatov, Z. (1990), 'Ekaterinoslav 1917–22 gg.', in *Literatura Russkogo Zarubezh'ia*, Vol. 1, Book 2, Moscow: Kniga, pp. 88–127.

Aris, B. (2003), 'Newspaper Shut for Lampoon of Putin', Telegraph.co.uk.

Avdasheva, S. (2000), *Khoziaistvennye sviazi v rossiiskoi promyshlennosti*, Moscow: Gosudarstvennyi universitet, Vysshaia shkola ekonomiki.

Baker, P. and S. Glasser (2005), *Kremlin Rising: Vladimir Putin's Russia and the End of Revolution*, New York: A Lisa Drew Book/Scribner.

Ball, A.M. (1987), *Russia's Last Capitalists: The Nepmen, 1921–1929*, Los Angeles, CA: University of California Press.

Banerji, A. (1997), *Merchants and Markets in Revolutionary Russia*, New York: St. Martin's Press in association with the Centre for Russian and East European Studies, University of Birmingham.

Barghoorn, F. (1960), 'Some Russian Images of the West', in Cyril E. Black (ed.), *The Transformation of Russian Society: Aspects of Social Change since 1861*, Cambridge, MA: Harvard University Press, pp. 574–87.

Baron, Samuel H. (1978), 'Entrepreneurs and Entrepreneurship in Sixteenth/Seventeenth-century Russia', *Conference on Entrepreneurship and Economic Innovation in Russia/Soviet Union*, **49**, 16–18 November, Washington, DC.

Baron, Samuel H. (1980), *Muscovite Russia: Collected Essays*, London: Variorum Reprints.

Baron, Samuel H. (1983), 'Entrepreneurs and Entrepreneurship in Sixteenth/Seventeenth-century Russia', in Gregory Guroff and Fred V. Carstensen (eds), *Entrepreneurship in Imperial Russia and the Soviet Union*, Princeton, NJ: Princeton University Press, pp. 27–58.

Batjargal, B. (December 2000), 'Social Capital and Entrepreneurial Performance in Russia: A Panel Study', Davidson Institute Working Papers, No. 352, http://www.bus.umich.edu/KresgeLibrary/Collections/Workingpapers/wdi/wp352.pdf.

Baumol, William J., Robert E. Litan and Carl J. Schramm (2007), *Good Capitalism, Bad Capitalism, and the Economics of Growth and Prosperity*, New Haven, CT: Yale University Press.

BBC News World Edition (2003), 'Red Tape is Receding, Russian Firms Say', 6 February.

Beliaev, S. (2001), 'Funded Loans in Petersburg and the Development of the Municipal Infrastructure, 1875–1916', in William Craft Brumfield, Boris V. Anan'ich and Yuri A. Petrov (eds), *Commerce in Russian Urban Culture, 1861–1914*, Washington, DC: Woodrow Wilson Center Press, Chapter 3.

Berglof, E., A. Kunov, Y. Shvets and K. Yudaeva (2003), *The New Political Economy of Russia*, Cambridge, MA: The MIT Press.

Berliner, J.S. (1952), 'The Informal Organization of the Soviet Firm', *Quarterly Journal of Economics*, **66** (3), 342–65.

Berliner, J.S. (1957), *Factory and Manager in the USSR*, Cambridge, MA: Harvard University Press.

Berliner, J.S. (1962), 'The Informal Organization of the Soviet Firm', Franklyn D. Holzman (ed.), *Readings on the Soviet Economy*, Chicago: Rand McNally & Company, pp. 408–31.

Berliner, J.S. (1976), *The Innovation Decision in Soviet Industry*, Cambridge, MA: MIT Press.

Birman, I. (1983), *Ekonomika nedostach*, New York: Chalidze Publications.

Birman, I. (1988), 'The Imbalance of the Soviet Economy', *Soviet Studies*, **40** (2), 210–21.

Birman, I. (1989), *Personal Consumption in the USSR and the USA*, New York: St. Martin's Press.

Blackwell, W.L. (1976), 'Modernization and Urbanization in Russia: A Comparative View', in M. Hamm (ed.), *The City in Russian History*, Lexington, KY: The University Press of Kentucky, pp. 291–330.

Cochrane, John H. and Barry W. Ickes (1995), 'Macroeconomics in Russia', in Edward P. Lazear (ed.), *Economic Transition in Eastern Europe and Russia: Realities of Reform*, Stanford, CA: Hoover Institution Press, pp. 65–106.

Coulloudon, V. (2001), 'Moscow City Management: A New Form of Russian Capitalism?', in P. Rutland (ed.), *Business and State in Contemporary Russia*, Boulder, CO: Westview Press, pp. 89–100.

Country Report, Russia (2007), New Zealand Ministry of Foreign Affairs & Trade, http://www.mfat.govt.nz/Foreign-Relations/Europe/0-russiaecoreport-dec07.php, December.

Demidova, N.F. (1987), *Sluzhilaia biurokratiia v Rossii XVII v. i ee rol' v formirovanii absolutisma*, Moscow: Nauka.

Demkin, A.V. (1999), *Kupechestvo i gorodskoi rynok v Rossii vo vtoroi chetverti XVIII veka*, Moscow: Institut rossiiskoi istorii RAN.

de Soto, Hernando (1990), *The Other Path: The Invisible Revolution in the Third World*, New York: Perennial Library.

de Soto, Hernando (2000), *The Mystery of Capital*, New York: Basic Books.

Di Tella, R., S. Galiani and E. Schargrodsky (2005), 'Property Rights and Beliefs: Evidence from the Allocation of Land Titles to Squatters', draft of a paper presented at a Public Choice Center Seminar Series, George Mason University, Fairfax, VA, 1 February.

Ditiatin, I.I. (1875–77), *Ustroistvo i upravlenie gorodov Rossii*, 2 vols, St Petersburg.

Dixit, A.K. (2004), *Lawlessness and Economics: Alternative Modes of Governance*, Princeton, NJ: Princeton University Press.

Djilas, M. ([1957] 1958), *The New Class: An Analysis of the Communist System*, New York: Frederick A. Praeger, Inc.

Dobb, M. (1948), *Soviet Economic Development since 1917*, New York: International Publishers.

Easter, G. (2000), *Reconstructing the State: Personal Networks and Elite Identity in Soviet Russia*, New York: Cambridge University Press.

Eaton, H.L. (1967), 'Cadastres and Censuses of Muscovy', *Slavic Review*, **26** (1), 54–69.

Economist (1983), 'Living on the Left in Russia', 15 October.

Edeen, A. (1960), 'The Civil Service: Its Composition and Status', in Cyril E. Black (ed.), *The Transformation of Russian Society: Aspects of Social Change since 1861*, Cambridge, MA: Harvard University Press, pp. 274–92.

Elfimov, A. (2003), *Russian Intellectual Culture in Transition: The Future in the Past*, Munster: Lit Verlag and Piscataway, NJ: Transaction Publishers.

Emerson, Richard M. (1972), 'Exchange Theory Part II: Exchange Relations and Network Structures', in Joseph Berger, Morris Zelditch, Jr. and Bo Anderson (eds), *Sociological Theories in Progress* Vol. 2, Boston, MA: Houghton Mifflin Company, pp. 58–87.

Emmons, T. (1968), 'The Peasant and the Emancipation', in Wayne S. Vucinich (ed.), *The Peasant in Nineteenth-century Russia*, Stanford, CA: Stanford University Press, pp. 41–71.

Fainsod, M. (1953), *How Russia is Ruled*, Cambridge, MA: Harvard University Press.

Faulconbridge, G. (2007), 'Putin Says Russian Jury System Discredited', Reuters, http://www.reuters.com/article/latestCrisis/idUSL1167606, 11 January.

Fisher, Ralph T., Jr. (1960), 'The Soviet Model of the Ideal Youth', in Cyril E. Black (ed.), *The Transformation of Russian Society: Aspects of Social Change since 1861*, Cambridge, MA: Harvard University Press, pp. 625–35.

Fitzpatrick, S. (1999), *Everyday Stalinism: Ordinary Life in Extraordinary Times: Soviet Russia in the 1930s*, New York: Oxford University Press.

Fitzpatrick, S. (2000), '*Blat* in Stalin's Time', in S. Lovell, A. Ledeneva and A. Rogachevskii (eds), *Bribery and Blat in Russia: Negotiating Reciprocity from the Middle Ages to the 1990s*, New York: St. Martin's Press, Inc., pp. 166–82.

Freeze, G.L. (1989), 'The Orthodox Church and Serfdom in Prereform Russia', *Slavic Review*, **48** (3), 361–87.

Fukuyama, Francis (1995), *Trust: The Social Virtues and the Creation of Prosperity*, New York: The Free Press.

Galeotti, M. (2000), '"Who's the Boss: Us or the Law?" The Corrupt Art of Governing Russia', in S. Lovell, A. Ledeneva and A. Rogachevskii (eds), *Bribery and Blat in Russia: Negotiating Reciprocity from the Middle Ages to the 1990s*, New York: St. Martin's Press, Inc., pp. 270–87.

Ganiushkina, Y. (2005), 'Peterburzhtsy ne otdaut svoi cherdaki', *Moi raion, Moskovskii*, **23** (119), 6, 17 June.

Gerschenkron, A. (1970), *Europe in the Russian Mirror: Four Lectures in Economic History*, Cambridge, UK: Cambridge University Press.

Gerschenkron, A. and D. Marx (1950), 'Comments on Naum Jasny's "Soviet Statistics"', *The Review of Economics and Statistics*, **32** (3), 250–52.

Gimpel'son E.G. (1997), 'Sovetskie upravlentsy: politicheskii i nravstvennyi oblik, 1917–1920 gg.', *Otechestvennaia istoriia*, **5**, Moscow, 44–54.

Gimpel'son, V.E. (2002), *Chislennost' i sostav rossiiskoi biurokratii: mezhdu sovetskoi nomenklaturoi i gossluzhboi grazhdanskogo obshchestva*, Moscow: GU-VSHE; also http://www.hse.ru/science/preprint/ WP3_2002_05.htm.

Gippius, Z. (1990), 'Peterburgskie dnevniki', in *Literatura Russkogo Zarubezh'ia*, Vol. 1, Book 2, Moscow: Kniga, pp. 176–332.

Gliksman, Jerzy, G. (1960), 'The Russian Urban Worker', in Cyril E. Black (ed.), *The Transformation of Russian Society: Aspects of Social Change since 1861*, Cambridge, MA: Harvard University Press, pp. 311–23.

Granovetter, M.S. (1973), 'The Strength of Weak Ties', *American Journal of Sociology*, **78** (6), 1360–80.

Granovetter, M.S. (1983), 'The Strength of Weak Ties: A Network Theory Revisited', *Sociological Theory*, **1**, 201–33.

Gregory, Paul R. (1990), *Restructuring the Soviet Economic Bureaucracy*, Cambridge, UK and New York: Cambridge University Press.

Gregory, Paul R. (1994), *Before Command: An Economic History of Russia from Emancipation to the First Five-year Plan*, Princeton, NJ: Princeton University Press.

Gregory, Paul R. (ed.) (2001), *Behind the Façade of Stalin's Command Economy: Evidence from the Soviet State and Party Archives*, Stanford, CA: Hoover Institution Press.

Gregory, Paul R. (2004), *The Political Economy of Stalinism: Evidence from the Soviet Secret Archives*, Cambridge, UK; New York: Cambridge University Press.

Gregory, Paul R. and Robert C. Stuart (1986), *Soviet Economic Structure and Performance*, New York: Harper & Row.

Grossman, G. (1987), 'The Second Economy: Boon or Bane for the Reform of the First Economy?', in G. Grossman and V.G. Treml (eds), 'Studies on the Soviet Second Economy', in *Berkeley–Duke Occasional Papers on the Second Economy in the USSR*, No. 11, December.

Haimson, Leopold H. (1960), 'The Parties and the State', in Cyril E. Black (ed.), *The Transformation of Russian Society: Aspects of Social Change since 1861*, Cambridge, MA: Harvard University Press, pp. 110–45.

Halpin, T. (2008), 'Dmitri Medvedev Votes Were Rigged, Says Computer Boffin', in *Times Online*, http://www.timesonline.co.uk/tol/news/world/ europe/article3768223.ece, 18 April.

Hamm, M. (ed.) (1976a), *The City in Russian History*, Lexington, KY: The University Press of Kentucky.

Hamm, M. (1976b), 'The Breakdown of Urban Modernization: A Prelude to the Revolutions of 1917', in M. Hamm (ed.), *The City in Russian History*, Lexington, KY: The University Press of Kentucky, pp. 182–200.

Hanchett, W. (1976), 'Tsarist Statutory Regulation of Municipal Government in the Nineteenth Century', in M. Hamm (ed.), *The City in Russian History*, Lexington, KY: The University Press of Kentucky, pp. 91–114.

Hanson, Philip (1974), *Advertising and Socialism: The Nature and Extent of Consumer Advertising in the Soviet Union, Poland, Hungary and Yugoslavia*, White Plains, NY: International Arts and Science Press.

Harper, Samuel N. (1937), *The Government of the Soviet Union*, New York: D. Van Nostrand Company, Inc.

Harrison, M. (2001), 'Providing for Defense', in Paul R. Gregory (ed.), *Behind the Façade of Stalin's Command Economy: Evidence from the Soviet State and Party Archives*, Stanford, CA: Hoover Institution Press, pp. 81–110.

Hartley, J. (1999), *A Social History of the Russian Empire, 1650–1825*, New York: Longman.

Hellie, R. (1971), *Enserfment and Military Change in Muscovy*, Chicago: The University of Chicago Press.

Hellie, R. (1982), *Slavery in Russia, 1450–1725*, Chicago: The University of Chicago Press.

Hellie, R. (1999), *The Economy and Material Culture of Russia, 1600–1725*, Chicago: The University of Chicago Press.

Hittle, J. (1976), 'The Service City in the Eighteenth Century', in M. Hamm (ed.), *The City in Russian History*, Lexington, KY: The University Press of Kentucky, pp. 53–68.

Hittle, J. (1979), *The Service City: State and Townsmen in Russia, 1600–1800*, Cambridge, MA: Harvard University Press.

Hoeffding, O. (1962), 'Soviet Economic Planning', in Franklyn D. Holzman (ed.), *Readings on the Soviet Economy*, Chicago: Rand McNally & Company, pp. 475–87.

Hoffman, D.E. (2002), *The Oligarchs*, New York: Public Affairs.

Hogarth, C.J. (transl. and ed.) (1911), *A History of Russia*, Vol. 1, New York: E.P. Dutton & Co.

Hogarth, C.J. (transl. and ed.) (1912), *A History of Russia*, Vol. 2, New York: E.P. Dutton & Co.

Hogarth, C.J. (transl. and ed.) (1913), *A History of Russia*, Vol. 3, New York: E.P. Dutton & Co.

Hogarth, C.J. (transl. and ed.) (1926), *A History of Russia*, Vol. 4, New York: E.P. Dutton & Co.

Hogarth, C.J. (transl. and ed.) (1931), *A History of Russia*, Vol. 5, New York: E.P. Dutton & Co.

Hollander, P. (1978), *Soviet and American Society: A Comparison*, Chicago: The University of Chicago Press.

Hough, J. (1977), *The Soviet Union and Social Science Theory*, Cambridge, MA: Harvard University Press.

Human Development Report, Russian Federation (2007/2008), United Nations Development Programme, http://hdrstats.undp.org/countries/data_sheets/cty_ds_RUS.html.

Illarionov, A. (2006), 'The Rise of the Corporate State in Russia', Cato Institute, Washington, DC, Policy Forum, http://www.cato.org/people/andrei-illarionov/.

Informatsiia o sotsial'no-ekonomicheskom polozhenii Rossii (Russian Socio-Economic Data) (2008), Moscow: Federal'naia sluzhba gosugarstvennoi statistiki, http://www.infostat.ru/, January–March.

Itogi (2000), No. 51, December.

Ivanova, N. (2002), *Nastol'iashchee (Nowstalgia)*, Moscow: 'Raduga'.

Jack, A. (2004) *Inside Putin's Russia: Can There Be Reform Without Democracy?*, Oxford: Oxford University Press.

Jasny, N. (1950a), 'Soviet Statistics', *The Review of Economics and Statistics*, **32** (1), pp. 92–9.

Jasny, N. (1950b), 'International Organizations and Soviet Statistics', *Journal of the American Statistical Association*, **45** (249), 48–64.

Jasny, N. (October 1951), 'Labor and Output in Soviet Concentration Camps', *The Journal of Political Economy*, **59** (5), 405–19.

Jones, R.E. (1977), 'Jacob Sievers, Enlightened Reform and the Development of a "Third Estate" in Russia', *Russian Review*, **36** (4), 424–37.

Kahan, A. (1985), *The Plow, the Hammer, and the Knout: An Economic History of Eighteenth-century Russia*, Chicago: The University of Chicago Press.

Kara-Murza, S. (2002), *Manipuliatsiia soznaniem (Manipulation of Minds)*, Moscow: Eksmo-Press.

Karamzin, N.M. (1988–89), *Istoriia gosudarstva Rossiiskogo*, 4 vols, Moscow: Kniga.

Karpova, E. (2001), in Grani.ru, http://www.grani.ru/jobs/articles/post/, 25 January.

Katsenelinboigen, A. (1978), *Studies in Soviet Economic Planning*, White Plains, NY: M.E. Sharpe.

Kaufman, A. (1962), *Small-scale Industry in the Soviet Union*, New York: National Bureau of Economic Research.

Kaufmann, D. and A. Kaliberda (1996), 'Integrating the Unofficial Economy into the Dynamics of Post-socialist Economies: A Framework of Analysis and Evidence', The World Bank, Country Department IV, *Policy Research Working Paper* No. 1691.

Kelly, C. (2000), 'Self-interested Giving: Bribery and Etiquette in Late Imperial Russia', in S. Lovell, A. Ledeneva and A. Rogachevskii (eds), *Bribery and Blat in Russia: Negotiating Reciprocity from the Middle Ages to the 1990s*, New York: St. Martin's Press, Inc., pp. 65–94.

Khlevnyuk, O. (2001), 'The Economy of the Gulag', in Paul R. Gregory (ed.), *Behind the Façade of Stalin's Command Economy: Evidence from the Soviet State and Party Archives*, Stanford, CA: Hoover Institution Press, pp. 111–29.

Klebnikov, P. (2001), *Krestnyi otets Kremlia Boris Beresovski ili istoriia rasgrableniia Rossii*, Moscow: 'Detektiv-Press'.

Kliger, S. (1999), 'The Future Belongs to Me: Russian Students and Their Religious Views', in V. Shlapentokh, C. Vanderpool and B. Doktorov (eds), *The New Elite in Post-Communist Eastern Europe*, College Station, TX: Texas A&M University Press, Chapter 22.

Kline, George L. (1960), 'Changing Attitudes Toward the Individual', in C.E. Black (ed.), *The Transformation of Russian Society: Aspects of Social Change since 1861*, Cambridge, MA: Harvard University Press, pp. 606–25.

Kliuchevskii, V.O. (1956), *Sochineniia*, Vol. 1, Moscow: Gosudarstvennoe izdatel'stvo politicheskoi literatury.

Kliuchevskii, V.O. (1957), *Sochineniia*, Vols 2–3, Moscow: Gosudarstvennoe izdatel'stvo politicheskoi literatury.

Kliuchevskii, V.O. (1958), *Sochineniia*, Vols 4–5, Moscow: Gosudarstvennoe izdatel'stvo politicheskoi literatury.

Kliuchevskii, V.O. (1959), *Sochineniia*, Vols 6, 8, Moscow: Gosudarstvennoe izdatel'stvo politicheskoi literatury.

Klugman, J. (1989), *The New Soviet Elite: How They Think and What They Want*, New York: Praeger.

Klyamkin, I. and L. Timofeev (2000), *Tenevaia Rossiia: ekonomiko-sotsiologicheskoe issledovanie*, Moscow: RGGU, also at http://www.liberal.ru/book1.asp?Rel=9.

Kolle, H. (1995), 'The Russian Post-emancipation Household: Two Villages in the Moscow Area', http://www.ub.uib.no/elpub/1995/h/506006/ and http://www.ub.uib.no/elpub/1995/h/506006/Hovedoppgave.pdf.

Kornai, J. (1980), *Economics of Shortage*, Vols A and B, New York: North-Holland Publishing Company.

Koslow, J. (1972), *The Despised and the Damned: The Russian Peasant through the Ages*, New York: The Macmillan Company.

Kostikov, V. (2005), 'Osliki vo vlasti', *Argumenty i fakty*, No. 28.

Krishtanovskaia, O. and S. White (1999), 'From *Nomenklatura* to New Elite', in V. Shlapentokh, C. Vanderpool and B. Doktorov (eds), *The New Elite in Post-Communist Eastern Europe*, College Station, TX: Texas A&M University Press, Chapter 1.

Krueger, A.O. (1974), 'The Political Economy of the Rent-seeking Society', *American Economic Review*, **64** (3), 291–303.

Kukolev, I. (1999), 'Formation of the Business Elite in Russia', in V. Shlapentokh, C. Vanderpool and B. Doktorov (eds), *The New Elite in Post-Communist Eastern Europe*, College Station, TX: Texas A&M University Press, Chapter 18.

Kupriianov, A.I. (1996), 'Predstavleniia o trude i bogatstve russkogo kupechestva doreformennoi epokhi', in L.N. Pushkarev et al. (eds), *Mentalitet i kul'tura predprinimatelei Rossii XVII-XIX vv.: Sbornik statei*, Moscow: Institut rossiiskoi istorii RAN, pp. 83–107.

Landa, Janet Tai (1994), *Trust, Ethnicity, and Identity: Beyond the New Institutional Economics of Ethnic Trading Networks, Contract Law, and Gift-Exchange*, Ann Arbor, MI: The University of Michigan Press.

Lane, D. (2001), 'The Political Economy of Russian Oil', in P. Rutland (ed.), *Business and State in Contemporary Russia*, Boulder, CO: Westview Press, pp. 101–28.

Langer, L. (1976), 'The Medieval Russian Town', in M. Hamm (ed.), *The City in Russian History*, Lexington, KY: The University Press of Kentucky, pp. 11–33.

Lapina, N. (1998), 'Business and Power in the Russian Regions', *Bericht des BIOst*, 41/1998, 4 September.

Latov, Y.V. (1999), 'Neformal'naia ekonomika kak global'no-istoricheskoe iavlenie', in *Tenevaia ekonomika: ekonomichesii i sotsial'nyi aspekty. Problemno-tematicheskii sbornik*, Moscow: INION.

Latov, Y.V. (2001), *Ekonomika vne zakona: Ocherki po istorii i teorii tenevoi ekonomiki*, Moscow, Chapter 6, http://ie.boom.ru/Latov/Monograph/Chapter6.htm.

Lebedev, S. (2001), 'European Business Culture and St. Petersburg Banks', in William Craft Brumfield, Boris V. Anan'ich and Yuri A. Petrov (eds), *Commerce in Russian Urban Culture, 1861–1914*, Washington, DC: Woodrow Wilson Center Press, Chapter 2.

Ledeneva, A. (1998), *Russia's Economy of Favours: Blat, Networking, and Informal Exchange*, Cambridge, UK: Cambridge University Press.

Liashchenko, P.I. (1949), *History of the National Economy of Russia to the 1917 Revolution*, New York: Macmillan.

Litwack, J.M. (1991), 'Legality and Market Reform in Soviet-type Economies', *The Journal of Economic Perspectives*, **5** (4), 77–89, Autumn.

Los, M. (ed.) (1990), The *Second Economy in Marxist States*, New York: St. Martin's Press.

Losskii, N.O. (1991), *Usloviia absoliutnogo dobra*, Moscow: Izdatel'stvo politicheskoi literatury.

Lovell, S. (2000), 'Reciprocity and the Soviet Cultural Revolution: The Literary Perspective', in S. Lovell, A. Ledeneva and A. Rogachevskii (eds), *Bribery and Blat in Russia: Negotiating Reciprocity from the Middle Ages to the 1990s*, New York: St. Martin's Press, Inc., pp. 141–65.

Lovell, S., A. Ledeneva and A. Rogachevskii (eds) (2000), *Bribery and Blat in Russia: Negotiating Reciprocity from the Middle Ages to the 1990s*, New York: St. Martin's Press, Inc.

Luneev, V. (1999), 'Crime and the Formation of a New Elite', in V. Shlapentokh, C. Vanderpool and B. Doktorov (eds), *The New Elite in Post-Communist Eastern Europe*, College Station, TX: Texas A&M University Press, Chapter 4.

Maleva, T.M. (ed.) (2003), *Srednie klassy v Rossii: ekonomicheskie i sotsial'nye strategii*, Moscow: Gendal'f.

Maly, Matthew (2004), 'My Comment on a Normal Country by Andrei Shleifer and Daniel Treisman', *Johnson's Russia List* No. 8081, also at http://matthew-maly.ru/articles/eng25.shtml.

Matthews, M. (1978), *Privilege in the Soviet Union*, London: George Allen and Unwin.

Matthews, M. (1986), 'Poverty and Patterns of Deprivation in the Soviet Union', in *Berkeley–Duke Occasional Papers on the Second Economy in the USSR*, No. 6, June.

Matusevich, V. (1992), 'Cooperatives: The Seeds of the Market Economy?', in Michael P. Claudon and Tamar L. Gutner (eds), *Putting Food on What Was the Soviet Table*, New York: Geonomics Special Report and Policy Statement, pp. 49–59.

Mavor, J. (1925), *An Economic History of Russia*, Vol. 2, 2nd edition, New York: E.P. Dutton & Co.

Mavor, J. ([1925] 1965), *An Economic History of Russia*, Vol. 1, reprint, 2nd edition, New York: Russell & Russell.

McChesney, F.S. (1997), *Money for Nothing. Politicians, Rent Extraction, and Political Extortion*, Cambridge, MA: Harvard University Press.

McGuire, Martin C. and Mancur Olson, Jr. (1996), 'The Economics of Autocracy and Majority Rule: The Invisible Hand and the Use of Force', *Journal of Economic Literature*, **34** (1), 72–96, March.

McKay, John P. (1970), *Pioneers for Profit: Foreign Entrepreneurship and Russian Industrialization, 1885–1913*, Chicago: University of Chicago Press.

McLure, Charles E., Jr. (1995), 'Revenue Assignment and Intergovernmental Fiscal Relations in Russia', in Edward P. Lazear (ed.), *Economic Transition in Eastern Europe and Russia: Realities of Reform*, Stanford, CA: Hoover Institution Press, pp. 199–246.

Medvedev, Roy (2000), *Post-Soviet Russia: A Journey through the Yeltsin Era*, transl. by George Shriver, New York: Columbia University Press.

Merl, S. (1993), 'Social Mobility in the Countryside', in William G. Rosenberg and Lewis H. Siegelbaum (eds), *Social Dimensions of Soviet Industrialization*, Bloomington, IN: Indiana University Press, pp. 41–62.

Metro (2005), 'Reestr firm pochistiat', 18 July.

Miliukov, P.N. (1913), *Glavnye techeniia russkoi istoricheskoi mysli*, St Petersburg: Izdatel'stvo M.V. Aver'ianova.

Miller, D. (1976), 'State and City in the Seventeenth-century Muscovy', in M. Hamm (ed.), *The City in Russian History*, Lexington, KY: The University Press of Kentucky, pp. 34–52.

Mironov, B.N. (2000), *The Social History of Imperial Russia, 1700–1917. Volume One*, Boulder, CO: Westview Press.

Morton, H.W. (1979), 'The Soviet Quest for Better Housing – An Impossible Dream?', in *Soviet Economy in a Time of Change*, US Congress, Joint Economic Committee, Washington, DC: GPO, Vol. 1, pp. 790–811, 10 October.

Mroz, T., L. Henderson and B.M. Popkin (2005), 'Monitoring Economic Conditions in the Russian Federation: The Russia Longitudinal Monitoring Survey 1992–2004', report submitted to the US Agency for International Development, Carolina Population Center, NC: University of North Carolina at Chapel Hill, http://www.cpc.unc.edu/projects/rlms/papers/econ_04.pdf, April.

Nikolaeva, O. (2002), 'Dol'shchiki b'iutsia za kachestvo novostroek', *Novyi Peterburg*, **47** (571), 14 November.

Nove, A. ([1969] 1984), *An Economic History of the U.S.S.R.*, New York: Penguin Books.

Novgorodskaia pervaia letopis' (*The First Chronicle of Novgorod*) (1950), ed. A.N. Nasonov, Moscow and Leningrad: Akademiia nauk SSSR.

Nutter, G.W. (1962), *Growth of Industrial Production in the Soviet Union*, Princeton, NJ: Princeton University Press.

Ofer, G. (1987), 'Soviet Economic Growth: 1928–1985', *Journal of Economic Literature*, **25** (4), 1767–1833, December.

Osokina, E. (2001), *Our Daily Bread: Socialist Distribution and the Art of Survival in Stalin's Russia, 1927–1941*, Armonk, NY: M.E. Sharpe, Inc. In Russian: Osokina, E. (1999), *Za fasadom 'Stalinskogo izobiliia': Raspredelinie i rynok v snabzhenii naseleniia v gody industrializatsii, 1927–1941*, Moscow: ROSSPEN.

Ostrom, Elinor and James Walker (eds) (2003), *Trust and Reciprocity: Interdisciplinary Lessons from Experimental Research*, New York: Russell Sage Foundation.

Owen, Thomas C. (1981), *Capitalism and Politics in Russia: A Social History of the Moscow Merchants, 1855–1905*, New York: Cambridge University Press.

Pavlov-Sil'vanskii, N.P. (1988), *Feodalizm v Rossii*, Moscow: Nauka.

Perel'man, V. (1977), *Pokinutaia Rossiia. Krushenie*, Tel-a-Viv: 'Vremia i my'.

Petrov, Y. (2001), 'The Banking Network of Moscow at the Turn of the Twentieth Century', in William Craft Brumfield, Boris V. Anan'ich and Yuri A. Petrov (eds), *Commerce in Russian Urban Culture, 1861–1914*, Washington, DC: Woodrow Wilson Center Press, Chapter 4.

Petviashvili, Joseph (2007), graphs and discussion of the Russian Duma elections in December 2007, http://krotty.livejournal.com/2007/12/06/.

Pipes, R. (1974), *Russia under the Old Regime*, New York: Charles Scribner's Sons.

Pipes, R. (1995), *A Concise History of the Russian Revolution*, London: The Harvill Press.

Platonova, O. (ed.) (1995), *1000 let russkogo predprinimatel'stva: Iz istorii kupecheskikh rodov*, Moscow: Sovremennik.

Podmoskovnik (2008a), graphs and discussion of the 2007–08 elections in Russia, http://podmoskovnik.livejournal.com/tag/elections, Jan.–Feb.

Podmoskovnik (2008b), graphs and discussion of the Russian presidential elections in March 2008, http://podmoskovnik.livejournal.com/, 18 April.

Polianskii, F.Y. (1983), *Tsena i stoimost' v usloviiah feodalizma*, Moscow: Izdatel'stvo Moskovskogo universiteta.

Politkovskaya, A. (2007), *A Russian Diary*, transl. by A. Tait, New York: Random House.

Posner, R.A. (1975), 'The Social Costs of Monopoly and Regulation', *Journal of Political Economy*, **83** (4), 807–27.

Pososhkov, I. (1987), *The Book of Poverty and Wealth*, ed. and transl. by A.P. Vlasto and L.R. Lewitter, Stanford, CA: Stanford University Press.

Potter, Cathy J. (2000), 'Payment, Gift or Bribe?', in S. Lovell, A. Ledeneva and A. Rogachevski (eds), *Bribery and Blat in Russia: Negotiating Reciprocity from the Middle Ages to the 1990s*, New York: St. Martin's Press, Inc., pp. 20–34.

Powers, Charles H. (1985), 'Clarification and Extension of Emerson and Cook's Exchange Theory', *Sociological Theory*, **3** (2), Autumn, 58–65.

Pshenichnikov, Maxim (2008), graphs and discussion of the Russian Duma elections in December 2007, http://oude-rus.livejournal.com/52935.html, 18 January.

Putnam, R.D. (1993a), *Making Democracy Work*, Princeton, NJ: Princeton University Press.

Putnam, R.D. (1993b), 'The Prosperous Community', *The American Prospect*, **4** (13), 21 March.

Radaev, Valerii V. (1993), 'Novye predprinimateli: sotsial'nyi portret', in Valerii V. Radaev (ed.), *Stanovlenie novogo rossiiskogo predprinimatel'stva: sotsiologicheskii aspect*, Moscow: Institut ekonomiki RAN, pp. 65–80.

Reshetar, John S., Jr. (1960), 'Russian Ethnic Values', in Cyril E. Black (ed.), *The Transformation of Russian Society: Aspects of Social Change since 1861*, Cambridge, MA: Harvard University Press, pp. 559–73.

Rezun, D.I. and D.M. Tereshkov (eds) (1994–98), *Kratkaia entsiklopediia po istorii kupechestva i kommertsii Sibiri: v chetyrekh tomakh*, 4 vols, Novosibirsk: Institut istorii SO RAN.

Riasanovsky, Nicholas V. (1968), 'Afterword: The Problem of the Peasant', in Wayne S. Vucinich (ed.), *The Peasant in Nineteenth-century Russia*, Stanford, CA: Stanford University Press, pp. 263–84.

Rieber, Alfred J. (1982), *Merchants and Entrepreneurs in Imperial Russia*, Chapel Hill, NC: University of North Carolina Press.

Rigby, T.H. (1999), 'Russia's Business Elite', *Russian and Euro-Asian Bulletin*, **8** (7), http://www.cerc.unimelb.edu.au/bulletin/99sep.htm, Aug.–Sept.

Rowley, C.K. (1993), 'The Limits of Democracy', in C.K. Rowley (ed.), *Property Rights and the Limits of Democracy*, Aldershot, UK and Brookfield, VT: Edward Elgar Publishing, pp. 1–23.

Rowley, C.K. (1996), 'What is Living and What is Dead in Classical Liberalism', in C.K. Rowley (ed.), *The Political Economy of the Minimal State*, Cheltenham, UK and Brookfield, VT: Edward Elgar Publishing, pp. 1–23.

Rowney, D. (1993), 'The Scope, Authority and Personnel of the New Industrial Commissariats in Historical Context', in William G. Rosenberg and Lewis H. Siegelbaum (eds), *Social Dimensions of Soviet Industrialization*, Bloomington, IN: Indiana University Press, pp. 124–45.

Rozman, G. (1976a), *Urban Networks in Russia, 1750–1800, and Premodern Periodization*, Princeton, NJ: Princeton University Press.

Rozman, G. (1976b), 'Comparative Approaches to Urbanization', in M. Hamm (ed.), *The City in Russian History*, Lexington, KY: The University Press of Kentucky, pp. 69–85.

Rubin, P.H. (1997), *Promises, Promises: Contracts in Russia and Other Post-Communist Economies*, Cheltenham, UK and Brookfield, VT: Edward Elgar Publishing.

Ruckman, Jo Ann (1984), *The Moscow Business Elite: A Social and Cultural Portrait of Two Generations, 1840–1905*, DeKalb, IL: Northern Illinois University Press.

Russia'2007: Statistical Pocketbook (2007), Moscow: Federal State Statistics Service (Rosstat), http://www.statrus.info/.

Rutgaizer, V.M. (1992), 'The Shadow Economy in the USSR', in *Berkeley-Duke Occasional Papers on the Second Economy in the USSR*, No. 34, February.

Rutland, P. (1993), *The Politics of Economic Stagnation in the Soviet Union*, New York: Cambridge University Press.

Rutland, P. (ed.) (2001), *Business and State in Contemporary Russia*, Boulder, CO: Westview Press.

Ryavec, K.W. (2003), *Russian Bureaucracy: Power and Pathology*, Lanham, MD: Rowman & Littlefield Publishers, Inc.

Ryvkina, R.V. (2001), *Drama peremen*, Moscow: 'Delo'.

Sakharov, A.M. (1959), *Goroda severo-vostochnoi Rusi XIV-XV vekov*, Moscow: Izdatel'stvo Moskovskogo universiteta.

Satter, D. (2003), *Darkness at Dawn: The Rise of the Russian Criminal State*, New Haven, CT: Yale University Press.

Scott, J.C. (1998), *Seeing Like a State*, New Haven, CT: Yale University Press.

Sedik, D.J. (1989), 'Connections and Consumption in the USSR', in *Berkeley–Duke Occasional Papers on the Second Economy in the USSR*, No. 16, September.

Semenova, A.V. et al. (eds) (2000), *Istoriia predprinimatel'stva v Rossii*, Moscow: ROSSPEN.

Shanin, T. (1972), *The Awkward Class: Political Sociology of Peasantry in a Developing Society: Russia 1910–1925*, Oxford: Clarendon Press.

Shanin, T. (1986), *Russia as a 'Developing Society'. The Roots of Otherness: Russia's Turn of Century*, Center for Peasant Studies and Agrarian Reforms of the Moscow School of Social and Economic Science, http://old.msses.ru/ruralworlds/eng/shanin-develop/glava2.html.

Shatsillo, K.F. (1968), *Russkii imperializm i razvitie flota*, Moscow: Nauka.

Shchapov, A.P. (2001), *Izbrannoe*, Irkutsk: Ottisk.

Shearer, David R. (1993), 'Factories within Factories: Changes in the Structure of Work and Management in Soviet Machine Building Factories, 1926–1934', in William G. Rosenberg and Lewis H. Siegelbaum (eds), *Social Dimensions of Soviet Industrialization*, Bloomington, IN: Indiana University Press, pp. 193–222.

Shelley, Louise I. (1990), 'The Second Economy in the Soviet Union', in M. Los (ed.), *The Second Economy in Marxist States*, New York: St. Martin's Press, pp. 11–26.

Shevchenko, I. (2004), *The Central Government of Russia: From Gorbachev to Putin*, Burlington, VT: Ashgate.

Shiller, R.J., M. Boycko and V. Korobov (1991), 'Popular Attitudes Toward Free Markets: The Soviet Union and the United States Compared', *American Economic Review*, **81** (3), 385–400, June.

Shipler, D.K. (1983), *Russia: Broken Idols, Solemn Dreams*, New York: Penguin Books.

Shleifer, A. and D. Treisman (2004), 'A Normal Country', in *Foreign Affairs* **83** (2), March/April, http://www.foreignaffairs.org/2004/2.html. Also published as a book: Shleifer, A. and D. Treisman (2005), *Normal Country: Russia after Communism*, Cambridge, MA: Harvard University Press.

Shul'gin, V. (1991), 'Tri stolitsy', in *Literatura Russkogo Zarubezh'ia*, Vol. 2, Moscow: Kniga, pp. 161–238.

Simis, Konstantin M. (1977–78), 'The Machinery of Corruption in the Soviet Union', *Survey*, **23** (4), 35–55.

Simis, Konstantin M. (1982), *USSR: The Corrupt Society*, New York: Simon and Schuster.

Smith, Ronald S. (2002), 'Freedom and the Tragedy of the Commons: How Social Capital and Interpersonal Networks Enable Collective Action', *Humane Studies Review*, **14** (2).

Solomon, G. (1991), 'Sredi krasnyh vozhdei', in *Literatura Russkogo Zarubezh'ia*, Vol. 2, Moscow: Kniga, pp. 271–88.

Solov'ev, S.M. (1959), *Istoriia Rossii s drevneishih vremen* (*History of Russia from Early Times*), Book I, Vols 1–2, Moscow: Izdatel'stvo sotsial'no-ekonomicheskoi literatury.

Solov'ev, S.M. (1960), *Istoriia Rossii s drevneishih vremen* (*History of Russia from Early Times*), Books II–IV, Vols 3–8, Moscow: Izdatel'stvo sotsial'no-ekonomicheskoi literatury.

Solov'eva, A.M. (1975), *Zheleznodorozhnyi transport Rossii vo vtoroi polovine deviatnadtsatogo v.*, Moscow: Nauka.

Sorokin, P. (1990), 'Nravstvennoe i umstvennoe sostoianie sovremennoi Rossii', in *Literatura Russkogo Zarubezh'ia*, Vol. 1, Book 1, Moscow: Kniga, pp. 406–16.

Steen, A. (2000), 'Decision-making in Russia: From Hierarchy to Networks?', 28th Annual ECPR Joint Session of Workshops 14–19 April, Copenhagen, http://www.essex.ac.uk/ecpr/jointsessions/Copenhagen/papers/ws23/steen.pdf.

Struve, P.B., K.I. Zaitsev, N.V. Dolinsky and S.S. Demosthenov (1930), *Food Supply in Russia During the World War*, New Haven, CT: Yale University Press.

Stykow, P. (1999), 'Elite Transformation in the Saratov Region', in V. Shlapentokh, C. Vanderpool and B. Doktorov (eds), *The New Elite in Post-Communist Eastern Europe*, College Station, TX: Texas A&M University Press, Chapter 12.

The *Other* Russia (2008a), 'Moscow Workers Pressured to Vote', http://www.theotherrussia.org/2008/02/29/moscow-workers-pressured-to-vote/, 29 February.

The *Other* Russia (2008b), 'Russian Vote Inundated with Violations and Fraud – Observers', http://www.theotherrussia.org/2008/03/03/russian-vote-inundated-with-violations-and-fraud-observers/, 3 March.

Thiede, R. (1976), 'Industry and Urbanization in New Russia from 1860 to 1910', in M. Hamm (ed.), *The City in Russian History*, Lexington, KY: The University Press of Kentucky, pp. 125–38.

Tikhomirov, M.N. (1956), *Drevnerusskie goroda*, Moscow: Gosudarstvennoe izdatel'stvo politicheskoi literatury.

Tikhomirov, V. (2000), *The Political Economy of Post-Soviet Russia*, New York: Palgrave.

Tollison, Robert D. and Richard E. Wagner (1995), 'Romance, Realism, and Economic Reform', in Robert D. Tollison and Roger D. Congleton (eds), *The Economic Analysis of Rent Seeking*, Aldershot, UK and Brookfield, VT: Edward Elgar, pp. 380–93.

Treml, V.G. (1992), 'A Study of Labour Inputs into the Second Economy of the USSR', in *Berkeley–Duke Occasional Papers on the Second Economy in the USSR*, No. 33, January.

Tullock, G. (1967), 'The Welfare Costs of Tariffs, Monopolies, and Theft', *Western Economic Journal*, **5** (3), 224–32.

Tullock, G. (1987), *Autocracy*, Hingham, MA: Kluwer Academic Publishers.

Tullock, G. (1998), 'The Fundamentals of Rent-Seeking', *The Locke Luminary*, **1** (2) (Winter), Part 2, available at: http://www.thelocke institute.org/journals/luminary_v1_n2_p2.html.

Varshavskaia, E. (2001), 'Chto tam "v teni"?', interview in *Chelovek i trud*, No. 11, http://www.chelt.ru/2001/11/varshavskaja_11.html.

Vladykin, K. (2002), 'Chekharda iz-za "Stolichnoi"', *Grani.ru*, http://grani.ru/brands/articles/stolichnaya/.

Volin, L. (1960), 'The Russian Peasant', in Cyril E. Black (ed.), *The Transformation of Russian Society: Aspects of Social Change since 1861*, Cambridge, MA: Harvard University Press, pp. 292–311.

Volin, L. (1962), 'The Peasant Household under the Mir and the Kolkhoz in Modern Russian History', in Franklyn D. Holzman (ed.), *Readings on the Soviet Economy*, Chicago: Rand McNally & Company, pp. 491–505.

Volkov, M.Y. (1979), *Ocherki promyslov Rossii. Vtoraia polovina XVI – pervaia polovina XVIII veka. Vinokurennoe proizvodstvo*, Moscow: Nauka.

Vucinich, A. (1960), 'The State and the Local Community', in Cyril E. Black (ed.), *The Transformation of Russian Society: Aspects of Social*

Change since 1861, Cambridge, MA: Harvard University Press, pp. 191–209.

Watters, Francis M. (1968), 'The Peasant and the Village Commune', in Wayne S. Vucinich (ed.), *The Peasant in Nineteenth-century Russia*, Stanford, CA: Stanford University Press, pp. 133–57.

Weber, M. (1958a), *The City*, transl. and ed. by Don Martindale and Gertrud Neuwirth, Glencoe, IL: The Free Press.

Weber, M. (1958b), *The Protestant Ethic and the Spirit of Capitalism*, New York: Scribner.

Whitmore, B. (2008a), 'The Two-headed Tsar: Who Will Really Be in Charge in Russia?', in RFE/RL, http://www.rferl.org/featuresarticle/2008/03/f208b6ef-844f-438b-8251-e2e105c97cfe.html, 2 March.

Whitmore, B. (2008b), 'Russia: The New and Improved Single-Party State', in RFE/RL, http://www.rferl.org/featuresarticle/2008/04/2c6fc8db-a136-4a06-ab69-f53f7a4fd015.html, 15 April.

Williamson, Oliver E. (1985), *The Economic Institutions of Capitalism: Firms, Markets, Relational Contracting*, New York: The Free Press.

Willis, D.K. (1987), *Klass: How Russians Really Live*, New York: Avon Books.

Wintrobe, Ronald (1998), *The Political Economy of Dictatorship*, Cambridge, UK and New York: Cambridge University Press.

Wirtschafter, E.K. (1997), *Social Identity in Imperial Russia*, Dekalb, IL: Northern Illinois University Press.

World Bank Russian Economic Report (2007), No. 15, www.worldbank.org/ru, November.

World Economic Outlook (2008), IMF, http://www.imf.org/external/pubs/ft/weo/2008/01/weodata/index.aspx, April.

Yakovlev, A. (2001), 'Black Cash Tax Evasion in Russia: Its Forms, Incentives and Consequences at Firm Level', *Europe-Asia Studies*, **52** (1), January.

Yanin, V. (1985), 'Medieval Novgorod: Fifty Years' Experience of Digging up the Past', in H.B. Clarke and Anngret Simms (eds), *The Comparative History of Urban Origins in Non-Roman Europe: Ireland, Wales, Denmark, Germany, Poland and Russia from the Ninth to the Thirteenth Century*, Oxford: British Archaeological Reports.

Yeltsin, B. (1990), *Ispoved' na zadannuiu temu*, Moscow: Assotsiatsiia 'Novyi Stil'.

Yergin, D. and J. Stanislaw (1998), *The Commanding Heights: The Battle Between Government and the Marketplace that is Remaking the Modern World*, New York: Simon & Schuster.

Zabelin, I.E. ([1876] 1908), *Istoriia russkoi zhisni s drevneishih vremen*, Vol. 1, Moscow: Tipografiia Gracheva.

Zabelin, I.E. ([1879] 1912), *Istoriia russkoi zhisni s drevneishih vremen*, Vol. 2, Moscow: Tipografiia Gracheva.

Zarakhovich, Y. (2002), 'Fighting Spirits', *Time Europe Magazine*, **160** (1), 1 July.

Zelnik, Reginald E. (1968), 'The Peasant and the Factory', in Wayne S. Vucinich (ed.), *The Peasant in Nineteenth-century Russia*, Stanford, CA: Stanford University Press, pp. 158–90.

Zherebin, V.M. and A.N. Romanov (2002), *Uroven' zhizni naseleniia*, Moscow: Unity.

Zigfeld, K. (2008), 'Annals of Russian Elections Fraud', post on Publius Pundit, http://www.publiuspundit.com/2008/02/annals_of_russian_elections_fr.php, 29 February.

Index

abuse of social networks 12
Adams, Mark 143
administration, reforms of 50
agriculture as feature of urban life 38
Ancient Chronicle 20, 52
Anderson, G.M. 11
Andropov, Yuri 153
apartments, privatization of 199, 202, 203
appanage system 22, 23, 24, 30, 50
Arbatov, Z. 124, 140
artisan cooperatives 36–7
asset specificity 3, 4
authoritarianism and social networks 8–10, 14
autocracy 8–10
Autocracy (Tullock) 9

backwardness of urbanization 35, 58
bad ties 7
banking 95
Baumol, J. 184
beliefs in 1990s and 2000s 194–6
Berezovsky, Boris 160
Berliner, J. 116, 141
Birman, I. 132
black cash businesses 185–6, 192
black markets 110, 154–5
Boettke, Peter 11, 14, 108, 109, 112, 115, 141, 155
Bolshevik Revolution and government
    dual power period 107, 127
    economy prior to 108–9
    industrialization 114–17
    meshochnichestvo (small bread speculation) 109–10
    New Economic Policy (NEP) 110–13
    policies following NEP 113–17
    shortages 113–14, 117, 127, 128
    trading during 110–13
    see also Soviet state

bounded rationality 3
boyars 23–4, 54
Boycko, M.A. 159
bread speculation 109–10
bribery and corruption 75–8, 84
Brovkin, V. 118, 140
bureaucracy
    and businesses 181–3, 190
    and merchants 95–6
    and network relationships 120–22
bureaucratization in the 16th century 25
businesses
    black cash 185–6, 192
    and bureaucracy 190
    and politics 159, 164

capitalism 204–5
categorization of the population 28–9, 55
Catherine II 38, 41, 51
centralization of the Muscovite state 22–4
character, Russian 140–41
Church, Russian Orthodox
    and economic development 71–4, 83
    and merchants 87–8
    ownership of land 83
church peasants 56
cities
    administrative and commercial functions 41–2, 60
    creation of new 38
    distance between 38
    population of 35–6
    population of industrial/trade 45, 46
    as service element of the state 37–8
    slow growth of industry 39–4
civil service sector and network relationships 120–22; *see also* bureaucracy